Ballparks of the Deadball Era
A Comprehensive Study

Ballparks of the Deadball Era

A Comprehensive Study of Their Dimensions, Configurations and Effects on Batting, 1901–1919

RONALD M. SELTER
with a foreword by Philip J. Lowry

McFarland & Company, Inc., Publishers
Jefferson, North Carolina, and London

The present work is a reprint of the illustrated case bound edition of Ballparks of the Deadball Era: A Comprehensive Study of Their Dimensions, Configurations and Effects on Batting, 1901–1919, *first published in 2008 by McFarland.*

LIBRARY OF CONGRESS CATALOGUING-IN-PUBLICATION DATA

Selter, Ronald M.
Ballparks of the deadball era : a comprehensive study of their dimensions, configurations and effects on batting, 1901–1919 / Ronald M. Selter ; with a foreword by Philip J. Lowry.
p. cm.
Includes bibliographical references and index.

ISBN 978-0-7864-6625-2
softcover : 50# alkaline paper ∞

1. Baseball fields — United States — History.
2. Stadiums — United States — History.
3. Baseball — United States — History. I. Title.

GV879.5.S45 2012   796.3570973 — dc22   2008033961

BRITISH LIBRARY CATALOGUING DATA ARE AVAILABLE

© 2008 Ronald M. Selter. All rights reserved

No part of this book may be reproduced or transmitted in any form or by any means, electronic or mechanical, including photocopying or recording, or by any information storage and retrieval system, without permission in writing from the publisher.

On the cover: "Brooklyn Base Ball Park, 1909,"
The Pictorial News Co., New York (vintage postcard, PicturesNow)

Manufactured in the United States of America

McFarland & Company, Inc., Publishers
Box 611, Jefferson, North Carolina 28640
www.mcfarlandpub.com

Foreword
by Philip J. Lowry

It is an honor to write a foreword for Ron Selter's book on Deadball Era ballparks and batting. When I needed an editor last year for the fourth edition of my ballparks book *Green Cathedrals*, he was the obvious choice, because nobody knows more about the details of old ballparks than does Ron.

Ron takes us on a journey through the ballparks of the Deadball Era, that roughly 20-year period of low scores, few homers and dominant pitching that ran from 1901 to 1919. We all remember of course the 16 major league teams that composed the two major leagues from 1903 until 1952. Ron covers each of these franchises, most of which played in three or more ballparks in the era's two decades. He also includes the Milwaukee Brewers of 1901, who moved to St. Louis to become the Browns in 1902, and the Baltimore Orioles of 1901–1902, who moved to New York to become the Yankees in 1903. Even Burns Park, used by the Detroit Tigers for Sunday games in 1901 and 1902 is included.

In the tradition of "ballpark effects," invented by Bill James in his early baseball statistical work, Ron analyzes the effects of ballpark size and configuration on batting by determining in great detail the difference between team batting records at home and on the road. The resulting information makes important new contributions to our treasure house of sabermetric data, statistics which analyze and explain the "why" behind the "how many" of baseball statistics.

If you want to know why certain teams had the highest batting averages and others had the lowest ones, why the all-time triples record was set by a Pirate in Forbes Field, and other similar questions, look no further. You have found the ballpark book which combines analysis and facts to help us understand why certain records almost had to be set in certain parks. Perhaps it was because of long power alleys, short or distant outfield fences, or huge amounts of foul territory. Either way, the answers are here.

Congratulations to Ron for breaking new ground in the analysis of Deadball Era ballpark effects.

Philip J. Lowry is the author of *Green Cathedrals*.

Contents

Foreword by Philip J. Lowry v
Preface 1
Introduction: Baseball in the Deadball Era 5
Abbreviations 11

1. **BALTIMORE** 13
   Oriole Park IV 13
2. **BOSTON** 17
   South End Grounds III 17
   Huntington Avenue Baseball Grounds 22
   Fenway Park 28
   Braves Field 33
3. **BROOKLYN** 37
   Washington Park III 38
   Ebbets Field 42
4. **CHICAGO** 47
   West Side Grounds 48
   South Side Park III 53
   Comiskey Park I 59
   Weeghman Park / Cubs Park 63
5. **CINCINNATI** 71
   League Park II 72
   Palace of the Fans 74
   Redland Field 78
6. **CLEVELAND** 81
   League Park III 82
   League Park IV 86

7. DETROIT ... 90
   Bennett Park ... 90
   Burns Park ... 97
   Navin Field ... 100

8. MILWAUKEE ... 103
   Lloyd Street Grounds ... 103

9. NEW YORK ... 107
   Polo Grounds IV ... 108
   Hilltop Park ... 113
   Polo Grounds V ... 121

10. PHILADELPHIA ... 125
   Baker Bowl ... 126
   Columbia Park II ... 132
   Shibe Park ... 135

11. PITTSBURGH ... 140
   Exposition Park III ... 141
   Forbes Field ... 145

12. ST. LOUIS ... 151
   Robison Field ... 152
   Sportsman's Park III ... 157
   Sportsman's Park IV ... 161

13. WASHINGTON ... 167
   American League Park I ... 167
   American League Park II ... 171
   Griffith Stadium ... 174

14. SUMMARY
   The Impact of Ballparks on Batting in the Deadball Era ... 180

Chapter Notes ... 183
Bibliography ... 187
Index ... 189

Preface

I am a baseball researcher with a long-time interest in ballparks. My principal research has been in the area of twentieth century major league ballparks. This book seeks to answer three inter-related questions: (1) what ballparks were used in the Deadball Era, (2) what were the configurations and dimensions of each of the ballparks, and (3) what impact did the greatly varied ballpark dimensions have on batting. The scope of this book covers all American League (AL) and National League (NL) regular-use ballparks in the Deadball Era, defined as 1901 through 1919. Included in the group of regular-use ballparks are all full-season ballparks and Burns Park, used by the Detroit Tigers for 23 Sunday home games in the 1901 and 1902 seasons. Excluded are ballparks used exclusively by the 1914–1915 Federal League and neutral-site ballparks used primarily for Sunday games or as emergency venues.[1]

Ballpark dimensional data from long ago are often difficult to interpret. There are obvious mistakes, such as typos in team guides and incorrect measurements. Then there are other mistakes that are not so obvious, as when team guides failed to record ballpark changes from the previous off-season, or when sources listed only "power alley" measurements rather than specifying left-center or right-center. In *this* book, the following dimensional definitions are used: left field (LF) and right field (RF) mean the distance from home to the foul poles; straightaway left field (SLF) and straightaway right field (SRF) mean 15 degrees from the foul line; left-center (LC) and right-center (RC) mean 30 degrees from the foul line; and center field (CF), as in dead center, means 45 degrees from the foul line. The center field corner dimensions are provided for rectangular ballparks. One dimension found for many contemporary parks, the *power alleys* (22.5 degrees), is not used, as this term and associated dimensions were not in use in the Deadball Era. In some cases dimensional data necessarily reflect the researcher's best judgment.

The ballparks are organized by city, with a separate chapter for each of 13 major league (ML) cities. Within each chapter, the ballparks are arranged in chronological order according to the year of first use. The following items of data are provided for each park:

Dimensions expressed in feet for LF, SLF, LC, CF, RC, SRF, and RF.
Fence Heights expressed in feet for LF, CF, and RF.
Average Outfield Distances expressed in feet for LF, CF, and RF–the average, for each field, of all points in that field.
Architect is identified for approximately half of the parks.
Capacity as defined by permanent seating only. In the Deadball Era, capacity was an elastic concept. The seating capacity of bleachers, for example, varied as without individual seats the size of the crowd in the bleachers was limited only by the maximum endurable

crowding. Permanent seating capacity excludes by definition any standees either in the stands or on the field. Also excluded are temporary stands, often called circus bleachers, and usually used for Opening Days and World Series. Where the capacity was estimated by the author, the capacity figure is denoted as Est. (e.g., 9,000 Est.).

Park Size/Composite Outfield Distance is the average outfield distance for the entire park, defined as the un-weighted average of the LF, CF, and RF average distances.

Park Site Area is the acreage of the land plat or property parcel.

Deadball Era Run Park Factor (Rank) measures a park's relative offensive characteristics. The average park in each league for any given season is defined as having a park factor of 100. Ballparks with run factors of noticeably less than 100 are pitcher's parks, and ballparks with run factors of noticeably greater than 100 are hitter's parks. The park factor for runs was only calculated for the seasons the park was used in the specified league during the Deadball Era. Thus the Fenway Park AL run factor excludes the NL usage of the park in 1914–1915. Parks are ranked by league among the 20 regular-use Deadball Era AL ballparks or the 15 regular-use NL ballparks. The sources for the run factors are (1) *Total Baseball* (for ballparks used only in the Deadball Era [e.g., Columbia Park in Philadelphia]), and (2) Retrosheet seasonal run factors computed as an un-weighted average of run factors for the Deadball Era seasons (for ballparks not used exclusively in the Deadball Era [e.g. Shibe Park in Philadelphia]).

Batting Park Factor measures the impact of the park's configuration and dimensions on batting. A top-level measurement of this is illustrated by each team's home-road batting data. A more meaningful comparison is batting data for particular ballparks vs. the other league parks. The best measure is the batting data for home team and visitors for each park compared to the batting data in games involving the same teams in the other parks. This comparison is measured by batting park factors. Park factors represent the relative batting (home team and visitors) in a given ballpark vs. the batting by the home team and opponents in road games (and are adjusted to compare with the theoretical league average ballpark). Thus park factors take into account the batting and pitching potential of both the home team and opponents. Park factors are already shown in baseball encyclopedias for home runs and runs. In this book, park factors are presented for a number of offensive statistics, including doubles, triples and home runs per at bat in addition to batting average, on-base and slugging percentage. This is the first time such park factor data has been available for the Deadball Era. Park factors are defined with the average park in the league for a given season set to 100. Batting park factors for the general offensive statistics of batting average, on-base, and slugging of greater than 100 indicate a hitter's ballpark, and park factors less than 100 indicate a pitcher's ballpark. Extra-base hit park factors of greater than 100 indicate that ballpark is better than the average ballpark in that league that season for that category (e.g., doubles). Note that park factors are relative measures, therefore direct comparisons of park factors between leagues are invalid, and comparisons of different seasons within the same league are only valid if all of the league's ballparks remained unchanged between seasons. If a change in ballparks in the league results in the replacement of a hitter's ballpark (with park factors noticeably greater than 100) with a pitcher's ballpark in the next season, then if all other variables are equal, all of the other parks in the league will experience an increase in their batting park factors. This theoretical effect actually happened in the AL between the 1902 and the 1903 seasons when the Baltimore ballpark (Oriole Park IV), a hitter's park, was replaced by the New York ballpark (Hilltop Park), a pitcher's park.

Park Size Methodology

Ballparks vary substantially in their outfield dimensions. While the variations in dimensions have diminished among major league ballparks built since World War II, recent ballpark construction may be reversing this trend. When comparing ballparks in the Deadball Era, substantial variations in park size are apparent. In New York City, the three ML ballparks — Ebbets Field, the Polo Grounds, and Yankee Stadium — had very little dimensional commonality. The following method was used to compute average outfield dimensions for the purpose of estimating park size.

Average Outfield Distances

1. Definition of terms: the LF and RF distances mean at the LF and RF foul poles respectively. CF means dead center field. RC is at a point 30 degrees off the RF foul line. LC is at a point 30 degrees off the LF foul line. RC and LC are points only. The only actual fields are LF, CF, and RF. RF is between the RF foul line and RC. LF is between the LF foul line and LC. CF is the area between the RC and LC points. Thus each field accounts for 30 degrees. By this definition there are no left-center or right-center fields, only left-center and right-center points.

2. To determine the average outfield distance for LF, CF, and RF, find the RF and LF (foul line) distances. This data is nearly always available. Determine the RC and LC distances. In many pre–World War II parks, the outfield walls were at 90 degrees to the foul line, and the left-center/right-center distances were 115 percent of the foul-line distances. If this is not the case for RF and LF fences, obtain as many points with known distances (3–10) for each field as possible. It is desirable to know the distance at each change of direction in the fence or substantial change in fence height. For each of the points selected, one needs to know the angle relative to the foul line (e.g., 15 degrees for straightaway RF) for each distance. The use of a ballpark diagram and a protractor to measure each angle makes this possible. An example: RF = 300 feet, 10 degrees = 350, 18 degrees = 370, and RC = 380. Compute the average distance for each angular interval: 0–10 degrees = (300+350)/2=325, 10–18 degrees = (350+370)/2=360, 18–30 degrees = (370+380)/2 = 375. Compute the weighted average RF distance by using the number of degrees in each interval as the weights. In the above example, the average RF distance is: ((325 x 10) + (360 x 8) + (375 x 12))/30 = 354.

3. For parks with straight and square fences (that is with the LF and RF fences at 90 degrees to the foul lines) all the way to the LC/RC point, the average LF/RF distance is equal to 1.052 times the foul-line distance.

Estimating Home/Road Batting Data

Team batting data (except for at bats and hits) by game does not exist for the AL for 1905–1909 and the NL for 1903–1909. To work around this problem of missing team batting data, a method was developed to estimate the home-road breakdown for each team's batting data and for their opponent's batting data. Combining the two sets of estimated home-road data permitted the calculation of batting statistics by park and thus the calculation of batting park factors. The methodology employed to produce estimated home/road batting data is provided in the Introduction.

Introduction: Baseball in the Deadball Era

The Game

The major league (ML) baseball season was shorter in the Deadball Era. The American League (AL) and National League (NL) both played a 140-game schedule from 1901 to 1903, and with expansion to the well-known 154-game schedule adopted in 1904. Exceptions were the 1918 season that was ended earlier than scheduled because of World War I (at about 126 games per team), and the 1919 season that was scheduled for 140 games. In the Deadball Era, teams often played a few more games than scheduled to make up tie games. A Deadball Era team could have as many as five tie games in a season. Because all games were played in ballparks without lights, there were often complete games of less than nine innings. These less-than-nine inning games were usually cut short by darkness (a frequent occurrence both early and late in the season) or, in a few colorful cases, by prior mutual agreement to limit the time of a game so one or both teams could catch a train.

A few rules were different in the Deadball Era. During the 1901–02 AL seasons, foul balls were *not* strikes. Before the 1931 season, batted balls that landed in fair territory before leaving the field of play (including into the stands in foul territory) were called bounce home runs. Thus it was possible for a batter to hit a 100-foot home run, such minimum-distance home runs actually did occur on a few occasions. Batted balls passing the fair side of a foul pole and landing foul were only foul balls, *not* home runs. Overflow crowds standing in the outfield sometimes necessitated temporary ground rules on balls hit into the crowds of on-the-field spectators. These ground rules usually called for balls hit into the overflow crowds to be ground-rule doubles (or in some parks triples). Such rules could inflate extra-base hits in the smaller parks by turning catchable fly balls into doubles, while they could decrease home runs in the larger parks by turning potential inside-the-park home runs into doubles. Such variations in the ground rules and the variations in the frequency of overflow crowds by park make the underlying relationship between a ballpark's configuration and batting far more difficult to ascertain.

Sunday games were very important as teams drew much better on Sundays than on any other day of the week, but Sunday baseball games were illegal in several ML cities. In Detroit and Cleveland in the early years of the AL, Sunday baseball was prohibited; that is why the Tigers played all their 1901 and 1902 Sunday home games in Burns Park, which was located just outside the Detroit city limits. The Pennsylvania teams (Philadelphia and Pittsburgh), all three New York City teams (Yankees, Giants and Dodgers until the 1919 season), as well as the Braves and Red Sox in Boston, were prevented by law from playing Sunday home games. This led to persistent league scheduling problems and, for the teams located in the aforementioned cities, frequent one-day road trips to play a legal Sunday game in another league city. Some teams that faced these prohibitions scheduled a few Sunday home games at neutral sites a considerable distance away. This explains why Detroit (1903 and 1905) and Cleveland (1902, 1903, and 1905) played a few "home" games in places like Columbus, Ohio, and Fort Wayne, Indiana.

The game was played in a different manner during the Deadball Era. First of all, the ball was dead and often dirty as well. If the cork-center ball introduced in 1910 was not noticeably dead at the start of a game, it would be by the time it had to be replaced. In nearly every ML ballpark in the Deadball Era, foul balls hit into the stands were supposed to be returned to the playing field. However, fans in some parks often could not be forced to return foul balls. Thus except for balls hit out of the park or foul balls not returned, the same ball continued in use inning after inning. The prevalent strategy was to play for one run at a time. There were lots of sacrifices and many stolen base attempts. The suicide squeeze was introduced early in the Deadball Era. Double-steal attempts with runners on first and third were a common offensive tactic.

As a result there was generally less offense and noticeably fewer runs per game. Batting as measured by league batting average (BA) in the Deadball Era was only slightly lower (5 percent) than in today's game where the ML average includes the beneficial effect of the designated hitter in the AL. What was markedly different was the significantly lower level of extra base hits, especially home runs, and to a lesser extent walks in the Deadball Era. Home runs in the Deadball Era were also far less homogenous than in today's game. In addition to bounce home runs, there were large numbers of inside-the-park home runs. In fact, during the first decade of the Deadball Era, inside-the-park home runs were the predominant type of home runs, accounting for 54 percent and 52 percent of total home runs in the AL and NL respectively, while bounce home runs accounted for another five percent. The standard over-the-fence-on-the-fly home run of the modern era was actually in the minority from 1901 to 1910. The lower levels of offense were partially offset by more errors per game, as Deadball Era gloves were downright primitive. The following table compares batting statistics between the Deadball Era (1901–1919) and today's modern era (2004–2006). All per-game data includes the total of both teams.

	Deadball Era	*Modern Era*
BA	.254	.267
Runs/G	7.84	9.51
2B/G	2.38	3.79
3B/G	0.93	0.38
HR/G	0.30	2.23
BB/G	5.44	6.69
Errors/G	3.53	1.30

One interesting aspect of baseball in the Deadball Era is the profusion of unearned runs. Fully 31 percent of all runs scored in the Deadball seasons were unearned; by contrast, in contemporary ML games only eight percent of total runs scored are unearned. Thus if one measures the average offense output by earned runs/game, there is 61 percent more offense in today's game than in the Deadball Era.

The Ball

The major leagues first used a new ball in 1910 that had a cork center wrapped by a rubber core. This new ball was known as the cork-center ball. The AL used this ball on a trial basis in many but not all games that season. The NL is known to have used the ball in at least some 1910 games. Inferring from the home run data (1909 vs. 1910), both leagues appear to have made widespread use of the new livelier ball in the 1910 season. Although not adopted officially and used regularly by both leagues until 1911, the effects of this livelier ball can be seen in the home-run rate. In 1910, home runs per 100 at bats increased 32 percent in the AL (0.273 to 0.357) and 42 percent in the NL (0.371 to 0.527) compared with the prior season. In 1911, the home-run rate jumped an additional 34 percent in the AL and 46 percent in the NL. This new cork-center ball is the primary reason for the increased number of home runs in the early teens.

Researcher and author David Vincent looked into the baseballs used during World War I and the post-war seasons in his recent book, *Home Run: The Definitive History of Baseball's Ultimate Weapon.*[1]

> The last change in 1920 involved the baseball itself. At the time, each league used a ball from a different manufacturer. The A. G. Spalding Company manufactured the National League baseball while Reach & Company made the sphere for the Junior Circuit. They were all made to the same specifications, the only difference being that the stitching on the cover of the National League ball had two colors, red and blue, while the American League ball had red yarn holding the outer cover on the ball.
>
> The league presidents and representatives of the manufacturers all agreed during the 1921 season that no changes had been made to the specifications of the baseball. The primary theory discussed at the time as the cause of the "rabbit" ball was the fact that during World War I the government took the best quality wool for its own use and commercial enterprises, such as Reach and Spalding, had to use wool of lower quality than they had previously used. With the end of the war, importers brought better quality wool from Australia into the United States. The yarn made from this wool was of better quality and was able to be wound tighter around the core of the baseball by the machines that completed that part of the process. The tighter winding was as a result of the better-quality yarn, not a change to the machines, and created a slightly harder, more elastic ball — one that batters could hit farther than the old baseball.
>
> The entry of the United States into the war had also depleted the ranks of workers in baseball factories, just as it had on the ball field. With new, inexperienced workers in the factories, the quality of the product was sure to deteriorate until the veteran laborers returned after the end of the war. Although machines performed the first part of the manufacturing process, workers hand-stitched the cover on the ball, and the post-war covers were probably more uniform in their quality than those used at the end of the Deadball Era.

It is not known exactly when, after the United States' entry into the war in April 1917, Australian wool became unavailable for the manufacture of baseballs. What is known is that the rate of home runs (per 100 at bats) dropped 17 percent in the AL and 20 percent in the NL for the 1917–1918 seasons compared to 1915–1916. The deterioration of the quality of the ball due to sub-standard manufacturing materials and less-skilled labor during World War I is likely the principal reason for the decrease in the home-run rate during the 1917–1918 seasons.

In 1919, the AL home-run rate exploded with a 125 percent increase over 1918 (.642 per 100 at bats vs. .286). In that same season, the NL home-run rate increased by a very noticeable but less spectacular 33 percent (.555 vs. .416). As the AL and NL baseballs had different manufacturers, the AL ball (made by Reach & Company) could have benefited by the availability of the higher-quality Australian wool. One interesting footnote to history: with the tremendous jump in the home-run rate during the 1919 AL season, the greatest home-run hitter in baseball, Babe Ruth, had an increase in his home-run rate of 93 percent, while the AL as a whole increased by 125 percent.

The Ballparks

Before 1900, most major league ballparks were simple small wooden grandstands hastily constructed around recreation fields, in some cases not even entirely enclosed by fences. At the start of the Deadball Era in 1901, all ML ballparks were built of wood, and all except two had only single deck grandstands. Only the grandstands in the Polo Grounds in New York, in the Baker Bowl in Philadelphia, and in the West Side Grounds in Chicago were double-decked. In addition to grandstands, all ML ballparks had one or more sets of flanking pavilions (covered bleachers) and/or foul-line bleachers, and some also had additional sets of outfield bleachers. These early ML wooden ballparks were confined by the street patterns of turn-of-the-century urban America. These ballparks were privately owned and thus could not use eminent domain to secure adjacent properties to expand the parks. Because of the limitations imposed by the pre-existing street patterns, Deadball Era ballparks were nearly always asymmetrical (only Chicago's Comiskey Park, built in 1910, was symmetrical). The pattern of urban streets in the East and Midwest (where all ML teams were located) resulted in city blocks generally having larger north-south than east-west dimensions. As the majority of these ballparks were oriented with the LF line running north-south, the smaller east-west dimensions of the ballpark's land parcels limited the park's RF dimension. As an example, the three Deadball ballparks in Philadelphia (Columbia Park II, Shibe Park, and Baker Bowl) had Opening Day left field dimensions that were between 38 and 118 feet greater than their right field dimensions. In addition Deadball ballpark dimensions varied tremendously from ballpark to ballpark; in 1901, left field dimensions measured 290 at American League Park I (Washington AL) and 410 at Robison Field (St. Louis NL).

Beginning with the erection of Shibe Park and Forbes Field in 1909, however, concrete-and-steel ballparks (often with some limited non-structural use of wood) became the rule. The new steel-and-concrete ballparks made up the Classic American ballparks. The definition of Classic ballparks are those steel-and-concrete ML parks built between 1909 (Shibe Park) and 1923 (Yankee Stadium). These big baseball palaces signaled the growing prominence of baseball and represent the golden era in ballpark design. By the start of the 1919 season, Robison Field, the NL ballpark in St. Louis, was the only wooden ballpark still being used in the majors. During the 19 years of the Deadball Era a total of 16 teams located in 13 cities used 34 different ballparks for one or more seasons, and these 34 ballparks had a total of over 50 different configurations.

The average size of the Deadball Era ballpark sites (the entirety of the land parcels including playing field, access ramps, and stands) was not large by today's standards. Deadball Era ML ballpark sites averaged 5.6 acres for the pre–Classic wooden parks, and only slightly larger (6.8 acres) for the Classic ballparks. Contemporary ML ballpark sites, typically with their sprawling parking lots, are much larger.

In this book, comparisons of ballpark dimensions are often made to the dimensions listed in the revised edition (1992) of *Green Cathedrals*. In late 2006, an updated edition of *Green Cathedrals* was published.[2] Comparisons of ballpark dimensions are not made with the 2006 edition, because the author served as an editor of the 2006 edition and was a major contributor of Deadball Era ballpark dimensions to that edition. To clarify situations of multiple ballparks with the same name in the same city (an example being Sportsman's Park I, II, III, and IV in St. Louis), this book uses the ballpark nomenclature of *Green Cathedrals* 2006 edition.

The Players

ML rosters during the Deadball Era were made up almost entirely of white players from the East, the Midwest, and the West; relatively few players were from the South. A number of American Indians (invariably called "Chief") and an occasional Cuban played in the majors, but African-Americans were uniformly excluded from the minor leagues as well as from ML baseball. Players with college baseball experience were rare. Roster limits were smaller than today's 25-player limit, which led to using far fewer pitchers per game, and complete games by starting pitchers were the norm (about 75 percent of all games were complete games). In addition, because of the small rosters, pitchers were often used as pinchhitters. In the Deadball Era, ML players were shorter and weighed less than today's players.

The Statistics

The Deadball Era Official AL and NL team batting data generally consist of ledgers that are a handwritten, inconsistent, and eye-straining statistical quagmire. The Official AL and NL data sheets are known as Day-By-Days (DBD), as each line on the team and individual player sheets is for a single game. For the 1901–1904 AL and 1901–1902 NL seasons there are no official team batting DBD records. For these seasons, the group Information Concepts Inc. (known as ICI in the baseball statistics literature) was charged with compiling team batting data for each game from primary sources for use in the pioneering Macmillan baseball encyclopedia. This data set is available in computer printouts and includes at bats, hits, doubles, triples, home runs, and base on balls. The Official DBD team batting data for the AL 1905–1909 and NL 1903–1909 consists of only at bats and hits. For the 1910–1912 AL seasons, the team DBD also includes doubles, triples, and home runs. For 1913–1919 AL and 1910–1919 NL seasons, the team batting DBD data added base on balls. However, the base-on-balls data for the 1918 AL season were illegible. Team home-road hit-by-pitcher data were compiled from individual player data provided by Pete Palmer for the 1901–1904 AL and 1910–1919 NL. In all cases where one or more categories of team batting were missing for individual seasons, the home-road splits of the data were estimated from the known team seasonal totals.

Home-run data (by season, by park, by type, and by field) for every home run in the Deadball Era were compiled by the author from newspaper game accounts and supplemented with home-run data from the SABR Home Run Log.

Estimated Home/Road Batting Data

To work around the problem outlined above of missing team home/road batting data, a method was developed to estimate the home/road breakdown of each team's and their opponent's full season batting data. Combining the two sets of estimated home/road data (team and opponents) permitted the compilation of batting data by park, and thus the calculation of batting park factors.

Data for runs scored and home runs are available by team for home and road game.[3] Offensive innings (for batters) were calculated from the All Games database, which lists the number of innings played for every ML Deadball Era game.[4] Adjustments in the number of home-game innings were made for home-team victories where the home team did not bat in the last inning and for walk-off home-team victories where there were partial home-team innings. This innings and batting data for the AL for the 1901 and 1902 seasons were used to develop a relationship between runs and hits above the seasonal average per inning. The known numbers of team runs in home and in road games were adjusted by subtracting 1.4 times the number of home or road home runs from each team's home or road runs. The 1.4 factor for the run value of home runs is the estimated run value (from Pete Palmer's linear weights) of home runs in the Deadball Era. Each team's full-season runs average (defined as runs per inning) was multiplied times the number of home-game innings to produce the expected number of runs for home games. The same method was used to compute the expected number of hits in home games. The actual number of runs scored and hits in home games were known for selected seasons. For each team in the 1901–1902 AL, home/road hits were compiled from the Official AL team DBD batting records. The actual and expected numbers of runs and hits in home games were compared; the differences between actual and expected runs and hits were called delta runs and delta hits. On average, the delta runs and delta hits — those above (or below) the expected level in home games — had an average relationship of 1.21 delta hits per delta run. This means that in the fixed number of innings played, it took on average 1.21 delta hits to produce one delta run in the 1901–1902 AL.

The same methodology was employed for road games. The delta at bats for home/road games were set equal to delta hits, as generally each additional hit in an inning would result in one additional at bat. The estimation of doubles and triples was based on the full-season proportion of each team's doubles and triples to hits and the applicable estimated park factor. These park factors were derived from other Deadball seasons for which complete home/road batting data were available. For walks, the full-season ratios of team walks to innings and the park factors were used to estimate the home/road allocation of the full-season team walks. Team data for hit by pitcher for the full season were divided between home/road on the basis of innings adjusted by the historical league average ratio of home-to-road hit by pitcher per inning.

How good are these estimates of batting data by park? The above methodology was used to estimate the home/road batting data for all AL teams and ballparks for the 1901 and 1902 seasons. The average error for each category of batting data was computed by dividing the estimated batting data for each ballpark (sum of team and opponents by park) by the actual value. The Average Error is independent of sign. The results follow:

Batting Category	Average Error
At Bats	0.7%
Hits	1.5%
Doubles*	7.3%
Triples*	11.8%
Home Runs*	0.2%
Base on Balls**	3.6%
Batting Average	1.6%
On-Base	1.2%
Slugging	1.3%

*Per At Bat
**Per Total Plate Appearance (AB+BB+HP)

Thus, the estimated values for each of the batting categories by ballpark are quite good for all categories except doubles (only fair) and triples (noticeably poor). The estimates for home-runs-per-at-bat must be quite good, as the actual number of home runs at home and on the road are already known.

Abbreviations

AB: At Bats
AL: American League
BA: Batting Average
BAL: Baltimore
BB: Base on Balls
BOS: Boston
Bounce: Bounce Home Runs
BRO: Brooklyn
CF: Center Field
CHI: Chicago
CIN: Cincinnati
CLE: Cleveland
DET: Detroit
G: Games (Games played; unplayed forfeits are omitted)
H: Hits
HP: Hit by Pitcher
HR: Home Runs
IPHR: Inside-the-Park Home Runs
LC: Left Center Field; for IPHR distributions it is the area in between LF and CF
LF: Left Field Line
MIL: Milwaukee
ML: Major League

NL: National League
NY: New York
OBP: On-Base Percentage
OPP: Opponents
OTF: Over-The-Fence; a category of home runs; includes Bounce home runs
OTHER: Other AL or NL Ballparks
PHL: Philadelphia
PIT: Pittsburgh
RC: Right Center Field; for IPHR distributions it is the area in between CF and RF
RF: Right Field Line
SABR: Society for American Baseball Research
SLF: Straightaway Left Field; 15 degrees off the LF line
SRF: Straightaway Right Field; 15 degrees off the RF line
SLUG: Slugging Percentage
STL: St. Louis
TPA: Total Plate Appearances (AB+BB+HP)
WAS: Washington, D.C.
2B: Doubles
3B: Triples

1

Baltimore

Previously a top NL franchise in the 1890s, Baltimore had fallen on hard times in 1898 and 1899. The NL then abandoned Baltimore after the 1899 season when the league contracted from twelve to eight teams. Without a team in the city after the 1899 season, the NL kept control of Union Park (also known as Oriole Park III), the ballpark used by the NL Baltimore Orioles in the 1890s. The absence of ML baseball in Baltimore made the city a prime target for the newly formed AL. The AL moved one of its original eight franchises to Baltimore for the 1901 season. As the AL was an outlaw league (but a self-proclaimed ML) in 1901, the AL had to build a new ballpark for its Baltimore team (also named the Orioles) to use for its home games. In the Deadball Era, playing Sunday baseball was not an option in Baltimore; it was illegal as late as the 1930s.[1]

After only two seasons, the Baltimore AL franchise was transferred to New York City for the 1903 season, where they became the Highlanders and later the Yankees. AL baseball did not return to Baltimore until 1954 when the St. Louis Browns moved and became the third version of the Baltimore Orioles. In the intervening years, ML baseball made a second brief appearance in Baltimore as the Federal League Terrapins played at Terrapin Park, a new ballpark located across the street from Oriole Parks III and IV, for the two years the league operated (1914–1915).

Oriole Park IV

Baltimore American League: 1901–1902

There were four wooden ballparks in Baltimore called Oriole Park. The first (Oriole Park I) was used by the American Association Baltimore Orioles in 1883–1889, and was located at the southeast corner of Barclay and 25th St.[2] The second one (denoted Oriole Park II) was used by the same American Association Baltimore Orioles from 1890 until May 1891. This second Oriole Park was nearby at the southwest corner of Greenmount Ave. and 29th St., a location that later became the site of Oriole Park IV. A third Oriole Park (Oriole Park III) was at the southwest corner of Barclay and 25th St. This park was home to the American Association Baltimore Orioles from May to October 1891 and the NL Baltimore Orioles for the 1892–1899 seasons. Oriole Park IV was built before the 1901 season for the new AL Baltimore franchise on the same site as Oriole Park II.

Oriole Park IV was located with Greenmount Ave. on the east, Barclay St. on the west, and 29th St. on the north, not far from downtown Baltimore. The wooden park consisted of three sections of covered grandstand that extended from about first base to about third base, with bleachers down each of the foul lines. Home plate and the grandstand were located near the northwest corner of the park site. As a result, the batters faced east-southeast. The playing field was laid out in a manner similar to Ebbets Field in Brooklyn, with the left field foul line meeting the left field perimeter fence at noticeably less than 90 degrees. With a rectangular park site, the right field foul line necessarily met the right field fence at more than 90 degrees. A result was the first-base and third-base bleachers converged with the foul lines. In addition there was a distant right-center field corner where the right and left field fences met. This right-center field corner was thus located at the corner of Greenmount Avenue and 29th Street.

The Basis of Oriole Park IV's Configuration and Dimensions

The basis of the park's configuration and dimensions were a 1902 Sanborn fire insurance map of the park,[3] and a photo of the park from *Diamonds*.[4] The 1902 Sanborn map showed the entirety of the depth along the north-south axis of the park site (about 490 feet). The eastern boundary (LF) as shown on the Sanborn was Greenmount Ave. However, the far western portion of the park site was cut off on the Sanborn map and therefore the park's western boundary (RF) was not shown. The width of the park site (about 480 feet) was estimated from photos and game accounts. A 1901 photo in *Baseball Memories: 1900–1909*[5] shows a moderate amount of foul territory adjacent to both first base and third base, and this was used to estimate the home plate to backstop distance (60 feet). As the location of home plate and the width of the park site had to be estimated, all of the park's outfield dimensions are estimates. The outfield fence in RF was angled much like the fence at Ebbets Field in Brooklyn; the lower two-thirds of the fence angled back away from the plate, and the top third of the fence was vertical.

Park data and dimensions for Oriole Park IV are shown below.

DIMENSIONS (estimated)

Years	LF	SLF	LC	CF	RC	SRF	RF
1901–1902	414	384	384	405	480	386	330

AVERAGE OUTFIELD DISTANCES

Years	LF	CF	RF
1901–1902	391	416	396

FENCE HEIGHTS (estimated from photographs)

Years	LF	CF	RF
1901–1902	10	10	10

CAPACITY: 8,000 (EST.)

PARK SIZE/COMPOSITE AVERAGE OUTFIELD DISTANCE: 401

PARK SITE AREA: 5.5 ACRES (EST.)

DEADBALL ERA RUN FACTOR: 115 (RANK: AL 3)

The Impact of the Park's Configuration and Dimensions on Batting

The home-road batting data showed the 1901 Baltimore Orioles with a team batting average of .325 at home, an astounding 61 points higher than the team's batting average on the road that season. The .325 mark for Baltimore at home in 1901 is the highest team average in the Deadball Era and the highest documented team home average in AL history.[6] On first impression, it seems that the Oriole's home park must have been an extremely good hitter's park. However, visitors to Oriole Park in 1901 hit .271 at Baltimore compared with .285 in their home parks. In 1902, the visitors hit .307 at Baltimore and .310 at home. Part of the explanation for these extreme home-road batting marks is the remarkable level of home-park advantage in the early years of the AL. For the 1901–1903 AL seasons, home teams won between 58 and 62 percent of their home games (excluding ties), teams on average had 10.9 percent better batting averages at home than on the road. In contrast, the typical home-road batting average differential in the 20th century has amounted to 4–5 percent (e.g., AL 1931–1939 was 4.9 percent; the NL 1920–1941 was 3.8 percent). It is the author's belief the reason for the extreme levels of home-park advantage in the early years of the AL was due to umpire intimidation. From newspaper game accounts, umpire baiting in the early years of the AL was a popular pastime for fans, players, and managers.

A study of home runs hit at Oriole Park IV during the 1901–02 seasons showed that 85 percent of the total home runs were inside-the-park home runs (IPHR). This proportion of IPHR at Oriole Park IV was far above the ML average (54 percent) for the first decade of the Deadball Era. This home-run data is consistent with the estimated dimensions that show Oriole Park IV to have been the second largest ballpark in the AL. There were only eight OTF home runs (excluding one bounce home run) hit at Oriole Park IV in the two seasons the AL used the park. Of these eight OTF home runs, five were to RF and three were to an unknown field. This home-run evidence supports the estimated RF distance (330) as being substantially less than the LF distance (414) derived from the Sanborn map. Home-road AL batting data for the 1901–1902 seasons showed Oriole Park IV to have been a noticeably above-average offensive park. Data for seven offensive categories were compiled and are provided below. Oriole Park IV in 1901–1902 was a better-than-average park for triples and below average for doubles, a finding that is consistent with the average outfield distance of 401 feet. Overall, the run factor (115) of Oriole Park IV in the Deadball Era was the second highest in the AL among full-season ballparks. The home-road batting data, the home-run data, and batting park factors are shown below in eight tables:

Home Runs by Type at Oriole Park IV

Year	Total	OTF	Bounce	IPHR
1901	21	1	1	20
1902	34	8	0	26

OTF Home Runs by Field at Oriole Park IV (excludes Bounce)

Year	Total	LF	CF	RF	Unknown
1901	0				
1902	8	0	0	5	3

Inside-the-Park Home Runs by Field at Oriole Park IV

Years	Total	LF	LC	CF	RC	RF	Unknown
1901	20	1	1	2	0	13	3
1902	26	7	0	3	0	13	3

Team Batting 1901 Baltimore

	G*	AB	H	2B	3B	HR	BB	HP	BA	OBP	SLUG
HOME	65	2244	730	89	75	10	178	25	.325	.381	.445
ROAD	69	2345	618	90	36	14	191	30	.264	.327	.351

*Excludes one game won by forfeit and not played

Team Batting 1902 Baltimore

	G	AB	H	2B	3B	HR	BB	HP	BA	OBP	SLUG
HOME	63	2125	655	92	63	17	194	24	.308	.373	.435
ROAD	77	2635	663	110	44	16	223	34	.252	.318	.345

Team Batting 1901 Baltimore & Opponents

PARK	G	AB	H	2B	3B	HR	BB	HP	BA	OBP	SLUG
BAL	65	4632	1376	183	111	21	332	50	.297	.351	.398
OTHER	69	4688	1285	195	86	24	381	51	.274	.335	.368

Team Batting 1902 Baltimore & Opponents

PARK	G	AB	H	2B	3B	HR	BB	HP	BA	OBP	SLUG
BAL	63	4445	1368	175	100	35	325	45	.308	.361	.416
OTHER	77	5274	1481	251	88	28	446	50	.281	.343	.378

Batting Park Factors at Oriole Park IV

Years	BA	OBP	SLUG	2B*	3B*	HR*	BB**
1901–1902	108	104	108	90	128	115	90

*Per AB
**Per Total Plate Appearance (AB+BB+HP)

2

Boston

The NL had a franchise in Boston since 1876, the first year of the NL's existence. In the 1890s the NL team, then called the Beaneaters, played in three ballparks. The first, South End Grounds II (1888–May 1894), was called the Grand Pavilion because of it ornate and distinctive grandstand. Unfortunately, the ballpark burned down in May 1894. The Beaneaters then played their home games at Congress Street Grounds until June 1894, while a new ballpark was being built on the burned-out site of South End Grounds II. This new ballpark was also called South End Grounds (denoted as South End III); however, it had a smaller and less impressive pavilion for its grandstand. The Beaneaters (later called the Braves) moved into South End Grounds III in July 1894, and they played there until late in the 1914 season.

After the 1900 season, the AL moved one of its franchises to Boston, and the team (one of the original eight franchises in the AL) built a new ballpark just north of South End Grounds III called (due to its location) Huntington Avenue Baseball Grounds. The AL team, known as the Boston Americans for the 1901–1907 seasons and as the Red Sox thereafter, played at Huntington Avenue Grounds for eleven years. Starting with the 1912 season, the Red Sox moved into a newly constructed Classic ballpark, Fenway Park. The Braves (as the NL team was now known) occasionally played big games in the much larger Fenway Park before they decided to build a new ballpark, Braves Field. While Braves Field was under construction, the Braves shared Fenway Park with the Red Sox from September 1914 through July 1915. This situation created an unusual home park effect; in the 1914 World Series, the AL's Fenway Park was actually the NL's home park during the Series.

During the Deadball Era, the Red Sox were the number-one baseball team in Boston and the dominant team in the AL, winning six pennants in 19 seasons. The Braves, on the other hand, won only one pennant (the 1914 Miracle Braves). Another constant in baseball in Deadball Era Boston was the prohibition on Sunday baseball. Not until 1928 was baseball on Sunday legal in Boston.

South End Grounds III

Boston National League: 1894–1914

The South End Grounds III ballpark was quickly built during the 1894 season to replace the South End Grounds II ballpark that had burned to the ground. Opening Day for the park was July 20, 1894. All three of the South End Grounds ballparks were located on the same site, at Walpole and Columbus Avenues in the Roxbury section of Boston, just south across the railroad tracks from the site of the AL's Huntington Avenue Grounds.

South End Grounds II, from the infield in 1888. After the fire in 1894, the grandstand was rebuilt in a similar but smaller fashion. Note the ornate spires on top of the grandstand, known as the Grand Pavilion, and the small number of figures in the team photo-that included players, coaches and the manager.

The LF dimension at South End Grounds was limited by the railroad tracks and yards (New York, New Haven, and Hartford Railroad) beyond the LF fence. In the same manner, the RF dimension was limited by Columbus Ave. Thus the park site was wedged into the space between the railroad yards and Columbus Ave. With the original location of home plate, the only variations in the dimensions that could occur were between straightaway LF and straightaway RF. As originally built, there was a small single-deck roofed grandstand (called a pavilion with 900 seats) and both first-base and third-base bleachers. At the time of the July 1894 opening of the park, the only stands in the outfield were a small set of bleachers in RF called the pie bleachers because they were triangular shaped, like a piece of pie. These pie bleachers ran from the Columbus Ave. fence in RF to beyond right center. Total seating capacity was about 5,000.[1] It was not long before the first expansion of the park occurred. After the 1894 season, two iron wings were added to the pavilion, and the capacity of the enlarged pavilion was now 2,300.[2] This expansion raised the park's total seating capacity to about 6,600. The next change to the ballpark occurred before the 1908 season. The pie bleachers were removed, and new and larger bleachers were built in the outfield, from the Columbus Ave. fence in RF to the railroad tracks fence in LF, with a gap in CF where the flagpole stood.[3] This CF gap was fenced off flush with the left and right sections of the outfield bleachers. Total capacity was now something less than 10,000. The final expansion of the park occurred before the 1912 season and involved three changes: (1) home plate and the left field foul line were moved about 10 feet to the west (and thus closer to the stands) and the field was re-oriented to the right, (2) two sections were added to the grandstand, and (3) the bleachers in LF-CF were dismantled and rebuilt as additions to the third-base bleachers. The re-orientation of the field was done such that the LF foul line intersected the LF railroad fence at 275 feet. The resulting RF foul line distance was 235, which was the major league minimum at that time. Two objectives were accomplished by these moves: (1) more seats (ones commanding higher prices) along the foul lines were added, and (2) the average LF distance was greatly increased. The new capacity of the park was about 11,000. At the same time, the flagpole, previously located in CF between the two sections of outfield bleachers, was moved to an in-play location in LC.

The Boston Braves (known at various times during the Deadball Era as the Beaneaters, Doves, and Rustlers) stayed at South End Grounds III until August 11, 1914. They then moved to Fenway Park to finish the 1914 season, and they played there for most of the 1915 season.

The Basis of South End Grounds' Configurations and Dimensions

The configurations and dimensions shown below are estimates based on park diagrams. Where possible, ballpark photos have been used to prove or disprove reported dimensions. The listed outfield dimensions for South End Grounds III were taken from *Green Cathedrals*; they are: LF 250 (1894), LC 445, deepest left-center 450, CF 440, RC 440, and RF 255.[4] The basis for the configuration and dimensions of South End Grounds III was a Sanborn Fire Insurance map of the park in 1895.[5] The Sanborn map showed the pavilion, first-base and third-base bleachers, and perimeter fences, but no bleachers in the outfield. This map permitted the location of home plate and the foul lines at unique locations such that they matched exactly the listed LF and RF dimensions for 1894. The location of home plate resulted in a home-plate-to-backstop distance of 80 feet. A new larger diagram was drawn using all of the above data from the Sanborn map. Based on numerous game accounts in the *Boston Globe*, the pie bleachers were added to the park diagram. The estimated extent and depth of the pie bleachers was based on a photo of 1903 Huntington Ave Grounds which showed the outfield and pie bleachers of South End Grounds III in the background.[6] The 1894 outfield dimensions, other than at the LF and RF lines, and all subsequent ballpark dimensions for 1901–1911 were derived from this diagram.

The second configuration of the ballpark came about with the construction of new LF-CF bleachers before the 1908 season. These new bleachers had a depth of 40 feet as reported in the *Boston Globe*.[7] The left end of the bleachers was at the junction with the LF fence at a point to the left of straightaway LF. The right end of the bleachers was at the junction with the RF Columbus Ave. fence and was to the left of straightaway RF. The park diagram, with the addition of the LC and RC sections of bleacher, was used to estimate the dimensions (other than the foul lines) for the park's second (1908–1911) configuration. For the 1909 season, the LF railroad fence was raised ten feet higher than in previous years.[8] In later years, descriptions of home runs over the LF fence mentioned a screen in LF.

The park's third and final configuration came about due to the 1912 relocation of the LF bleachers and the addition of two sections to the third-base side of the grandstand.[9] Descriptions of these relocated bleachers, that were rebuilt and added to the existing set of third-base bleachers, were contained in articles in the *Boston Globe*.[10] The reorientation of the playing field required the shortening of the first-base bleachers. The extent of the remaining section of bleachers in RF was taken from a 1914 Sanborn fire insurance map.[11] The new 1912 LF distance (275) and the new RF distance (235) were provided by the late ballpark researcher Larry

Zuckerman from reports in the Boston newspapers. A new ballpark diagram was developed with home plate being relocated and the field shifted to the right to fit the new LF and RF dimensions. All other dimensions were then calculated using this new park diagram. The dimensions and other ballpark data for South End Grounds III are shown below.

DIMENSIONS (calculated from park diagrams)

Years	LF	SLF	LC	CF	RC	SRF	RF
1894–1907	250	424	430	416	392	347	255
1908–1911	250	385	387	378	392	347	255
1912–1914	275	430	435	386	400	304	235

AVERAGE OUTFIELD DISTANCES

Years	LF	CF	RF
1894–1907	363	413	327
1908–1911	344	382	330
1912–1914	387	407	308

FENCE HEIGHTS (from *Green Cathedrals* and estimated from photos)

Years	LF	CF	RF
1894–1896	10	10	6–14*
1897–1907	10	10	6–20**
1908	6–10	6	6–20**
1909–1911	6–20	6	6–20**
1912–1914	6–20	6–10	6–20**

*The 14 foot height was the Columbus Ave. fence
**The 20 foot height was the Columbus Ave. fence

CAPACITY: 6,600 (1901–1907 Est.), 9,800 (1908–1911 Est.), 11,000 (1912–1914)

PARK SIZE/COMPOSITE AVERAGE OUTFIELD DISTANCE: 368 (1901–1907), 352 (1908–1911), 370 (1912–1914)

PARK SITE AREA: 4.5 ACRES

DEADBALL ERA RUN FACTOR: 107 (RANK: NL 3)

The Impact of the Ballpark's Configurations and Dimensions on Batting

South End Grounds III was one of the three top NL offensive ballparks in the Deadball Era. In the three configurations of the ballpark, the batting average park factors ranged from 99 to 103. The park factors for on-base and slugging were also slightly better than average at the ballpark. It was in home runs that the park made its impact on scoring. The home run park factor, 145 for 1901–1907, rose to 181 in the park's second configuration with the installation of the LF and CF bleachers. This second configuration (in place 1908–1911) also boosted doubles as the doubles park factor rose from 96 to 115. Never much of a park for three-base hits, none of the park's reconfiguration seemed to matter as the triples park factor varied only from 60 to 64. The third configuration (1912–1914) reduced the home run park factor from 181 to 132, still noticeably better than the average NL ballpark. At the same time, the park factor for doubles increased to 132.

While a far above average park for home runs, South End Grounds III was relatively unique for the Deadball Era in that nearly all home runs were of the OTF variety. Unlike nearly all other ML ballparks in the first decade of the Deadball Era, it was a poor park for IPHR, averaging a mere one IPHR per season. For OTF home runs, it was a far different story. The park averaged better than 29 OTF home runs per season (1901–1910) with a high of 48 in 1910. What is curious is that in the park's original configuration with straightaway LF distance of 424 and LC of 430, there were so few IPHR (nine in seven years). Perhaps in the park's original configuration there was an embankment in LF and left-center such as there was at Baker Bowl in Philadelphia and at the contemporary AL Boston ballpark, Huntington Ave Grounds. Such an embankment, if in fact it existed, would have cut down on the number of IPHR by causing well-hit balls to roll back toward the outfielders.

The effect of the 1912 reconfiguration of the playing field on home runs was both immediate and substantial. In the 1912 season, with the reorientation of the field and the removal of the LF bleachers, the number of OTF home runs to LF dropped from 40 in the prior season to just five! In the last season (1911) of the park's prior configuration, nearly all (97 percent) of the home runs were OTF home runs. Of these, 40 were to LF, five to CF, and 24 to RF (four were field unknown). For the 1912 season, there were 48 OTF home runs; five were to LF, 11 to CF, and 28 to RF (four were field unknown).

The home-run data and batting park factors for all of the Deadball seasons at South End Grounds III are shown in four tables below.

HOME RUNS BY TYPE AT SOUTH END GROUNDS III

Years	Total	OTF	Bounce	IPHR
1901–1907	202	193	0	9
1908–1911	177	175	2	2
1912–1914	106	100	1	6

OTF HOME RUNS BY FIELD AT SOUTH END GROUNDS III
(EXCLUDES BOUNCE)

Years	Total	LF	CF	RF	Unknown
1901–1907	191	119	0	51	17
1908–1911	173	104	6	54	9
1912–1914	99	7	25	60	7

INSIDE-THE-PARK HOME RUNS BY FIELD AT SOUTH END GROUNDS III

Years	Total	LF	LC	CF	RC	RF	Unknown
1901–1907	10	3	0	2	2	1	2
1908–1911	2	0	1	1	0	0	0
1912–1914	6	1	0	3	0	0	2

BATTING PARK FACTORS AT SOUTH END GROUNDS III

Years	BA	OBP	SLUG	2B*	3B*	HR*	BB**
1901–1907	99	100	97	96	60	145	101
1908–1911	103	103	104	115	63	181	104

Years	BA	OBP	SLUG	2B*	3B*	HR*	BB**
1912–1914	103	102	104	127	64	132	98

*Per AB
**Per total plate appearance (AB+BB+HP)

Huntington Avenue Baseball Grounds

Boston American League: 1901–1911

Before the 1901 season, Huntington Avenue Baseball Grounds was built for the new Boston AL team (known the Boston Americans for their first seven seasons and thereafter as the Red Sox). Located at Huntington and Rodgers Avenues in the Roxbury section of Boston, the ballpark site was just north, across the railroad tracks and yards, from the NL's South End Grounds. The Huntington Ave. site had previously been used as a temporary location for carnivals and traveling circuses, and as a result the area was dubbed the Huntington Carnival Lot.[12] The site was leased by Charles Somers, who, in addition to being the owner of the Cleveland franchise in 1901, was the financial backer of the Boston AL entry.[13]

The story of the selection of the site and the acquisition of the lease is told in Bill Nowlin's recent book *Red Sox Threads*.[14]

> Connie Mack, owner of the Athletics, was involved with the Boston Americans, too; he headed the small group selected to find a suitable site for the AL's Boston franchise. They visited possible locations in Cambridge, Charlestown, and Boston, but finally settled on a site not far from the National League park, the South End Grounds. The site was owned by Durand Associates and leased to the Boston Elevated Railway Company. Mack's committee (which comprised Hugh Duffy and Tommy McCarthy) asked John Dooley to speak with his partner in the J. R. Prendergast Company, a cotton brokerage. Daniel Prendergast was also a director of Boston Elevated Railway, and Dooley recalls an old newspaperman named Peter Kelley coming to his office on behalf of team owner Charles Somers to ask that Prendergast help convince the railway company to accept the site. Dooley says he prevailed upon Prendergast to have the Elevated accept the offer of $5,000 for the rights to use the land. It was Connie Mack who signed the lease on the Huntington Avenue land.
>
> To say the site was unimproved was an understatement. It was, in the words of Ed Walton, "no more than an expansive wasteland made up of heavily weeded bumps and lumps." It had been used as a circus lot—even the temporary home to Buffalo Bill's traveling Wild West Circus when a show would come to town. There was a fairly large pond on the property that children would splash into during summer months from a number of chutes they would slide down, as a water slide. In the winter, of course, people could ice skate there, but this was no high society skating pond. The area was largely bounded by rail yards, a huge Boston Storage Warehouse behind the length of the left-field bleachers, some stables, breweries, and a pickle factory. The United Drug Company was situated near enough to the park that one could often smell the chemicals at work.

Plans for the park were completed in February 1901, and called for a covered grandstand and uncovered bleachers located down the first and third base lines. Total seating capacity was to be 9,000.[15] Groundbreaking for the park occurred on March 7, 1901. The structure of the grandstand was built with expanded metal and roughcast concrete.[16] The rest of the park was built of wood, and the roof rested on a number of 28-foot-high columns. There were four entrances to the park, two on Huntington Ave. and two on Rodgers Ave. One of the two entrances on Huntington Ave., the one near the LF corner, was the access point for a wide walkway into the park which was at an angle to both the LF foul line and the Huntington Ave. fence. This diagonal walkway limited the LF distance and made the LF dimension necessarily less than the distance from home plate to the Huntington Ave. fence. There was a sloping embankment in LF in front of the Huntington Ave. fence that started about 50 feet in front of the fence and was used to accommodate overflow crowds. At the time of the 1901 opening of the park, there were no stands or bleachers in the outfield. The grandstand and home plate were in the southwest corner of the park site. An odd feature of the park was a large in-play tool shed located in CF. In addition, there was an in-play scoreboard mounted above the fence in RC.

After the 1904 season, a rectangular set of bleachers was added in LF.[17] These bleachers ran from a short distance left of the CF corner to nearly the junction of the entrance walkway fence and the Huntington Ave. fence. These bleachers could not run all the way to the LF foul line. These bleachers consisted of 14 rows of seats and had a low fence in front, and this last feature contributed to a number of bounce home runs into the LF bleachers starting with the 1905 season. The addition of these LF bleachers increased the park's capacity by an estimated 3,500 seats. According to the *Boston Globe*, the park's total capacity, reported as 9,000 when the park opened in 1901, was now surprisingly reported to be about 17,000. The next change to the ballpark occurred before the 1909 season. A 1909 game account in the *Chicago Tribune* observed, "President Taylor (of the Boston Red Sox) improved the park-new bleachers in CF, and moved the press box to the roof."[18] There was no mention of any increase in seating capacity. The next expansion was before the 1910 season and involved the extension of the third-base bleachers into fair territory in LF. This new section of bleachers crossed the LF foul line at about a 45 degree angle and extended to within 20–25 feet of the pre-existing LF bleachers. Having two set of bleachers referred to as LF bleachers starting with the 1910 season, led in the newspaper game accounts to numerous ambiguous references to home runs hit into the "LF bleachers."

The Red Sox stayed at Huntington Avenue Grounds until the end of the 1911 season, when they moved into one of the first Classic ballparks, Fenway Park. The Red Sox took the sod with them from Huntington Avenue Grounds to use in the infield at Fenway Park.

The Basis of Huntington Ave. Grounds' Configurations and Dimensions

Unlike the case with many other Deadball Era ballparks, there is no shortage of dimensional data for Huntington Avenue Baseball Grounds. The problem is that the available dimensional data have the unfortunate characteristic of being in substantial disagreement. The configurations and dimensions shown below are estimates based on park diagrams. Where possible, ballpark photos have been used to confirm or disprove reported dimensions. The listed outfield dimensions for Huntington Avenue Grounds were taken from *Green Cathedrals*.[19] They are:

    1901   LF 350, LC 440, CF 530, RF 280
    1908   LF 350, LC 440, CF 635, RF 320

The original plans for the building and the configuration of Huntington Ave Grounds, as reported in the *Boston Globe*, included a park diagram and outfield dimensions.[20] This article and diagram gave the park's dimensions as LF 350, CF 530, and RF 320. One limitation of this diagram is that the diagram did not extend to the RF fence. The diagram ends in left

Huntington Avenue Grounds, 1903. A view of the ballpark from the third-base side of the grandstand. Note the first-base bleachers that extend almost to the right-field foul line, the field-level dugouts in the far right of the photo, and the puny-looking right-field foul pole in contrast to today's sizeable foul pole/screens. (Photograph by the G. Chantering & Co., American Memory Collection [6a28813], Library of Congress.)

center field at the 32 degree point along the Huntington Ave. fence, and also ends along the RF foul line about 75 feet before the RF corner. The alignment of the RF fence was derived from a 1904 photo in the *Boston Globe*.[21] In this photo, the fence at the back of the angled first-base bleachers extends, at an angle of noticeably more than 90 degrees to the foul line, into fair RF for about 30–40 feet. At this point there is a kink in the fence to the left as one moves away from the RF foul line. A second photo of the park, taken for the 1903 World Series, also shows the RF fence from the foul line to past the kink.[22] To meet the LF fence at the CF junction (at a home plate-to-CF distance of 530), the RF fence beyond the kink must have been aligned at 95 degrees to an extension of the RF foul line. A new diagram on a larger scale was drawn using all of the above data. All subsequent ballpark dimensions were derived using this diagram. The 1908 CF distance of 635, listed in *Green Cathedrals*, could only have been correct if the park was expanded towards the east and the RF fence realigned at much more than 95 degrees to the foul line. In addition, as the CF bleachers were added for the 1909 season, the CF dimension of 635 could have existed for only that one season. The 1901 RF dimension of 280 listed in *Green Cathedrals* bears closer examination. In the seven seasons that the Huntington Ave. Grounds' RF dimension of 280 was said to have been in effect (1901–1907), there were a grand total of only four home runs hit over the RF fence. This works out to be a rate of 0.6 OTF home runs to RF per season. By comparison, the RF distance at Columbia Park (Philadelphia AL) was known to have been 280. At Columbia Park in the 1901–1908 seasons, home runs over the RF fence averaged 9.8 per season — some 16 times the rate of comparable home runs at Huntington Ave. Grounds. Thus, in addition to being contradicted by the 1901 listed RF dimension, the home-run data show that it is most unlikely that the RF dimension at Huntington Ave. Grounds was ever 280.

The LF bleachers, built before the 1905 season, were located on the Huntington Ave. Grounds diagram based on a photo and story in the *Boston Globe*.[23] From this photo, the LF bleachers were determined to be 14 rows deep with a narrow walkway in front just behind a short fence. The depth of these bleachers at ground level was estimated at 27 feet. The front of the bleachers, if extended to the LF foul line, would have intersected the foul line at a distance of 348 feet from home plate. The horizontal extent of the LF bleachers was estimated from the photo in the *Boston Globe*. The left end of the bleachers was about 20 feet to the right of the junction of the walkway fence with the Huntington Ave. fence. The right end of the bleachers extended to nearly dead CF. The park diagram, with the LF bleachers added to it, was used to estimate the dimensions for the 1905–1908 time period for LF and CF (RF was unchanged during the life of the park). The location of the CF bleachers added for the 1909 season was based on two factors: game accounts of an IPHR hit "to the flagpole" during the 1910 season, which established that the flagpole was still in play, and photos that showed the location of the flagpole in front of the right side of the CF fence. Therefore, the CF bleachers must have been located behind the flagpole. The location and extent of the third-base bleachers, added for the 1910 season, was based on a photo in *Diamonds*.[24] The new 1910 LF distance of 305 was derived from a story in the *Boston Post* where sportswriter Paul Shannon commented that the LF distance at the new Fenway Park would be 19 feet more than LF at Huntington Ave. Grounds. The LF distance at Fenway Park when it opened in 1912 was 324 feet. Adding the third-base bleachers to the Huntington Ave. ballpark diagram, such that they cut the LF foul line 305 feet from home plate, established the location of the front of the bleachers. These new third base-LF bleachers extended about 50 feet past the foul line into fair territory in LF.

Park data and dimensions for Huntington Avenue Grounds are shown below.

DIMENSIONS

Years	LF	SLF	LC	CF	RC	SRF	RF
1901–1904	350	388	433	530	412	365	320
1905–1908	350	360	402	530	412	365	320
1909	350	360	402	456	412	365	320
1910–1911	305	360	402	456	412	365	320

AVERAGE OUTFIELD DISTANCES

Years	LF	CF	RF
1901–1904	393	470	366
1905–1908	370	457	366
1909	370	441	366
1910–1911	363	441	366

FENCE HEIGHTS (from *Green Cathedrals* and estimated from photos)

Years	LF	CF	RF
1901–1904	14	14	14–28*
1905–1908	6–14	6–14	14–28*
1909	6–14	6–14	14–28*
1910–1911	3–14	6–14	14–28*

*The 28-foot fence height was only at the scoreboard mounted above the RF fence

CAPACITY: 9,000 (1901–1904), 12,500 (1905–1908 Est.), 14,000 (1909–1911 Est.)

PARK SIZE/COMPOSITE AVERAGE OUTFIELD DISTANCE: 410 (1901–1904), 398 (1905–1908), 392 (1909), 390 (1910–1911)

PARK SITE AREA: 6.3 ACRES

DEADBALL ERA RUN FACTOR: 102 (RANK: AL 8)

The Impact of the Ballpark's Configurations and Dimensions on Batting

In the park's original 1901–1904 configuration, Huntington Ave. Grounds was the largest park in the AL. Unlike today when large parks (adjusted for altitude in the case of Coors Field) are known as pitcher's parks, this ballpark was average or above average in every offensive category except doubles (see data in the Batting Park Factors table below). In 1903, the AL adopted the foul-strike rule; foul balls with less than two strikes on a batter would now be counted as strikes. Despite this rule change, which reduced the overall batting average in the AL by about 15 points, the home batting average for the 1903 Boston Americans increased from .280 in 1902 to .296 in 1903. The batting average park factor (98 in 1901, and 97 in 1902) jumped to 108 for 1903. One possible contributing factor is that the negative impact of the adoption of the foul-strike rule affected Huntington Ave. Grounds much less than the other AL ballparks. Another indirect contributing factor was the elimination of Burns Park in Detroit and Oriole Park IV in Baltimore. Burns Park, which was an extreme hitter's park in 1902 (with a batting average park factor of 116), was not used in 1903. When the Baltimore franchise was transferred to New York, Oriole Park IV (with a 1902 batting average park factor of 108) was replaced by Hilltop Park in New York (1903 batting average park factor of 97). As these two changes made the other AL parks worse for hitters, the batting average park factor for Boston's Huntington Ave. Grounds and the other AL parks had to increase. However, these two factors are believed by the author to be only partial explanations for the large increase in the Huntington Ave. Grounds batting average park factor.

The large outfield dimensions at Huntington Ave. Grounds turned hits that would have been doubles at other parks into triples and IPHR. With the generous outfield dimensions in the park's original configuration, nearly all (96 percent) of the home runs were IPHR, as OTF home runs were rare; there only six such home runs. Despite being the biggest park in the AL, Huntington Ave. Grounds managed to post the third highest home run park factor in the 1901–1904 time period (only Washington 1901–1903 at 189 and New York 1903–1904 at 208 had higher home run park factors).

The effect on batting of the installation of the LF bleachers for the 1905 season was noticeable, but generally not very substantial. The 1905–1909 park factors decreased slightly for batting average, on-base, and slugging. The park factor for doubles increased slightly, while triples decreased (156 to 126) as one would expect with the shorter LF and LC dimensions. The small decrease in the batting average, on-base, and slugging park factors may have been due to the poorer batter's background that resulted from the new outfield bleachers which extended into CF. One noticeable effect of the installation of the new LF bleachers was more OTF home runs (an impressive-sounding 425 percent increase in OTF home runs-but still amounting to only four per season), most of which (15 of 21) were of the bounce variety. Thus, the LF bleachers led to the number of bounce home runs increasing from less than one per season (1901–1904) to about four per season (1905–1908). Nearly all of the bounce home runs hit in the 1905–1908 seasons were hit into the LF bleachers. For the 1909 season, with the construction of the CF bleachers, the proportion of IPHR declined to 58 percent of the total vs. 81 percent in 1905–1908. The park factor for doubles increased, while the triples park factor decreased (132 to 82), as one would expect with the shorter LF dimension. At the same time, total OTF home runs and OTF home runs to LF increased sharply. OTF home runs (excluding bounce home runs) were 2.0 per season in 1905–1909 and 18.5 in 1910–1911. OTF home runs to LF increased over the same time periods from 1.25 per year to 15 per year. As would be expected with the shorter LF and CF dimensions, the proportion of IPHR dropped again, this time to 47 percent of the total 1910–1911 home runs. In addition, the successive changes in the ballpark's configuration led to changes in the distribution by field of IPHR. The proportion of IPHR to CF increased with each change in configuration.

The home run and batting park factor data are shown below.

HOME RUNS BY TYPE AT HUNTINGTON AVE. GROUNDS

Years	Total	OTF	Bounce	IPHR
1901–1904	160	6	1	154
1905–1908	113	21	15	92
1909	31	13	9	18
1910–1911	88	47	10	41

OTF Home Runs by Field at Huntington Ave. Grounds
(Excludes Bounce)

Years	Total	LF	CF	RF	Unknown
1901–1904	5	1	1	3	0
1905–1908	6	4	0	2	0
1909	4	1	0	2	1
1910–1911	37	30	5	2	0

Inside-the-Park Home Runs by Field at Huntington Ave. Grounds

Years	Total	LF	LC	CF	RC	RF	Unknown
1901–1904	154	11	11	62	30	15	25
1905–1909	110	7	6	56	9	15	7
1910–1911	41	3	1	25	7	4	1

Batting Park Factors at Huntington Ave. Grounds

Years	BA	OBP	SLUG	2B*	3B*	HR*	BB**
1901–1904	101	101	104	71	156	139	105
1905–1909	100	100	103	85	126	168	102
1910–1911	95	98	98	103	82	191	108

*Per AB
**Per Total Plate Appearance (AB+BB+HP)

Fenway Park

Boston American League: 1912–19

Before the 1912 season, the Boston Red Sox built Fenway Park at Lansdowne Ave., Ipswich St., and Jersey St. (later Yawkey Way), a site located in the Fens only a half-mile from the Red Sox's prior park, Huntington Ave. Grounds. The term Fens referred to a marshy area in Boston on the south side of the Charles River from which Fenway Park got its name. In the building of Fenway Park, the Red Sox did make use of a portion of their Huntington Ave. Grounds' improvements; they took the sod from the old ballpark to use in the infield at Fenway Park. The announced plans for the park, published in October 1911, included a covered grandstand, a large first-base pavilion, and two sections (RF and CF) of outfield bleachers.[25] Noticeably missing were any stands (either bleachers or a covered pavilion) down the LF foul line. The multi-angled park site amounted to 365,308 square feet or 6.3 acres. Capacity was planned to be 28,000, with 15,000 in the grandstand, 8500 in the first-base pavilion, and 4500 in the bleachers. On Opening Day (April 20, 1912) the park actually consisted of (1) a concrete-and-steel single-deck covered grandstand extending about 50 feet beyond both first base and third base, (2) a first-base pavilion (with covered bench seats) that extended past the RF foul pole a short distance into fair RF, and (3) bleachers that started in the right side of CF and extended part way into RF. Total seating capacity was about 23,000, as the previously planned RF bleachers were not built.[26] The main entrance was behind home plate on Jersey St., with the entrance to the CF bleachers in deep RF, past the end of the first-base pavilion. There was a sloping six-foot-high embankment in LF that started about 10 feet in front in front of the 25-foot-high wall and was on occasion used as a place to erect temporary bleachers. Besides being a new ballpark built with the latest construction techniques (steel and concrete), Fenway Park was one of the first parks to have an electric scoreboard that was located in LF.

This configuration was substantially altered by features that were added just before the 1912 World Series. These new features consisted of (1) a new section of open bleachers (reserved seats for the World Series) extending from close to the third-base end of the grandstand to the LF wall, (2) a new section of open bleachers in RF that connected on the right edge to the existing first-base pavilion, and (3) temporary outfield seating in front of the existing CF stands/walls in LF, CF, and RF (1200 seats), as well as an additional row of boxes in front of the permanent grandstand (900 seats).[27] Note that the installation of the new outfield bleachers created an interesting in-play gap between the RF and the CF bleachers after the temporary World Series stands had been removed. The seating capacity for the 1912 World Series was estimated to have been about 34,100, although the announced attendance in two of the World Series games at Fenway Park exceeded 34,600. The removal of the temporary seats built for the World Series left the 1913–1919 regular season capacity at about 32,000.

A new entrance to the third-base bleachers on Lansdowne St. was added for the 1914 season. The park was completely rebuilt before the 1934 season and modified slightly in recent years. The Red Sox have stayed at Fenway Park to the present day.

The Basis of Fenway Park's Configurations and Dimensions

The configurations and dimensions shown below are based on park diagrams and are supplemented, in part, by an estimate for the straightaway RF distance in the 1912 regular season configuration. Where possible, ballpark photos have been used to confirm or disprove reported dimensions. The first plans for the configuration of Fenway Park, as reported in the *Boston Globe*, included an artist's impression of the park and outfield dimensions.[28] This article gave the park's planned dimensions as LF 325, CF 450, and RF 330. In the illustration of the ballpark, the stands consisted of a single-deck grandstand, and outfield seating included contiguous sections of bleachers in RF and CF. However, the Opening Day photos and the attendance (24,000 including standees) revealed that the RF bleachers had not been built.[29] The Opening Day photo of CF showed an open space adjacent to the right side of the CF bleachers. In addition, no interior fence is visible — only the high perimeter fence behind and to the right of the CF bleachers. The park's architect, Charles E. McLaughlin, produced a finely detailed diagram of Fenway Park for the 1912 World Series, which was published in the *Boston Globe*.[30] This diagram included the infield and baselines, which established the scale used to derive the park's Deadball Era dimensions: LF 324, CF 458, and RF 314. Since the originally planned RF bleachers were not built until September 1912, there was a large open space between the right side of the CF bleachers and the left edge of the first-base pavilion for the duration of the 1912 regular season. If, in this RF area, there was no interior fence in place during the 1912 regular season, then the limits of more than half of RF would have been the perimeter fence. The straightaway RF point at the perimeter fence (15 degrees off the foul line) was a distant 481 feet from home plate. The conclusion that there was no interior fence in RF is corroborated by the description in the *Boston Globe* of the new RF bleachers being built "in the large open space between the first base pavilion and the CF bleachers."[31] The 1912–1919 home-run data for Fenway Park support this conclusion. In the 1912 season, there were a total of 15 IPHR hit at the park, compared to an average of only 3.4 per season in the next seven years (1913–1919). Of these 15 IPHR, four were to RF or RC. In the next seven seasons, IPHR at Fenway Park to RF or right-center averaged 1.4 per year.

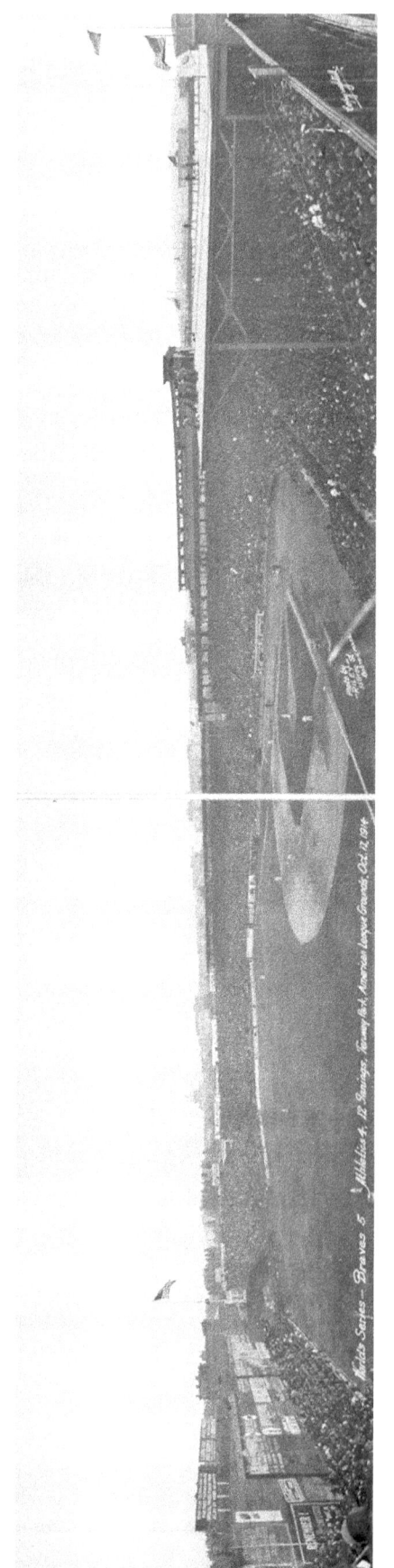

Fenway Park during the 1914 World Series. Surprisingly, Fenway Park was the home park of the NL Boston Braves in the 1914 World Series. The Red Sox graciously allowed the Braves to use their much larger ballpark. Note the temporary seats in front of both the left-field wall and center-field flagpole. During the regular season, there were no seats and these areas were in play. (Photograph by John F. Riley of Boston MA, Panoramic Photographs Collection [6a29764], Library of Congress.)

Another source of information about the park's original 1912 configuration and dimensions is from the Osborn Engineering Co. plans for Fenway Park.[32] These plans cover only the area of the grandstand and the area from the third-base end of the grandstand to the LF wall. Excluded are both the first-base pavilion and CF bleachers. On the Osborn plans, the planned LF dimension was 308, and the home-plate-to-backstop distance was 62. No other dimensions could be obtained. These Osborn Engineering Co. plans also show the third-base bleachers extending to the LF wall with the last two sections of these planned bleachers being flush against the LF foul line. The 1912 World Series newspaper coverage revealed that these stands had not been built for the 1912 regular season. When built for the World Series, photos show the last section of the third-base bleachers (nearest the LF wall) being cut off and out of alignment with the LF foul line.

A 1914 Sanborn fire insurance map of Fenway Park was used to compare dimensions with the 1912 World Series diagram. The known LF and RF dimensions were used to locate HP on the 1914 Sanborn map. Note that on both diagrams the LF wall is at 90 degrees to the foul line. The dimensions from the *Boston Globe's* World Series diagram were compared with the dimensions obtained using the Sanborn diagram. The following results list the angular location and the distance from home plate for various ballpark locations using each diagram.

Location	Globe Diagram	Sanborn Map
Junction 1B Pavilion–RF Bleachers	3 degrees/358	3 degrees/358
Left Front Corner RF Bleachers	15 degrees/404	18 degrees/404
Right Front Corner CF Bleachers	17 degrees/406	20 degrees/410
Left Front Corner CF Bleachers	38 degrees/404	41 degrees/406
Back of CF Notch	40 degrees/496	40 degrees/493
Dead CF	45 degrees/458	45 degrees/459
RF at 10 Degrees	10 degrees/378	10 degrees/374
RC at 30 Degrees	30 degrees/402	30 degrees/407

In comparing the two sets of dimensions, it is useful to note that a 1/16 inch measurement error on either of the diagrams would result in a dimension error of five-to-six feet.

All LF dimensions are exactly the same due to the LF distance being 324 on both diagrams and the geometry of the LF wall being at 90 degrees to the LF foul line on both diagrams. Which diagram is correct? A study of Fenway Park photos from the 1912–1917 time period revealed that the CF bleacher configuration and location on the Sanborn diagram appears to be correct. For sure, the rectangular shape of the CF bleachers shown in the *Globe* diagram is wrong, as a 1917 photo reveals the back left section of the CF bleachers to be cut off at a diagonal to the rest of the CF bleachers. In addition, the extent of the CF bleachers (to 41 degrees on the Sanborn vs. 38 degrees on the *Globe* diagram) appears to better match the 1917 CF photos. The location and alignment of the CF bleachers on the Sanborn map were used to modify the World Series diagram and the CF dimensions were then revised.

Park data and dimensions for Fenway Park are shown below.

DIMENSIONS (from the 1912 World Series and 1914 Sanborn diagrams)

Years	LF	SLF	LC	CF	RC	SRF	RF
1912	324	335	374	458*	407	481	314
1913–1919	324	335	374	458*	407	404	314

*Deepest point was 496 at the junction of the LF wall and the fence behind the CF bleachers

Average Outfield Distances

Years	LF	CF	RF
1912	341	419	439
1913–1919	341	419	387

Fence Heights (from *Green Cathedrals* and estimated from photos)

Years	LF	CF	RF
1912	25*	4–10*	4–20
1913–1919	25*	4–10*	4

*On top of six-foot embankment in LF and the left side of CF

PARK SIZE/COMPOSITE AVERAGE OUTFIELD DISTANCE:
400 (1912), 385 (1913–19)

ARCHITECT: Charles E. McLaughlin/Osborn Engineering

CAPACITY: 23,000 (1912 Est.), 32,000 (1913–1919)

PARK SITE AREA: 6.3 acres

DEADBALL ERA RUN FACTOR: 94 (Rank: AL 14)

The Impact of the Ballpark's Configurations and Dimensions on Batting

In the park's original 1912 configuration, Fenway Park was the largest ballpark in the AL. For the 1912 season, the home-road batting data showed Fenway Park to be a generally average hitter's park, and the 1912 batting park factors showed the park to have been very close to average in every offensive category except home runs (see data in the Batting Park Factors table below). The reduction in the RF dimensions for the 1913 season did nothing to improve the park's batting park factors. Fenway batting park factors for every offensive category, except for doubles and walks, were below average (less than 100) for the rest of the Deadball Era (1913–1919). Overall (measured by the run factor) in the Deadball Era, the park ranked near the bottom of the AL. This was a surprising finding, given the park's well-deserved reputation in the modern era as the best hitter's park in the AL.

With the generous CF and RF dimensions of the park's original configuration, the majority (75 percent) of 1912 home runs were of the inside-the-park variety. OTF home runs, despite the relatively close 324 LF dimension, averaged only 4.5 per season in the Deadball Era (at Fenway 1912–1919). The configuration change from 1912 to 1913 resulted in a large drop in the average RF distance from 439 to 387. A consequence was a drop in IPHRs from 15 to three, and a drop in the home-run park factor of more than 50 percent. Thus, in this Deadball Era ballpark, a reduction in outfield dimensions resulted in a drop in total home runs due to the reduced dimensions' negative impact on IPHR. Fenway Park in the Deadball Era was a far below average ballpark for home runs. In the 1916 season, the home team Red Sox managed only one home run at Fenway, while the visitors matched that total. In road games, the Red Sox hit 13 home runs, and their opponents hit seven, giving Fenway Park a home-run park factor for 1916 of 11. Overall, Fenway Park was the site of 75 home runs during the eight seasons from 1912–1919. Of these 75 home runs, 36 were OTF, a category that included three bounce home runs. Total home runs at Fenway averaged 9.4 per season (1912–1919), while the other seven parks in the AL averaged 20.7 home runs per season. Note that the Fenway Park home run totals for 1914 and 1915 were inflated because they include a few NL home runs since the Boston Braves used Fenway Park for about one full season between late 1914 and early 1915. Home runs at Fenway Park were below the levels at other AL parks because the LF wall (25 feet) on top of the six-foot height of Duffy's Cliff eliminated bounce home runs to LF, while sharply reducing OTF home runs to LF. In addition, the modest distances to LF precluded virtually any IPHR (only one in eight seasons). Of the three Deadball Era bounce home runs at Fenway Park, none were to LF; one was into the CF bleachers, and the other two were to RF. Unlike in the modern era, OTF home runs over what is now called the LF Green Monster (it was not green in the Deadball Era) were not numerous — a total of 18 in eight seasons. When they did occur, they were nearly always worthy of special mention in the newspaper game accounts. In the Deadball Era, only Babe Ruth and Tillie Walker hit two or more home runs over the LF wall at Fenway. In fact, in 1918 Walker, as a member of the visiting Philadelphia A's team, did it a fourth time! At Fenway Park, OTF home runs to CF and RF were even less common (15 over eight seasons); most of them by a well-known Boston Red Sox left-handed pitcher/outfielder. The home-run data and batting park factors for Fenway Park are shown below.

HOME RUNS BY TYPE AT FENWAY PARK

Years	Total	OTF	Bounce	IPHR
1912	20	5	0	15
1913–1919	55	31	3	24

OTF HOME RUNS BY FIELD AT FENWAY PARK (EXCLUDES BOUNCE)

Years	Total	LF	CF	RF	Unknown
1912	5	4	0	1	0
1913–1919	28	13	3	11	0

INSIDE-THE-PARK HOME RUNS BY FIELD AT FENWAY PARK

Years	Total	LF	LC	CF	RC	RF	Unknown
1912	15	0	0	11	1	3	0
1913–1919	24	1	0	16	2	5	0

BATTING PARK FACTORS AT FENWAY PARK

Years	BA	OBP	SLUG	2B*	3B*	HR*	BB**
1912	100	99	102	112	115	75	97
1913–1919	97	99	95	108	90	31	106

*Per AB
**Per Total Plate Appearance (AB+BB+HP)

Braves Field

Boston National League: 1915–1919

On August 18, 1915, the Boston Braves moved from Fenway Park to their new home park, Braves Field. The ballpark was located on Babcock St., near the Charles River and immediately south of the Boston and Albany railroad tracks. The park site was previously the home of the Allston Golf Club. Near Commonwealth Ave. and Gaffney St., the NL ballpark was only one mile from the AL ballpark (Fenway Park) that had opened three years earlier. As the Boston and Albany railroad tracks running west to east curved to the south, so did the perimeter LF wall. Thus the LF wall, which started at less than 90 degrees to the LF line, ran at a decreasing angle to the LF line as one moved toward CF. Also in LF was an in-play scoreboard set into the fence. Unlike most Classic ballparks, Braves Field was unconstrained in size by the pre-existing urban street pattern. The size of the original land plat (excluding the portion along Commonwealth Ave. that was sold off shortly after the purchase), was 10.5 acres; by comparison, the average Classic ballpark had a park site of 6.8 acres. This location also meant the ballpark was subject to cold winds blowing off the Charles River from LF towards home plate.

The steel-and-concrete Braves Field was one of the later Classic ballparks to be built. Unlike most Classic Era ballparks, Braves Field did not have a double-deck grandstand. Rather, the park consisted of a large single-deck grandstand and first-base and third-base pavilions (which were actually just uncovered bleachers down the foul lines) and a set of bleachers in right field. The right-field bleachers became known as the "Jury Box" when a sportswriter spotted exactly 12 (surely uncrowded) fans in the 2,500 seat bleachers. On the right side of the Jury Box was a ground-level runway that was the access route to the bleachers from the nearby park entrance. This bleacher's entrance to the park was located behind and to the right of the Jury Box. The front of the Jury Box extended from near (about 20 feet) the RF foul pole to about that same distance to the left of straightaway RF. To the left of the Jury Box, the fence ran along the left side of the Jury Box and went straight back to the RF perimeter fence. Thus any ball hit past the right-fielder to the left of the Jury Box could bounce or roll to the RF fence. At that point the fence was nearly 475 feet from home plate. In deep RC, an exit gate was available for fans in the grandstand and pavilions to use after the game. Other than the Jury Box, all of the seating was in foul territory. On Opening Day (August 18, 1915), Braves Field was the largest ballpark in the country, seating 45,000, a total made up of grandstand 18,000, pavilions 24,500, the RF bleachers (the Jury Box) 2,500.[33]

The original configuration of Braves Field was maintained until the start of the 1928 season, when an interior fence in LF and CF was erected that drastically reduced the park's once-generous dimensions.

The Basis of Braves Field's Configuration and Dimensions

The Opening Day dimensions listed in *Green Cathedrals* are LF 402, LC 402.5, CF 440, CF corner 550, RC 402, RF 402, and backstop 75.[34] The listed dimensions in *Lost Ballparks* are LF 402, CF 550, and RF 402.[35] A 1925 Sanborn fire insurance map of Braves Field was used to produce a park diagram with a backstop distance of 75 feet.[36] This derived location of home plate produced a LF dimension consistent with the above-listed LF dimensions. The dimensions derived from the Sanborn map were LF 400, LC 415, CF 461, RC 542, and RF 369. The diagram-based dimensions were compared with the listed dimensions above. All three sources agree that LF was 400–402, while the deepest part of the park, around 550, was somewhere in CF. The LC and dead CF distances were limited by the alignment of the LF-CF wall. The CF corner dimension listed in *Green Cathedrals* (550) was actually at the right-center field point. The RF dimension was more complex. Photos show the RF line passing the left edge of the first-base pavilion. Photos of the park in later years show a 20-foot gate connecting the left edge of the first-base pavilion with the right edge of the front of the Jury Box. If the gate were not in place or left open, then the RF foul line would have intersected at about the midpoint of the right side of the Jury Box. In that case, the Opening Day RF dimension would have been about 400. It is the author's judgment that the gate was always in place and the resulting RF dimension on Opening Day was 369 for the following two reasons: (1) If the gate were not in place or left open, then the crowd going to or from the Jury Box would have interfered with balls hit into the RF corner, and (2) a bounce home run in a game less than a week after the opening of the ballpark (on August 23, 1915) rolled under the gate between the first-base pavilion and the Jury Box.[37]

The park data and dimensions for Braves Field are shown below.

DIMENSIONS (calculated from park diagram)

Time Period	LF	SLF	LC	CF	RC	SRF	RF
1915–1919	400	400	415	461	542	390	369

FENCES HEIGHTS (from *Green Cathedrals*)

Years	LF	CF	RF
1915–1919	10	10	8–10*

*The 8-foot height was only at the exit gate in right-center

AVERAGE OUTFIELD DISTANCES

Time Period	LF	CF	RF
1915–1919	401	469	407

ARCHITECT: OSBORN ENGINEERING

CAPACITY: 45,000

PARK SIZE/AVERAGE OUTFIELD DISTANCE: 426

PARK SITE AREA: 10.5 ACRES

DEADBALL ERA RUN FACTOR: 89 (RANK: NL 16)

The Impact of the Ballpark's Configurations and Dimensions on Batting

Braves Field in the Deadball Era was the worst hitter's park in the NL (see the Batting Park Factors table below). The runs park factor was 89, meaning scoring was 11 percent below the average NL ballpark and the lowest in the NL. The park's large dimensions (it was the largest in either league) and the adverse pattern of winds made the ballpark the best pitcher's park in the NL. While Braves Field was good park for IPHRs, it consistently vied with Redland Field in Cincinnati for the lowest overall home run park factor in the NL (typically in the range of 30 to 70) averaging 52 during the Deadball seasons.

The owner of the Braves, James Gaffney, wanted to encourage IPHR, so the park was designed with ample dimensions.[38] The distance to LF was 400, CF 461, RC 542, and RF 369.[39] In passing, note that the intent to design the park to encourage IPHRs was a success; of the 235 home runs hit at Braves Field through the end of the 1927 season, 219 (93 percent) were IPHR. The first home run to clear the left-field fence was not hit until the 1925 season (by Frank Snyder of the NY Giants).[40] The only non-bounce OTF home run in the Deadball Era was hit into the Jury Box in right field (in 1917 by Walton Cruise). There were two bounce home runs during the Deadball Era; both were fluke home runs. One (August 23, 1915) rolled under the gate in the RF corner, and the second (July 11, 1919) bounced through a hole in the LF scoreboard.[41] The IPHR at Braves Field were mostly to CF and RC, the two deepest portions of the ballpark. The dimensions of the park, which essentially prevented OTF home runs and promoted IPHR, may have partly been motivated by self-interest; with the park's unique and generous dimensions, the Braves accounted for 80 percent more home runs than their opponents in the park's four-and-a-fraction seasons during the Deadball Era.

As would be expected for the worst offensive ballpark in the NL, Braves Field was below average in batting average, on-base, slugging, and doubles. Despite the very large outfield dimensions, the triples park factor was only slightly above average (112). Perhaps the very large dimension in RC (542) turned potential triples into IPHR.

HOME RUNS BY TYPE AT BRAVES FIELD

Years	Total	OTF	Bounce	IPHR
1915–1919	56	3	2	53

OTF HOME RUNS BY FIELD AT BRAVES FIELD (EXCLUDES BOUNCE)

Years	Total	LF	CF	RF	Unknown
1915–1919	1	0	0	1	0

INSIDE-THE-PARK HOME RUNS BY FIELD AT BRAVES FIELD

Years	Total	LF	LC	CF	RC	RF	Unknown
1915–1919	53	2	1	11	29	6	4

BATTING PARK FACTORS AT BRAVES FIELD

Years	BA	OBP	SLUG	2B*	3B*	HR*	BB**
1915–1919	94	96	93	87	111	52	102

*Per AB
**Per Total Plate Appearance (AB+BB+HP)

3

Brooklyn

Brooklyn had a franchise in the NL from 1890 to 1957. The Brooklyn team in the NL was called the Bridegrooms or Grooms (1890–1898) and the Superbas starting with the 1899 season. In addition, there was a Brooklyn entry in the American Association from 1884 to 1890. That meant there were two ML Brooklyn teams in the 1890 season. The NL used three ballparks in the 19th Century: (1) Washington Park II for the 1890 season, (2) Eastern Park for 1891–1897, and (3) Washington Park III for 1898–1912. Eastern Park was in the East New York section of Brooklyn, while all of the Washington Parks were in the Red Hook section. Washington Park III was located across the street from the location of the previous NL park, Washington Park II. Until 1898, Brooklyn was an independent city and was one of the largest cities in the United States. In 1898, Brooklyn was absorbed into New York City, and thereafter was one of five boroughs of the city. However, Brooklyn retained its separate cultural and sports identity into the latter half of the 20th Century. In the early part of the 20th Century, the Brooklyn team picked up the nickname Dodgers. This nickname came about because fans on the way to the ball games had to dodge the trolleys that operated on the many streetcar lines in that part of Brooklyn.

The Dodgers left Washington Park III after the 1912 season as it had become too small for the increasingly popular game of baseball. The Dodgers' new ballpark, Ebbets Field, was one of the most famous Classic ballparks, both larger and better built (steel-and-concrete) than the all-wooden Washington Park III. Ebbets Field was named for the principal owner of the Dodgers, Charles H. Ebbets. Built on a site in the Pigtown area of the Flatbush section of Brooklyn, Ebbets Field was considered to be a major improvement to the neighborhood, as the site was formerly the Pigtown garbage dump. The Dodgers used the ballpark until they moved to Los Angeles after the 1957 season.

After the Dodgers left Washington Park III for Ebbets Field following the 1912 season, Washington Park had a revival in 1914 with the Federal League coming to town. For the 1914 season, the Federal League placed a franchise in Brooklyn. The Brooklyn Federal League team (called either the Brook-Feds or the Tip Tops) took over and rebuilt the old wooden Washington Park III in steel and concrete. The architect for the rebuilt ballpark was Zachary Taylor Davis, who earlier had been the architect for two Classic ballparks in Chicago, Comiskey Park and Weeghman Park (later known as Wrigley Field). The Federal League ballpark (designated Washington Park IV) was used for only two seasons and was torn down in 1926.

New York state prohibited Sunday baseball until early in the 1919 season. After 1915, Brooklyn considered playing Sunday home games at Harrison Field in Newark, New Jersey, some 10–15 miles away, but such plans never materialized. One reason was the International League's Newark team had the territorial rights. During the 1907–1914 period, two innovative professional Sunday baseball games were played in New York City. One (July 4, 1909) was a charity function at Washington Park III to aid newsboys, and the other at the Polo Grounds was to aid survivors of the sinking of the *Titanic* (April 21, 1912). Both games skirted the prohibition on Sunday baseball by charging no admission. Instead, fans bought a program at the usual admission price. Finally, in 1919 the New York state legislature passed a bill legalizing Sunday baseball, and the bill was signed by the governor on April 19, 1919. The first completely legal ML Sunday baseball games in New York City were played on May 4, 1919. The response was tremendous. Brooklyn hosted the Braves at Ebbets Field before 22,000 fans, while 35,000 watched the Giants play the Phillies at the Polo Grounds.[1] These were the largest regular season crowds at both ballparks to that date.

Washington Park III

Brooklyn National League: 1898–1912

The fourth ballpark used by the NL in Brooklyn was called Washington Park III. Two prior ML ballparks had previously been in the area (on the other side of the intersection). These parks were also called Washington Park (denoted as Washington Park I and Washington Park II) as the site had been the headquarters of General Washington in the 1776 battle of Long Island during the Revolutionary War. Located in central Brooklyn between Third and Fourth Avenues and First and Third Streets, Washington Park III was an all-wooden ballpark built before the start of the 1898 season.[2] The park was not very large and especially not very grand; the cost of construction was between $60,000 and $100,000. The club shared construction costs with two streetcar companies that served the area. The street pattern in this area of Brooklyn had the avenues running southwest-northeast and the streets running northwest-southeast. The park site had dimensions of 500 feet northwest-southeast and 375 feet southwest-northeast, amounting to 4.2 acres. This park size was smaller-than-average for the wooden pre–Classic ML ballparks. Home plate and the main entrance to the covered grandstand were located close to the corner of Third St. and Fourth Ave. The LF line was parallel to Third St., and the RF line was parallel with Fourth Ave. As a result of this orientation, LF could be much deeper than RF as the RF dimension was always limited by the width of the park site along Fourth Ave. Another result of the park's orientation was that home plate-CF axis was about due north-south, and the afternoon sun shined into the eyes of the first baseman.

At the time of the park's opening in 1898, the seating areas consisted of (1) a covered grandstand that extended from about first base and beyond third base, (2) a pavilion (actually unroofed 50 cent seat bleachers) located down the LF foul line, and (3) bleachers in CF.[3] These CF bleachers were located along First St. and extended from about RC to the CF corner. These bleachers had a short life in that location, and they were torn down soon after Opening Day and moved to the RF foul area. The problem with the CF location was that white-shirted fans created a terrible batter's background.[4]

Because of the restricted depth of RF, the playing field was basically rectangular with LF much longer than RF. When opened in 1898, the planned seating capacity of Washington Park III was about 12,000, 5,000 in the grandstand and 3,200 each in the pavilion and in the bleachers. There was a clubhouse located behind the LF fence, but inside of the perimeter wall that abutted Third Ave. The perimeter wall in RF was along First St. On the other side of First St. was a row of apartments called Guinea Flats. These buildings were the site of rooftop and fire escape seating from which lucky fans could view the game without having to buy a ticket (at least not a ticket from the ball club). In 1901, the club added a 29-foot canvas screen on top of the RF wall to block the view of the fans the club considered "freeloaders."

The seating capacity of the park was expanded before the 1908 season by the construction of bleachers on the left side of CF. The bleachers ran diagonally from the right edge of the clubhouse near left-center field to the junction with the RF wall. In addition, over the years the club added more seats in front of the grandstand, such that the home plate-to-backstop distance in the last couple of seasons was reduced to 15 feet. With the new CF bleachers and the addition of seats in front of the grandstand, total capacity reached 16,000 by 1912.

The Basis of Washington Park III's Configurations and Dimensions

The basis for the configuration of Washington Park III was the ballpark perspective in *Baseball Memories: 1900–1909* and a Sanborn fire insurance map.[5] One month before the 1898 Opening Day, a story in the *Brooklyn Daily Eagle* provided a park diagram that showed the planned CF bleachers would have 15 rows or a depth of about 30 feet.[6] Using this information, the Opening Day 1898 dimensions (before the relocation of the CF bleachers) were estimated to have been LF 376, straightaway LF 389, LC 455, the CF corner 458, CF 375, RC 298, straightaway RF 305, and RF 295. Dimensional data for this ballpark has an interesting history. In 1898, a newspaper article (not in the *Daily Eagle*) reported the RF dimension to be all of 215 feet. This same story in the *Daily Eagle* reported the planned RF dimension as 310. The 1898 home-run data shows only 25 home runs at Washington Park that season. In addition, a review of numerous game accounts from the 1901 season showed no bleachers in fair RF.[7] If the RF dimension was truly 215 for the 1898 season, there should have been a much larger number of home runs at Washington Park. Both the ballpark configuration in *Baseball Memories: 1900–1909* and the 1906 Sanborn map are consistent with a RF dimension of 295, not 215. In addition, the RF dimension listed in *Green Cathedrals* for 1899 was 295.[8] The conclusion is that the reported 1898 RF dimension of 215 was likely a misprint and should have been 295. The RF dimension of 295 from *Green Cathedrals* was used on the Sanborn map to produce a ballpark diagram. The other dimensions (LF 376 and CF 417) were derived from the park diagram. Both the LF and RF fences were at 90 degrees to the foul lines and met in CF, but not at a right angle. In 1901–1907, the interior LF fence ran at 90 degrees to the foul line until the right edge of the LF clubhouse. At that point, the LF-CF fence ran at more than 90 degrees until the junction with the RF wall. In LC, at least a portion of the fence was made of pickets, likely to permit access to the clubhouse.[9] The deepest part of the park was the "CF corner" at the junction of the LF fence and RF wall (a distance of 500 feet). This CF corner (the corner angle was actually not 90 degrees) was in CF but was actually closer to LC than to dead CF.

After the 1901 season, the club removed the canvas screen on top of the RF wall, making the RF barrier 13 feet in height. Before the 1905 season, the RF wall was raised to a height of 20 feet. It appears that the club's motivation in varying the height of the RF wall was not to curb or encourage home runs, but to obstruct the view from the Guinea Flats across First St.

The addition of CF bleachers before the 1908 season changed the dimensions in LC and a portion of CF. The LF fence located to the right of the clubhouse, which in 1901–1907 had angled back towards the CF corner, now consisted of the front of the CF bleachers. The CF bleachers angled across CF at less than 90 degrees to the LF foul line until hitting the

RF-CF wall at a point that was actually to the left of dead CF. The estimated depth and alignment of the new CF bleachers were based on ballpark photos and were added to the Sanborn map to produce a second ballpark diagram. LC was now 415 instead of 445, and the deepest point in the ballpark, which had been 500 feet, was now 443. One interesting aspect of the alignment and location of the new CF bleachers is they did not affect the batter's background.

The dimensions and other ballpark data for Washington Park III are shown below.

DIMENSIONS (calculated from park diagrams)

Years	LF	SLF	LC	CF	RC	SRF	RF
1901–1907	376	389	455	417*	340	305	295
1908–1912	376	389	415	425**	349	313	302

*Deepest point was the CF corner at 500 feet
**Deepest point was to the left of dead CF at 443 feet

FENCES HEIGHTS (from *Green Cathedrals* and newspaper articles)

Years	LF	CF	RF
1901	12	12–20	42
1902–1904	12	12–13	13
1905–1907	12	12–20	20
1908–1912	12	8–20	20

AVERAGE OUTFIELD DISTANCES

Years	LF	CF	RF
1901–1907	398	419	310
1908–1912	396	409	318

ARCHITECT: COOTS

CAPACITY: 12,000 (1898–1907), 14,000 (1908–1911 EST.), 16,000 (1912)

PARK SIZE/AVERAGE OUTFIELD DISTANCE: 376 (1901–1907), 374 (1908–1912)

PARK SITE AREA: 4.2 ACRES

DEADBALL ERA RUN FACTOR: 93 (RANK: NL 14)

The Impact of the Park's Configurations and Dimensions on Batting

Washington Park III was generally not a good hitter's park. The runs park factor for 1901–1912 was 93, one of the lowest in the NL during the Deadball Era. For home runs, the park was moderately poorer than the average NL ballpark. A study of all home runs hit at Washington Park III during the 1901–1907 seasons showed that 57 percent of the total home runs were IPHR. This proportion of IPHR at Washington Park III was about the same as the

ML average (54 percent) in the first decade of the Deadball Era. This home-run data is consistent with the estimated dimensions that show Washington Park III in 1901–1907 to have been noticeably larger than the average NL ballpark in LF and CF, but noticeably smaller in RF. Changes in the configuration of the ballpark had little effect on batting. For the 1901 season when the RF wall and canvas screen was 42 feet in height, there were three OTF home runs to RF. In the next three seasons, when the removal of the canvas screen reduced the height of the RF barrier to 13 feet, there was a per season average of 4.3 OTF home runs to RF. The addition of CF bleachers for the 1908 season in front of the CF corner reduced the deepest CF point from 500 to 443, but had no noticeable effect on home runs. The only noticeable impact of the new 1908–1912 configuration was on triples. The park factor for triples went from 91 (1901–1907) to 110 (1908–1912). As would be expected in a park with an average LF distance of nearly 400 feet and RF at a much more hitter-friendly 310–318 average distance, nearly all OTF home runs were to RF. In the 12 seasons of use during the Deadball Era, there were no home runs hit over the LF fence and only two over the CF fence.

Home-run data and the batting park factors for Washington Park III are shown below in four tables.

Home Runs by Type at Washington Park III

Year	Total	OTF	Bounce	IPHR
1901	19	4	0	15
1902–1904	42	17	2	25
1905–1907	65	33	0	32
1908–1912	112	45	2	67

OTF Home Runs by Field at Washington Park III

Year	Total	LF	CF	RF	Unknown
1901	4	0	0	3	1
1902–1904	15	0	1	13	1
1905–1907	33	0	1	31	1
1908–1912	43	0	0	39	4

Inside-the-Park Home Runs by Field at Washington Park III

Year	Total	LF	LC	CF	RC	RF	Unknown
1901	15	2	1	10	0	0	2
1902–1904	25	11	4	10	0	0	0
1905–1907	32	6	2	19	0	0	5
1908–1912	67	34	11	18	1	1	2

Batting Park Factors at Washington Park III

Years	BA	OBP	SLUG	2B*	3B*	HR*	BB**
1901–1907	96	99	95	101	91	76	110
1908–1912	97	99	97	98	110	83	109

*Per AB
**Per Total Plate Appearance (AB+BB+HP)

Ebbets Field

Brooklyn National League: 1913–1919

The fifth ballpark used by the NL in Brooklyn was Ebbets Field. Prior to the building of the ballpark in 1912–1913, the site had been used as the Pigtown garbage dump. Ebbets Field was located on the outskirts of Brooklyn (at the time of its opening) in an area known as Flatbush. In 1913, the ballpark site was bounded by Montgomery St. on the north, by Franklin Ave. (later Cedar Place) on the west, Sullivan St. on the south, and Bedford Ave. behind the RF wall on the east.[10] Note that Sullivan St. did not run east-west, but had a slightly southwest-northeast orientation and thus did not form 90 degree angles with either Cedar Place or Bedford Ave. The dimensions of the park site were 478 feet along Sullivan St., 638 feet along Cedar Ave. and 474 feet along Bedford Ave. The east-west dimension of 450 feet along Montgomery St. on the north limited the RF dimensions for the life of the ballpark. The shape of the park site was thus not a rectangle, but a trapezoid. Because of the trapezoid shape, the first-base portion of the grandstand was parallel to Sullivan St. and that made the RF line intersect the RF wall at more than 90 degrees. On the west side, the third-base portion of the grandstand was parallel to Cedar Place, and the LF line converged with the third-base bleachers. The total area of the park site was 5.7 acres, less than average for the Classic ballparks. Home plate, the center of the grandstand, and the main entrance (a neo-classical rotunda) were all in the southwest corner of the park site at the intersection of Cedar Place and Sullivan St.

Ebbets Field, one of the most famous of the Classic ballparks, was built largely of steel and concrete, and had a capacity of 24,000 from 1913 to 1919. The ballpark's seating facilities in the Deadball Era consisted of a double-deck steel-and-concrete grandstand, which ran from the RF corner to beyond third base, and a large set of concrete bleachers that ran from the third-base end of the grandstand down the LF line. There was no seating in the outfield. The LF line was canted a few degrees to the west of a north-south orientation so that the LF foul line intersected the LF wall at 80 degrees. As the LF and RF walls intersected in the CF corner at 90 degrees, the RF foul line intersected the RF wall at 100 degrees. For the last 20–25 feet of the LF foul line nearest to the LF wall, there was zero foul territory. The foul line near the LF corner in 1913 was, in fact, the front of the bleachers.

The Basis of Ebbets Field's Configurations and Dimensions

The basis for the initial 1913 configuration of Ebbets Field was the original plans for the ballpark.[11] These plans included several ballpark diagrams that showed the park's boundaries, the location of the stands, and the perimeter fences. In addition, the location of home plate and the foul lines were included. Home plate was in the southwest portion of the park. The RF and LF dimensions derived from the park diagram in the original plans match exactly the LF and RF dimensions for 1913 Ebbets Field taken from *Green Cathedrals*: LF 419 and RF 301. Dead CF in the original plans was at the CF corner, a tremendous distance of 507 feet from home plate. There were generous amounts of foul area in the infield. From home plate to the backstop, the distance was 76 feet, and it was nearly as much (72 feet) from home plate to the grandstand along extensions of each foul line. The foul area narrowed down to 55 feet at both first and third base.

No sooner was the park opened (for an exhibition game vs. the Yankees on April 5, 1913), than a serious design flaw was discovered. The ballpark had only two entrances: the one on

First game at Ebbets Field, 1913. A view of Ebbets Field during a pre-season exhibition game vs. the New York Yankees (April 5, 1913). The notation at the bottom of the photo refers to the Yankee pitcher Ray Caldwell, who is on the mound in the photo. Note the famous kink in the right-field wall and the ample foul ground in the right-field corner. (American Memory Collection, Library of Congress.)

Cedar Place was for the LF bleachers, and the main entrance to the park and only entrance to the grandstand was the ornate and circular rotunda. The problem was the ticket windows were inside the rotunda, and fans with tickets had to push through the lines of other fans in line to buy tickets. In addition, at the end of the game the thousands of fans in the grandstand all tried to exit through the rotunda. Charlie Ebbets was quick to act. By April 29, 1913, four new entrances were added to the ballpark, two on Cedar Place and two on Sullivan St.[12] In addition, to help with the outflow of fans at the conclusion of the game, an exit gate was cut into the wall in right-center field.

For the 1914 season, a small change was made in the ballpark's configuration. Home plate was moved nine feet towards LF and about two feet towards RF. A revised park diagram for 1914–1919 was developed, and the new dimensions calculated. This move of home plate made the backstop distance 85 feet. The infield foul area was now asymmetrical. The LF dimension became 410 and RF 300. Dead CF, now just to the left of the CF corner, was 496. The deepest point in the park was still the CF corner at 500 feet. It appears the reason for this configuration change (at least the move of home plate towards RF) was to eliminate the absence of foul territory in the LF corner that had existed with the original configuration. Such a move would have eliminated disputes about balls hit into the LF corner being in or out of play.

Given the known dimensions from the original plans and the matching LF and RF dimensions in *Green Cathedrals*, the Deadball Era dimensions for Ebbets Field contain only a small amount of uncertainty. The following tables show the dimensions, fence heights, and average outfield distances in the Deadball Era for each configuration of Ebbets Field.

DIMENSIONS (calculated from park diagrams)

Years	LF	SLF	LC	CF	RC	SRF	RF
1913	419	417	441	507	388	326	301
1914–1919	410	408	431	496*	386	321	300

*The deepest point in the park, the CF corner, was 500

FENCES HEIGHTS (from *Green Cathedrals*)

Years	LF	CF	RF
1913–1919	20	20	19

AVERAGE OUTFIELD DISTANCES

Years	LF	CF	RF
1913	422	455	333
1914–1919	414	449	330

ARCHITECT: CLARENCE R. VAN BUSKIRK

CAPACITY: 24,000

PARK SIZE/COMPOSITE AVERAGE
OUTFIELD DISTANCE: 400 (1913), 394 (1914–19)

PARK SITE AREA: 5.7 ACRES

DEADBALL ERA RUN FACTOR: 102 (RANK: NL 6)

The Impact of the Park's Configuration and Dimensions on Batting

Ebbets Field in its Deadball seasons (1913–1919) was close to an average offensive park. The ballpark's run park factor was 102, or two percent above average, while the home run park factors were in a range of 40 to 85 (see Batting Park Factors in the fourth table below). This below-average home run park factor was definitely held down by the low level of OTF home runs. The ballpark had generous dimensions in LF and CF. In the history of the ballpark, no home runs were ever hit over the perimeter LF or CF walls. Unlike at most other ML ballparks in the second decade of the Deadball Era, the proportion of IPHR was and remained high, amounting to 68 percent of the total home runs hit in the ballpark's seven Deadball seasons.

Consistent with the Ebbets Field's run factor of 102, the batting average and on-base park factors were 98–99, and the slugging park factors were 93–95. Ebbets Field in 1915 had the second largest LF (Robison Field in St Louis was the largest) and the largest CF. Despite the ballpark's generous dimensions in LF, LC, and CF, Ebbets Field posted park factors for triples that averaged only 99 for the 1913–1919 seasons. Unlike many other Deadball Era parks with modest park factors for triples and home runs, Ebbets Field had a park factor for doubles of 85 for the 1913–1919 seasons.

Ebbets Field was a very asymmetrical ballpark with an average LF distance of 414 and an average RF distance of 330 in 1914–1919. To what extent did Ebbets Field favor left-handed batters over right-handed batters? Home-road batting data were compiled for all Brooklyn left-handed and switch-hitting batters in the Ebbets Field Deadball seasons of 1913–1919. The batting data for Brooklyn right-handed batters was obtained by subtracting left-handed and switch-hitting batters from the total team home and road batting data. In their home games played at Ebbets Field, Dodger left-handed batters had batting marks (batting average, on-base, and slugging) of .302, .360, and .411 vs. marks of .252, .295, and .329 for the right-handed batters. On the basis of this comparison one could say that Ebbets Field favored left-handed batters. One possible explanation is that the Dodgers had better left-handed batters than right-handed batters. Since the Dodgers' left-handed batters in these years included two-time batting champion Jake Daubert and Hall of Fame outfielder Zack Wheat, there may be merit to this argument. If the left-handed batters were better hitters than the right-handed batters, then the left-handed batters should have hit better at home and on the road. In fact, that is exactly what happened. The road batting marks for the Dodger left-handed batters were .282, .340, and .373 vs. .239, .277, and 306 for the right-handed batters. This established that the Dodger left-handed batters were, in fact, better hitters than the Dodger right-handed batters. A relative comparison was made of the home-road batting marks for both left-and-right handed batters. The Dodger left-handed batters had home-road batting ratios (batting average, on-base, and slugging) of 1.083, 1.074, and 1.104. The equivalent marks for the Dodger right-handed batters were 1.054, 1.060, and 1.078. Bear in mind that the above home-road batting ratios reflect the general home park advantage as well as the particular park effects unique to Ebbets Field. For comparison, the average NL home-road batting ratios in this decade (1910–1919) for batting average, on-base, and slugging were 1.044, 1.044, and 1.061. From this data, one can see that the Dodger left-handed batters had home-road batting ratios only two-to-four percent better than those of the Dodger right-handed batters. Not a very large difference for a strikingly asymmetrical ballpark such as Ebbets Field. There is one inherent problem with using home-road batting ratios in the Deadball Era. In the second decade of the Deadball Era, the average NL ballpark is believed to have favored left-handed batters. As evidence as to why this might have been true, consider that in 1915 the average LF distance for all NL ballparks was 383, while the average RF distance for all NL ballparks was 351. Thus, for the Dodger left-handed batters to have had home-road batting ratios better than the Dodger right-handed batters, Ebbets Field would have had to have favored left-handed batters more than the average NL park did. It is the author's conclusion that accurately measuring the impact of ballparks on left vs. right-handed batters would only be possible if all of the other parks in the league were roughly symmetrical. The complete 1913–1919 home-road batting data for Dodger left and right-handed batters are shown in the last table below.

The home-run data and batting park factors for Ebbets Field are shown below.

HOME RUNS BY TYPE AT EBBETS FIELD

Years	Total	OTF	Bounce	IPHR
1913	34	8	0	26
1914–1919	151	52	5	99

OTF Home Runs by Field at Ebbets Field (excluding Bounce)

Years	Total	LF	CF	RF	Unknown
1913	8	0	0	6	2
1914–1919	47	1*	0	44	2

*Into temporary bleachers in front of the LF wall

Inside-the-Park Home Runs by Field at Ebbets Field

Years	Total	LF	LC	CF	RC	RF	Unknown
1913	26	8	1	12	1	1	3
1914–1919	99	34	13	43	4	4	1

Batting Park Factors at Ebbets Field

Years	BA	OBP	SLUG	2B*	3B*	HR*	BB**
1913	98	98	93	100	85	85	100
1914–1919	100	99	95	82	101	40	103

*Per AB
**Per Total Plate Appearance (AB+BB+HP)

Home-Road Batting Data for the Brooklyn Dodgers, 1913–1919

Left-Handed Batters

	AB	H	2B	3B	HR	BB	HP	BA	OBP	SLUG
HOME	5025	1517	196	94	54	427	30	.302	.360	.411
ROAD	5398	1521	202	92	35	431	46	.282	.340	.373

Right-Handed Batters

	AB	H	2B	3B	HR	BB	HP	BA	OBP	SLUG
HOME	11644	2939	362	202	41	627	83	.252	.295	.329
ROAD	12190	1521	396	144	41	567	62	.239	.277	.306

4

Chicago

Chicago was one of the original NL franchises, starting play in 1876 as the White Stockings. The White Stockings were an immediate success, winning the first NL pennant. From 1876–1900, the NL team, called the White Stockings in the early years of the league, played in a total of six ballparks. The first, 23rd Street Grounds, was used from May 1876 to October 1877. The second and third ballparks were both called White Stockings Park and were used from 1878 to 1884. White Stockings Park was also known as Lake Front Park I, 1878–1882, and Lake Front Park II, 1883–1884. The fourth ballpark, West Side Park, was used from June 1885 to 1892. The NL team (by that time called the Colts) then played most of their home schedule at a fifth ballpark, South Side Park II, from 1891 to the end of the 1893 season. The Colts began using West Side Grounds during the 1893 season, but only for Sunday games. West Side Grounds became the only home field for the Colts starting in May 1895, and the team (called the Cubs beginning early in the twentieth Century) continued to use that ballpark until the end of the 1915 season. The names of several of the early Chicago ML ballparks (e.g., South Side Park and West Side Grounds) were taken from their relative location in the city.

In 1900, the still minor-league AL placed one of its eight franchises in Chicago, and the team built a new ballpark (South Side Park III) near the location of one of the former NL ballparks-South Side Park II. The Chicago AL team took the name of White Stockings, formerly used by the NL club, and played one minor league season at South Side Park III. The team later modified their name to the White Sox early in the first decade of the Deadball Era. The White Stockings/Sox played at South Side Park III for nine-and-a fraction ML seasons (1901–1910). In June 1910, the White Sox left South Side Park III and moved into the nearby and newly constructed Classic ballpark, Comiskey Park.

In 1914, a new ML came into being. The short-lived Federal League placed a franchise in Chicago, and the team was called the ChiFeds for the 1914 season (and the Chicago Whales in 1915). A new and largely steel-and-concrete ballpark was quickly built before the 1914 season on the north side of Chicago. Unlike earlier Chicago ballparks, this new ballpark was not named for the ballpark's location in the city of Chicago (following the pattern of earlier ballparks it could have been called North Side Park). Instead, the ballpark was named Weeghman Park, after the owner of the Chicago Federal League franchise, Charles A. Weeghman. The Federal League was essentially bought out by the AL and NL after the 1915 season. As part of the deal that ended the Federal League, Weeghman was allowed to buy the Chicago NL franchise. He promptly combined the rosters of the NL Cubs and the Federal League Whales and moved the team into Weeghman Park for the 1916 season. To this day, the Cubs still play in that ballpark, now much better known as Wrigley Field, one of the longest used and most beloved of the Classic ballparks.

Both the Cubs and White Sox were successful franchises in the Deadball Era. The Cubs were, usually contenders for the NL pennant and had a fierce rivalry with the New York Giants. In the AL, the White Sox had pennant-winning seasons in 1901, 1906 (the year the "Hitless Wonders" shocked the Cubs, winners of 116 regular-season game, by winning the all-Chicago 1906 World Series), 1917, and 1919.

West Side Grounds

Chicago National League: 1893–1915

The first use of West Side Grounds for major league baseball occurred when the NL club (called the Colts in the latter part of the 19th Century) played Sunday games there in the 1893 season. The ballpark, also known as West Side Park, was first used full-time by a ML team in the next season. That season, a fire started in the seventh inning of the game on August 5, 1894, and players Jimmy Ryan and Walt Wilmot used bats to chop through a barbed wire fence to permit over 1,000 fans to escape from the fire by moving onto the field. Despite the damage to the park caused by the fire, the Colts were able to play the remaining games of the season using the undamaged portion of the stands.

West Side Grounds occupied most but not all of a Chicago city block that was bounded by South Wood St., on the east, West Polk St. on the north, South Lincoln (later Wolcott) St. on the west, and West Taylor St. on the south. The park occupied the full width of the block between South Lincoln St. and South Wood St. (the east-west direction), but only a portion of the land between Polk St. and Taylor St. (in the north-south direction). The total size of the park site was 5.8 acres, with a 535 foot dimension in the east-west direction and 475 foot dimension in the north-south direction. As the grandstand and infield were located in the northwest portion of the site, the RF dimensions were always more limited than the LF dimensions.

The seating capacity of the park was 13,000 when it opened in 1893. Expanded in 1905 with additions to the grandstand, capacity reached 14,200. The final capacity of 16,000 was reached during the 1908 season with the roofing of the first-base and third-base bleachers and the installation of covered roof seats in these sections.

There was a moderate-sized scoreboard at the back of the bleachers in the RF corner in the early Deadball Era seasons. This scoreboard was replaced in the 1910 season with a larger steel scoreboard mounted at the back of the RF bleachers to the left of straightaway RF. The top of this scoreboard was an impressive 61 feet above the playing field.

After completing the 1915 season at West Side Grounds, the Cubs moved into one of the most famous Classic ballparks, Weeghman Park, later to be better known as Wrigley Field. West Side Grounds was torn down in 1920, and the site is now used for the Illinois State Hospital and Medical School.

The Basis of West Side Ground's Configurations and Dimensions

A 1917 Sanborn fire insurance map was used as the basis to derive a diagram of the ballpark.[1] Information on the changes in the park's configuration was obtained from a study of photos of the ballpark (from the Library of Congress, American Memory Collection). The covered grandstand (a wooden single-deck structure) extended from beyond first base to beyond third base. A set of bleachers reached from the third-base end of the grandstand and extended a short distance across the LF foul line at an angle of more than 90 degrees ending near the LF bleachers. Thus, the LF distances increased rapidly away from the LF foul pole as the fence angled towards the LF bleachers.

Covered roof seats were added to the grandstand before the 1905 season, making a sort of poor man's double-deck grandstand. These were not the only roof seats available to fans. There were "wildcat bleachers" erected on the tops of neighboring houses on both Wood St. and Taylor St. The use of these ad-hoc stands (called housetop grandstands) was to have tragic consequences.[2] During the Cubs-Giants game of July 18, 1908, a 14-year-old fan fell to his death. The next day, a judge issued an injunction prohibiting the continued usage of these rooftop stands. Within the ballpark, portions of the third-base and first-base bleachers nearest to the grandstand were roofed in 1908.[3] The new roof covered all of the 50 cent seats; only the 25 cent seats in the remaining bleachers were left uncovered. At the same time, the park's capacity was increased by adding covered seats on the new roof.

There were additional shallow bleachers in both LF and RF; the LF set had nine rows of seats and RF only seven rows of seats. Both the LF and RF bleachers were perpendicular to their respective foul line (RF) or an extension thereof (LF). The LF bleachers extended into LC, while the RF bleachers extended nearly to the flag pole in CF. There was only a modest amount of foul territory down the foul lines as both the first-base and third-base bleachers converged with the foul lines. The configuration history of CF at this ballpark was very curious. From 1901–1904, and perhaps in earlier seasons as well, an elevated walkway located in front of the flagpole in CF connected the LF and RF bleachers. This walkway, about 10 feet above ground, was in front of what appears to be a CF diagonal fence (in the Library of Congress photos). The new two-story clubhouse, built in CF before the 1905 season, replaced this ugly walkway. In 1905–1907, there was a large scoreboard mounted on top of the new CF clubhouse. For the 1908 season, the Cubs added a set of very steep bleachers extending above the roof of the clubhouse. The scoreboard was relocated to the back of the RF bleachers in RC. These CF bleachers reduced the CF dimension to about 418. In 1913, these bleachers were replaced by very large raised advertising billboards in CF. The top of these billboards were 40 feet high as listed on the 1917 Sanborn map. These monster billboards were mounted above the CF clubhouse and extended into (as inside of, not at the back of) both the LF and RF bleachers. The bottom of these huge advertising billboards were set back about 10 feet from the front of the LF and RF bleachers, and they were mounted on poles about 10–12 feet in the air. This strange arrangement meant the fans seated in the back rows of the bleachers had restricted sight lines and could not see many fly balls.

The location of home plate was fixed by the configuration of the LF and RF fences in combination with the LF and RF dimensions that never changed over the life of the park. Given the listed dimensions (LF 340 and RF 316), there was only one possible location of home plate on the Sanborn map.[4] Once the location of home plate was determined, the other outfield dimensions were derived from the park diagram.

The CF dimension for this ballpark must be considered a rather rough estimate for years before 1901. No nineteenth century photos of the ballpark exist in the huge collection of West Side Grounds photos at the Library of Congress. This is because all of the known West Side Grounds photos came from the files of the *Chicago Daily News* and covered the years 1901–1933. The 1901–1904 photos that show the CF area of the park suffer from the elevated walkway in CF blocking a clear view of a possible CF corner. In the 1901 and 1902 photos, it appears that there existed a CF diagonal fence or other buildings in CF behind the elevated walkway and in front of the CF corner. A 1905 *Chicago Tribune* article reported the old clubhouse was moved from its 1904 location (in LC or the left side of CF) back to the CF fence and was used temporarily at the start of the 1905 season while the new clubhouse was being

West Side Grounds, regular season, 1908. The large structure in center field beneath the scoreboard is the new clubhouse. Note the large sign at the back of the right-field bleachers, which is an ad for the *Chicago Tribune*. (American Memory Collection, the Library of Congress.)

completed.[5] It is possible the CF walkway and any CF buildings and interior fences did not exist before 1901. If so, the distance from home plate to the CF corner would have been about 500. The listed CF dimension of 560 in *Green Cathedrals* could never have existed. The CF corner was a fixed location (the junction of the LF and RF perimeter fences) and was bounded on the east by South Wood St. The location of home plate was likewise a fixed location. The home plate–LF perimeter fence distance was estimated to have been 385, and the home plate–RF perimeter fence distance was 316, then by geometry home plate to the CF corner would have been 499.

Park data and dimensions for West Side Grounds are shown below.

DIMENSIONS (calculated from Sanborn map)

Years	LF	SLF	LC	CF	RC	SRF	RF
1901–1904	340	398	443	448*	365	327	316
1905–1907	340	398	443	442	365	327	316
1908–1912	340	398	443	418	365	327	316
1913–1915	340	398	443	442	365	327	316

*The CF corner could have been about 500 in 1893–1900.

AVERAGE OUTFIELD DISTANCES

Years	LF	CF	RF
1901–1904	393	424	332
1905–1907	393	424	332
1908–1912	393	412	332
1913–1915	393	421	332

FENCE HEIGHTS

Years	LF	CF	RF
1901–1904	8	10	8
1905–1907	8	8	8
1908–1912	8	8	8
1913–1915	8	40	8

CAPACITY: 13,000 (1901–1904), 14,200 (1905–1907), 16,000 (1908–1915)

PARK SIZE/COMPOSITE AVERAGE OUTFIELD DISTANCE:
383 (1901–1907), 380 (1908–1912), 382 (1913–1915)

PARK SITE AREA: 5.8 ACRES

DEADBALL ERA RUN FACTOR: 98 (RANK: NL 11)

The Impact of the Park's Configurations and Dimensions on Batting

West Side Grounds had four configurations during its 15 seasons in the Deadball Era. However, the only changes were to CF, and all were minor. Part of the non-impact of these changes to CF can be seen in the fact that in no season were there any OTF home runs (excluding one bounce home run into the CF bleachers in 1912) hit to CF. The changes in configuration appear to have had no effect on the home-road batting data. Over the 15 years in the Deadball Era, the ballpark was slightly below average for NL parks in batting average, on-base, and slugging. In addition, the park was slightly above average for doubles (with a 15-year doubles park factor of 105) and below average for triples (a park factor of 83). The below-average park factor for triples was most likely due to the modest dimensions in RF and RC (316 and 365).

What appears to have had a substantial effect on home runs was the introduction of the cork-center ball during the 1910 season. In one game account during the 1910 season, the new cork-center ball was credited with assisting in a tremendous home run. Frank Schulte hit a home run that cleared the RF bleachers and sailed 20 feet over the new 61-foot-high steel scoreboard that was located 16 feet behind the front of the bleachers.[6] In the 1901–1909 time period, West Side Grounds averaged exactly one dozen home runs per season. With the introduction of the cork-center ball during the 1910 season, the park averaged 42.2 homeruns per season for the next six years. It was the combination of the livelier cork-center ball and the now easily reachable RF bleachers that led to the upsurge in home runs; in the 1910–1915 seasons, RF accounted for 76 percent of total OTF home runs at the park. On average between 1901–1909 and 1910–1915, the home run park factor nearly doubled (69 to 115). Bounce home runs at West Side Grounds were rare, less than one every two seasons. Despite the marked increase in OTF home runs that occurred with the introduction of the cork-center ball, the number of IPHR at West Side Grounds actually doubled over the 1910–1915 period. As would be expected in a park with generous LF dimensions and modest RF dimensions, nearly all IPHR were to LF, LC, and CF; there were only 12 IPHR to RF and RC in the 15 seasons the park was in use in the Deadball Era.

HOME RUNS BY TYPE AT WEST SIDE GROUNDS

Years	Total	OTF	Bounce	IPHR
1901–1909	108	37	1	71
1910–1915	253	159	6	94

OTF HOME RUNS BY FIELD AT WEST SIDE GROUNDS (EXCLUDING BOUNCE)

Years	Total	LF	CF	RF	Unknown
1901–1909	36	9	0	22	5
1910–1915	153	29	0	117	7

INSIDE-THE-PARK HOME RUNS BY FIELD AT WEST SIDE GROUNDS

Years	Total	LF	LC	CF	RC	RF	Unknown
1901–1909	70	9	24	29	3	3	2
1910–1915	95	14	35	39	1	5	1

BATTING PARK FACTORS AT WEST SIDE GROUNDS

Years	BA	OBP	SLUG	2B*	3B*	HR*	BB**
1901–1909	99	99	97	105	78	69	96
1910–1915	99	98	99	105	89	115	97

*Per AB
**Per Total Plate Appearance (AB+BB+HP)

South Side Park III

Chicago American League: 1901–1910

There were three ML ballparks in Chicago called South Side Park. All three were located in the same area on the south side of Chicago from whence they received their names. The first South Side Park was at South Wabash Ave. and West 39th St., and was used by the 1884 Union Association. The second South Side Park was at Wentworth Ave. and West 34th St. (across the street from the location of the future Comiskey Park I), and was used by the 1890 Players League and the 1891–1893 NL for selected games. The first use of South Side Park III for baseball was by the White Sox (initially called the White Stockings) in the 1900 minor league AL season. In 1901, major league baseball made its first appearance at South Side Park III. The park had previously been used by the Wanderers Cricket Club and was located only four blocks south of the future site of Comiskey Park.

South Side Park III was an all-wooden ballpark, located at West 39th St. and Princeton Ave. The park in 1900 consisted of only a grandstand and a set of first-base bleachers.[7] Configuration information about the ballpark was obtained from a study of photos of the ballpark.[8] In 1901, the covered grandstand extended in three separate sections from beyond first base to well beyond third base. The main section of the grandstand extended between halfway to third base and towards first base about 20 feet past home plate. Beyond the third base end of the main section of the grandstand, another section of the grandstand began after a gap and extended about halfway to the LF corner. For the opening of the 1901 AL season, there were bleachers in nearly every part of the park: (1) in fair LF, a set was parallel to the park's northern boundary and extended into CF, (2) in CF, a set of bleachers hooked over and ended in right center, (3) a third set of bleachers (in the third base-LF area) extended a moderate distance down the LF foul line, (4) additional bleachers reached from the first-base end of the grandstand towards the RF corner, and (5) RF bleachers that began in foul territory faced home plate and extended about 50 feet past the RF foul line into fair territory. In June 1901, covered rooftop box seats were added on the main and third-base sections of the grandstand. At the same time as the installation of the roof seats, the third-base bleachers were extended into fair LF at a diagonal angle to the LF foul line.[9] A scoreboard was mounted above the right-center field fence (which was about 10 feet high). The total area of the park was 5.0 acres, smaller than typical early twentieth century pre–Classic ML ballparks. There was a substantial amount of foul territory down the RF line. The White Sox added covered roof seats to the first-base section of the grandstand and to the first-base pavilion for the 1907 season. This addition increased the park's seating capacity to about 15,000. In April 1909, the park suffered a temporary reduction in capacity as a fire destroyed the first-base pavilion. The first-base pavilion was rebuilt later that season, this time with uncovered roof top seats.

The White Sox stayed at South Side Park III until June 1910, when after 28 home games they moved into one of the first Classic ballparks, Comiskey Park. The stands at South Side Park III were torn down in October 1910, and the lumber salvaged from the stands was hauled away. The park was later used by Negro league teams with a reduced set of newly erected stands.

The Basis of South Side Park's Configurations and Dimensions

A 1911 Sanborn fire insurance map of the park was found (in 1911 the park was no longer in ML use, and it was called American Giants Base Ball Park). Unlike the ballpark photos for 1902–1909, the 1911 Sanborn map showed the only seating remaining at that time to be the

South Side Park III, 1909. A view of the ballpark taken from the grandstand behind home plate during the City Championship Series. Note the extent of bleachers all around the outfield, and the rooftop box seats above the third base grandstand. (Photo Prints and Photographs Collection, PAN Subject: Sports No. 181 (P&P) L, Library of Congress)

grandstand and a set of first-base bleachers. There were no bleachers shown in the outfield or down the LF line.[10] The Sanborn map did provide the land plat of the park site that measured 445 feet east-west along 39th St. on the southern boundary, and 540 feet north-south on the western side along Princeton Ave. The park's irregular eastern boundary was set back about 150 feet from the nearest street to the east, Wentworth Ave. The J. F. Kidwell Greenhouse buildings intruded into a portion of the eastern boundary of the park about 250 feet north of the southern boundary (39th St.). As a result, a short section of the perimeter fence in the right-center field area ran nearly parallel with the southern boundary for about 60 feet and thus limited the distances in right-center field. The northern boundary of the park, parallel to the southern boundary, extended only 330 feet east from Princeton Ave. At that corner of the property, the eastern boundary ran south until meeting a short diagonal section that joined with the aforementioned section of fence that was nearly parallel with the southern boundary.

From game accounts, and notes on the White Stockings in the *Chicago Tribune*, it was learned that the RF fence was moved back in mid-season 1901 and again before the start of the 1903 season.[11] At the same time as the first move of the RF fence, the third-base bleachers were extended into fair LF to join the pre-existing LF bleachers. This addition to the seating capacity reduced the estimated LF dimension from 402 to 330. The first configuration was in use at the park for 31 games from April through June 1901. Then the RF fence was moved an unknown distance back in early July. This second configuration was in use from July 1901 through the end of the 1902 season. Before the start of the 1903 season, the RF fence was again moved back further from home plate.[12] Again, the distance of the move of the RF fence is unknown. The third configuration of the ballpark was in use until the White Sox moved to Comiskey Park in mid-season 1910.

The following dimensions must be generally considered rather rough estimates. The RF dimensions were based on an analysis of the number of OTF home runs (excluding bounce home runs) to RF at the ballpark vs. at other AL ballparks in the 1901–1908 seasons. The average RF distance at Sportsman's Park III in St. Louis was 335 feet, and OTF home runs to RF averaged 6.1/season. At New York's Hilltop Park in 1903, with the short RF configuration (average RF distance estimated at 305 feet), there were 12 OTF home runs to RF. Philadelphia's Columbia Park averaged 9.8 OTF home runs to RF for 1901–1908 while the average distance was 295. At South Side Park III in the first half of the 1901 season, OTF home runs to RF were on a pace to amount to 25 for the season. Thus, the early 1901 RF dimension at South Side Park must have been noticeably less than at any other AL park and was estimated to have been about 270. In the late 1901–1902 configuration during which OTF home runs to RF dropped to just two per season, the average RF distance must have more than before, and more than at 1903 Hilltop. The average RF distance (for home runs) in the July 1901–1902 configuration was estimated to have been 327. In the 7.5 seasons (1903–1910) at South Side Park, OTF home runs to RF averaged 1.3 per season. This rate of home runs was more than at Bennett Park in Detroit (average RF distance of 366) or AL Park II in Washington (average RF distance of 384), where for both parks OTF home runs to RF were known to have been less than one per season. The higher rate of OTF home runs at South Side Park in 1903–1910 is consistent with the lesser estimated RF average distance of 355.

The estimated LF distances were developed consistent with an analysis of AL home run data for the 1904–1910 seasons. For all eight AL ballparks, data on OTF home runs were compiled using the SABR Home Run Log and game accounts in Deadball Era newspapers. Information was obtained for each AL ballpark on the number of OTF home runs to LF, CF, and RF. The time period for each park was selected such that there were no changes in the average LF distances. The results are shown below.

City–Park	Time Period	OTF HRs to LF*	Average LF Distance**
BOS–Huntington Ave.	1904–1909	1.0	370
CHI–South Side III	1903–1909	0.9	378
CLE–League III	1904–1909	5.0	349
DET–Bennett	1901–1909	0.8	392
NY–Hilltop	1903–1909	1.1	367
PHL–Columbia II	1904–1908	4.8	358
STL–Sportsman's III	1902–1908	7.3	355
WAS–American League II	1904–1910	0.7	384

*Per Season Excluding Bounce Home Runs
**Adjusted for Fence Height, Average of all LF points

From the home run data, it was established that the number of OTF home runs/season to LF at South Side Park was similar to the numbers of home runs at Boston, Detroit, New York and Washington. The locations of the LF bleachers and of the angled third base-LF bleachers were estimated consistent with an average LF distance of 378. On the Sanborn map, the LF dimension for South Side Park was derived as 330 feet. Because of the angle of these third base-LF bleachers, the home run distances increased rapidly as one moved away from the foul pole. The average LF distance at South Side Park was estimated at 378, which compares with the composite of Boston, Detroit, New York and Washington average LF distance of 376. On the Sanborn map, the LF distances could have been greater, as the derived location of the LF bleachers was not constrained by the park's northern boundary. This same LF bleacher configuration and location can be seen in *Baseball Memories: 1900–1909*.[13]

Once the LF and RF distances had been derived, the Sanborn-based ballpark diagram was completed with the RF fence (in its three locations) at more than 90 degrees to the foul line and the LF fence at less than 90 degrees to an extension of the LF line (excluding the short portion where it was limited by the front of the third base bleachers). The location of the CF bleachers was based on the relationships of the bleachers to the RC fence and to the LF bleachers in the ballpark photos from the Library of Congress. From the home run data and the study of photos of South Side Park, home plate was located on the Sanborn map, and the outfield dimensions were estimated.

There was a controversy surrounding the roof seats added to the first-base section of the grandstand for the 1907 season. In May of that year, the Chicago Building Commissioner ordered the new seats were a hazard to the public and should be removed.[14] The White Sox had previously obtained a permit, and the city's prior administration had conducted an inspection.[15] The seats were closed off, apparently only for a few games. A number of 1908 photos of South Side Park III show the seats back in use.[16] The 1907 configuration of the ballpark remained the same until the White Sox left the ballpark and the team moved to Comiskey Park in June 1910.

Park data and dimensions for South Side Park III are shown below.

DIMENSIONS (all estimated)

Time Period	LF	SLF	LC	CF	RC	SRF	RF
April–June 1901	402	398	397	386	360	308	270
July 1901–1902	330	398	397	386	360	336	300
1903–1910	330	398	397	386	360	358	325

AVERAGE OUTFIELD DISTANCES

Time Period	LF	CF	RF
April–June 1901	400	386	314
July 1901–1902	378	386	335
1903–1910	378	386	355

FENCE HEIGHTS (estimated from photos)

Time Period	LF	CF	RF
April–June 1901	6	6	8–20*
July 1901–1902	6	6	8–20*
1903–1910	6	6	8–20*

*20 foot height was only for the scoreboard

CAPACITY: 12,500 (April 1901), 14,000 (June 1901), 15,000 (1907–1910)

PARK SIZE/COMPOSITE AVERAGE OUTFIELD DISTANCE:
367 (April–June 1901), 366 (July 1901–1902), 373 (1903–June 1910)

PARK SITE AREA: 5.0 acres

DEADBALL ERA RUN FACTOR 89 (Rank: AL 20)

The Impact of the Park's Configurations and Dimensions on Batting

Despite having the very short RF fence, South Side Park III in its original configuration, was a very poor hitter's park, except for home runs and walks (see data in the Batting Park Factors table below). After the configuration change about midway through the 1901 season, the home run park factor fell by 65 percent, while the triples park factor jumped from 47 to 105. For the general offensive categories of batting average, on-base, and slugging, the batting park factors all fell. Over the next several seasons, park factors for batting average ranged from 90 to 96. In fact, the low batting park factors (for all categories except base on balls) continued from 1902 throughout the life of the park, as South Side Park continued to be the worst hitter's park in the AL. What caused South Side Park to be such a poor hitter's park? From 1903–1910, the average outfield distance of 373 made the park slightly below average in size amongst AL parks. The answer appears to have been the park's very poor batter's background. In the Deadball Era, clubs were becoming increasingly aware of the importance of hitting backgrounds. To quote Christy Mathewson in 1912 on this subject: "Frequently, backgrounds are tampered with if the home club is notably weak at the bat. The best background for the batter is a dull, solid green. Many clubs have painted backgrounds in several contrasting, broken colors so that the sunlight, shining on them, blinds the batter. The Chicago White Sox are said to have done this, and for several years the figures showed the batting of both the Chicago players and the visitors at their park was very light. The White Sox's hitting was weak anywhere, so the poor background was an advantage to them."[17] The home-road batting data compiled for this book bear this out. From 1903 to 1909, the White Sox had team batting averages at their home park (South Side Park III) that ranged from .225 to .256, while their opponent's team batting average ranged from a high of .233 to a low of

.207. In 1910, the final season at South Side Park III, the White Sox and the visiting teams did even worse. In the 28 home games before the White Sox moved into Comiskey Park, the home team's batting average was an anemic .171! The visiting teams did not do much better, compiling a batting average of .189. On a combined basis, the White Sox and their opponents hit .180, and together they combined for one home run and only four triples. The White Sox and their opponents had an on-base mark of only .246, and an incredibly low slugging mark of .211 (see the table below on 1910 South Side Park Batting Data). While the batting park factors for nearly all batting categories were shockingly poor, the 1902–1910 park factor for walks was the highest in the league. One possible explanation is that the hitting background was so poor many batters simply did not bother to swing! If batters do not swing at many pitches because of the poor background, one consequence will be more walks at that park.

South Side Park III was the scene of 63 home runs over the nine-and-a-fraction ML seasons (1901–1910) the park was used. Total home runs at South Side Park averaged 6.9 per season (1903–1909), while the other seven parks in the AL averaged 19.7 home runs per season. Of the 63 home runs at the ballpark, 42 were OTF, a category that included four bounce home runs. In the park's original 1901 configuration, South Side Park was the one of the smaller ballparks in the AL and had the league's shortest RF dimension. When the RF fence was moved back in mid-season 1901, the effect on home runs was both immediate and substantial. In the original configuration that was in place for the first 31 home games (April-June) of the 1901 season, 19 home runs were hit at South Side Park, most of them over the close RF fence. In the remaining 41 home games that season, only six additional home runs were hit. It is clear that the mid-season 1901 relocation of the RF fence led to a tremendous reduction in the rate of OTF home runs to RF (see table). The second move of the RF fence before the 1903 season led to a further but less dramatic fall in total home runs and OTF home runs to RF. With the very short RF dimension in early 1901, the majority (74 percent) of the park's home runs were OTF. Thereafter, OTF home runs accounted for a minority of the not very numerous seasonal totals of home runs at the park. The batting, home run, and batting park factor data are shown below.

1910 SOUTH SIDE PARK BATTING DATA

Team	G	AB	H	2B	3B	HR	BB	HP	BA	OBP	SLUG
CHI	28	883	151	23	3	0	86	9	.171	.252	.204
OPP	28	957	181	22	1	1	62	4	.189	.241	.217
Total	28	1840	332	45	4	0	148	13	.180	.246	.211

HOME RUNS AT SOUTH SIDE PARK III (EXCLUDES BOUNCE)

Time Period	Games	Total	OTF	OTF to RF	OTF to RF/G
April–June 1901	31	19	14	11	0.355
July 1901–1902	112	13	6	3	0.027
1903–June 1910	575	31	18	10	0.017

HOME RUNS BY TYPE AT SOUTH SIDE PARK III

Years	Total	OTF	Bounce	IPHR
1901–02	32	20	0	12
1903–1910	31	22	4	9

OTF Home Runs by Field at South Side Park III (Excludes Bounce)

Years	Total	LF	CF	RF	Unknown
1901–1902	20	2	0	14	4
1903–1910	18	7	0	10	1

Inside-the-Park Home Runs by Field at South Side Park III

Years	Total	LF	LC	CF	RC	RF	Unknown
1901–1902	12	0	4	3	2	2	1
1903–1910	9	1	2	4	1	1	0

Batting Park Factors for South Side Park III

Time Period	BA	OBP	SLUG	2B*	3B*	HR*	BB**
April–June 1901	93	99	91	100	47	114	125
Rest of 1901	91	91	90	94	105	39	93
1902	91	96	85	97	62	20	121
1903–1910	94	97	90	97	65	26	109

*Per AB
**Per total plate appearance (AB+BB+HP)

Comiskey Park I

Chicago American League: 1910–1919

Located only four blocks north of the site of the previous White Sox park, South Side-Park III, Comiskey Park I was the second park used by the White Sox and was built between February and June 1910 on a site recently purchased by the club for a reported $100,000. The site had been used for a truck garden and a city dump. Opening Day at Comiskey was July 1, 1910.

The largely steel-and-concrete park (only the bleachers were built of wood) was located at West 34th St. and Shields Ave. on the south side of Chicago. When opened in 1910, the park consisted of a large double-deck grandstand, covered pavilions down both foul lines, and separate sections of wooden bleachers in LF and in RF.[18] The grandstand and the detached foul line pavilions stretched from foul pole to foul pole and were 726 feet in overall length. The LF and RF fences were aligned at less than 90 degrees to the foul lines and connected to a moderate-length CF diagonal fence. A huge electric scoreboard (about 60–80 feet long and 25–30 feet high) was mounted behind and above the CF fence (which was about eight feet tall). A curious feature of the park's configuration was the iron fences that ran between the outfield bleachers and the foul line pavilions. In both the LF and RF corners, there were iron gates that had openings between their widely spaced pickets. As fair batted balls could bounce through or roll under these iron gates, the effective fence height in the corners was zero. This arrangement had an unintentional but substantial effect on home runs hit at the park. Like most other ML parks at that time, home plate was in the southwest corner of the field, and RF was the sun field. Configuration information about the ballpark was obtained from a study of photos of the park (from the Library of Congress, American Memory Collection) and from articles in the *Chicago Tribune*. The total seating capacity in 1910 was 35,000, with 19,000 in

Comiskey Park, 1910. A view of the infield and the entire outfield during a regular season game. This photo was taken from the upper deck of the grandstand behind home plate. Note the large center-field scoreboard and how both the left-field and right-field bleachers angle in (at less than 90 degrees to the foul lines). (Photo SDN-008839, Chicago History Museum.)

the grandstand, 8,000 in the two pavilions, and 8,000 in the two bleacher sections. The cost of construction was variously reported as between $500,000 and $750,000.

For the 1910 AL season, the park was perfectly symmetrical with equal-sized bleachers in LF and RF. The park site was a parcel 600 feet by 600 feet or 8.3 acres, one of the largest park sites of any Deadball Era ballpark. The LF and RF dimensions were reported as 362, 363, or 365 in various newspaper articles. All sources agreed CF was 420. There was a substantial amount of foul territory, as the distance to the backstop was a generous 82 feet. The park's only alteration during the Deadball Era was a reported modest expansion of the outfield bleachers in the last years of the 1910s.[19] This expansion increased capacity to about 38,000. Despite the expansion of the outfield bleachers, the Comiskey Park playing field remained perfectly symmetrical throughout the Deadball Era. The park remained unchanged until after the 1926 season when the pavilions and the LF and RF bleachers were replaced by double-deck stands and lower-deck CF bleachers were added. The White Sox stayed at Comiskey Park I through the 1990 season, when they moved next door into Comiskey Park II (or New Comiskey Park). The old park was demolished in January 1991 and now serves as a parking lot for Comiskey Park II.

The Basis of Comiskey Park's Configuration and Dimensions

The 1910 Opening Day dimensions were 363 for LF and RF and 420 to CF.[20] A park diagram was developed using these dimensions and a CF diagonal that was perpendicular to the home plate–CF axis. The alignment and length of the CF diagonal was estimated from a 1910 Comiskey Park photo from the Library of Congress.[21] Given the CF dimension of 420 and the estimated length of the CF diagonal, the LF and RF fences had to have been at 84 degrees to the foul lines. This alignment of the LF and RF fences is consistent with the Library of Congress photo. All other outfield dimensions for the park were calculated using the ballpark diagram.

A study of the home run data for Comiskey Park in the Deadball Era showed a drastic drop-off in bounce home runs after the 1912 season. In the two-and-a-half seasons (1910–1912) there were 17 bounce home runs, an average of seven a season. For the next seven seasons, the park averaged only one bounce home run per year. From this data, it appears clear that the iron gates and fences in the LF and RF corners must have been modified to sharply reduce bounce home runs. While game accounts in the 1913–1916 time period continued to mention the existence of the picket fences between the bleachers and the pavilions, there was only one bounce home run in these years through the picket fences.[22] Park data and dimensions for Comiskey Park are shown below.

DIMENSIONS (from park diagram)

Time Period	LF	SLF	LC	CF	RC	SRF	RF
June 1910–1919	363	368	402	420*	402	368	363

*Deepest points (422 at 35 degrees) were at the junctions of the LF and RF walls with the CF wall

AVERAGE OUTFIELD DISTANCES

Time Period	LF	CF	RF
June 1910–1919	374	418	374

FENCE HEIGHTS (estimated from photos)

Time Period	LF	CF	RF
1910–1912	0–8*	8	0–8*
1913–1919	8	8	8

*The zero height portions were the iron picket fences in the corners

ARCHITECT: ZACHARY TAYLOR DAVIS

CAPACITY: 35,000 (1910), 38,000 (1918–1919 EST.)

PARK SIZE/COMPOSITE AVERAGE OUTFIELD DISTANCE: 389

PARK SITE AREA: 8.3 ACRES

DEADBALL ERA RUN FACTOR 97 (RANK: AL 13)

The Impact of the Park's Configurations and Dimensions on Batting

In the first season at Comiskey Park, the White Sox and the visitors both compiled atrocious batting marks. In the 51 home games played in 1910 after the move to Comiskey Park, the White Sox posted an anemic .212 batting average. The visiting teams did even worse — an average of .200. Combined, the White Sox and their opponents hit .206 at Comiskey Park and put up power numbers of three home runs and a modest 41 triples. Overall, Comiskey Park, in its inaugural 1910 season, was a very poor hitter's park with batting park factors all far less than 100 (see the Batting Park Factors table below). With no change in the park's configuration, the Comiskey Park batting park factors in the remaining Deadball Era seasons (1911–1919) were only slightly below average. The park had park factors for batting average, on-base, and slugging only one-to-two percent below the AL average for the remainder of the Deadball Era. Only the home run park factor of 68 was noticeably below average

In Comiskey Park's first partial season (51 games in 1910), there were only three home runs hit, all of which were bounce home runs through the iron gates in the LF and RF corners. Over the nine-and-a-fraction Deadball seasons the park was used by the AL, Comiskey Park was the scene of 127 home runs. Total home runs at the park averaged 13.4 per season, while the other seven parks in the AL averaged 20.7 home runs per season. Of these 127 home runs, slightly more than half (67) were of the OTF type, a number that included 24 bounce home runs. As previously discussed, bounce home runs became rare after the 1912 season. In relative terms, Comiskey Park in the second decade of the Deadball Era (1911–1919) was a better-than-average venue for IPHR. This category accounted for 48 percent of the total home runs hit at Comiskey Park. This was above the AL average of 32 percent in the same time period. The home run data and batting park factors are shown below.

1910 COMISKEY PARK BATTING DATA

Team	G	AB	H	2B	3B	HR	BB	HP	BA	OBP	SLUG
CHI	51	1582	336	32	27	2	128	15	.212	.289	.271
OPP	51	1678	336	38	14	1	113	15	.200	.257	.241
Total	51	3260	672	70	41	3	241	25	.206	.267	.256

HOME RUNS BY TYPE AT COMISKEY PARK I

Time Period	Total	OTF	Bounce	IPHR
Late 1910*	3	3	3	0
1911–1912	44	25	14	19
1913–1919	80	39	7	41

*July 1 to end of season (51 Games)

OTF HOME RUNS BY FIELD AT COMISKEY PARK I
(EXCLUDES BOUNCE)

Time Period	Total	LF	CF	RF	Unknown
Late 1910*	0				
1911–1912	11	11	0	0	0
1913–1919	34	18	0	10	6

*July 1 to end of season

INSIDE-THE-PARK HOME RUNS BY FIELD AT COMISKEY PARK I

Time Period	Total	LF	LC	CF	RC	RF	Unknown
Late 1910	0						
1911–1912	19	1	1	9	2	6	0
1913–1919	41	8	5	21	4	2	1

Batting Park Factors at Comiskey Park I

Time Period	BA	OBP	SLUG	2B*	3B*	HR*	BB**
Late 1910	88	90	85	74	93	27	95
1911–1919	98	99	98	89	128	68	101

*Per AB
**Per Total Plate Appearance (AB+BB+HP)

Weeghman Park / Cubs Park

Chicago National League 1916–1919

Today, Wrigley Field is the second oldest ML ballpark. When built in 1914, it was known as Weeghman Park and was the new home park of the Chicago franchise of the upstart Federal League. Built in less than two months before the 1914 season, the park was named for the owner of the Chicago Federal League team, Charles H. Weeghman. The Federal League had operated in the 1913 season as a minor league with a franchise in Chicago. That franchise played its home games on the DePaul University athletic field.

Weeghman Park was situated in a north-side Chicago residential area not far from Lake Michigan, on a mostly vacant lot at the intersection of Clark St. and Addison Ave. This property was owned by E. M. Cantillion, Joe Cantillion, and Edmund Archambault, the principal stockholders of the American Association Minneapolis Millers.[23] These gentlemen, despite pressure from Organized Baseball, leased the property for use by the outlaw Federal League. The lease was signed in January 1914, and Charles Weeghman directed work on the ballpark to begin, which it did on March 4, 1914. Opening Day was scheduled for April 23, less than two months away. The original park site property was a rectangle bordered by on all sides by city streets: on the south Addison Ave., on the east Sheffield Ave., on the north Waveland Ave., and Seminary Avenue/Clark St. on the west). The southwest corner of the parcel was at the intersection of Clark and Addison. Note that Clark St. ran northwest-southeast, while Seminary Ave. ran north-south and terminated near the intersection of Clark and Addison. Note also that the block of Seminary Ave. between Addison and Waveland no longer exists.

The original ballpark site did not utilize the entire property. On the northern portion of the property, several large residential building stood on the south side of Waveland Ave. and abutted the ballpark's 1914 Opening Day northern boundary. These buildings supplied a substantial rental income and were left intact in the park's original construction. About a 60-foot strip of land along the park's western boundary (facing Seminary Ave. and Clark St.) was also not part of the original ballpark site. The plan was to use this strip of land for commercial purposes, a kind of ballpark shopping area. The early 1914 ballpark site's dimensions were estimated to have been about 515 feet east-west along Waveland Ave., and about 525 feet north-south along Sheffield Ave. The original ballpark site amounted to about 5.9 acres in size. This was smaller than the typical ML ballpark used in the Deadball Era (1901–1919). The size of the entire property leased by the Chicago Federal League team was 7.4 acres.

On Opening Day, April 23, 1914, the park consisted of (1) a single-deck covered steel-and-concrete grandstand that ran from beyond first base to beyond third base, (2) two pavilions (actually uncovered seating at this point in time) down the LF and RF lines, and (3) a section of wooden bleachers in the RC area, the only seating in fair territory. The seating capacity of the ballpark was variously estimated as between 14,000 and 20,000. The orientation of the field was conventional (home plate in the southwest portion of the field). Thus, the LF foul line ran north-south, and the RF foul line ran east-west and was parallel to Addi-

Weeghman Park, 1914. A view of the narrow Addison Avenue that made up the southern boundary of the ballpark. The ballpark was used by the Federal League for two seasons (1914–1915) before becoming the home of the NL Chicago Cubs in 1916. Note the first base wing of the single-deck roofed grandstand in the upper portion of the photograph. Weeghman Park (the ballpark was not called Wrigley Field until the 1920s) was not double-decked until after the 1926 season. (Photo SDN-059405, Chicago History Museum.)

son Ave. The single-deck grandstand and pavilions all angled towards the LF and RF foul lines, which meant the first-base stands diverged from Addison Ave. as the stands neared the RF fence.[24] The author's estimates of the 1914 Opening Day dimensions (see below for basis of estimate) were LF 302, CF 376, the CF corner (left of dead CF) 406, RF 298, and home plate to the backstop 62. A substantial brick wall enclosed most of the outfield, with a short fence topped by a low screen in front of the bleachers in RC. There were picket fences in both the LF and RF corners. A large scoreboard, an estimated 30 feet high and 40 feet wide, stood in LF. The configuration detailed above lasted for all of three games (April 23–26). The layout of the playing field meant the LF distance (at the foul pole) was only 302 feet. In the three games played in this configuration, nine home runs were hit. First of all, nine home runs in three games were unheard of in the Deadball Era. In addition, all nine were OTF home runs, and eight of the nine were over the short LF fence. Newspaper accounts spoke of these home runs to LF as "cheap shots." The team's president, Charles Weeghman, admitted that the LF distance was too short and took immediate steps to correct the problem. An additional strip of land, already part of the lease, was added to the northern part of the ballpark (moving the northern boundary towards but not all the way to Waveland Ave.). This required the demolition of at least one back porch that had been attached to one of the houses on Waveland Ave. This additional property allowed the LF distance to be increased 25 feet, while LC was increased by nearly 50 feet.[25] The new and expanded LF dimensions, along with a new LF-CF fence were in place when the team next played on April 28. The large scoreboard located in LF was moved to LC three days later. Interestingly, the even shorter RF distance (estimated at 298 feet) attracted no discussion. As Sheffield Ave. was the eastern boundary of the park, there was no way to increase the RF distance unless the brand new grandstand and third-base pavilion were to be somehow lifted up and moved to the west. The bleachers, located in RC, reduced even further the in-play area of the ballpark.

Before the 1915 season, the park was again modified and expanded. The residential buildings on the north edge of the ballpark were torn down and the occupants relocated (hopefully in the reverse sequence). The ballpark's northern boundary now extended all the way to Waveland Ave. The purpose of this additional northern expansion was to permit the replacement of the RC bleachers with a new and larger set of bleachers that were built behind the new LF-CF fence. This also required the second relocation of the scoreboard, this time from LC to CF. The new bleachers ran from the LF foul pole to the left edge of the scoreboard, which was now in CF. The CF scoreboard was located at a diagonal to the LF-CF bleachers and faced home plate. The left edge of the scoreboard joined the back of the right edge of the LF-CF bleachers, and the scoreboard was entirely behind the RF-CF fence, and thus was completely out of play. The new LF bleachers provided a net increase in capacity of several hundred seats. The removal of the RC bleachers also increased the area of fair territory in RC and CF as the estimated RC distance was increased by 35–40 feet. The park now had an estimated north-south dimension of about 565 feet, while the east-west distance along Addison Ave. remained unchanged. The total size of the park site was now about 6.7 acres.

The next change in the ballpark's configuration occurred in 1916 and was caused by a mid-season installation of an in-play screen on top of the RF wall in response to the large number of home runs to RF and RC. This 10-foot-high screen ran from the RF foul pole nearly to the right edge of the CF scoreboard and raised the RF barrier to an estimated height of 22 feet.[26] This was the last change to the configuration of the park until the 1922–1923 off season. After the 1915 season, Charles Weeghman acquired the Cubs NL franchise as part of the agreement shutting down the Federal League. After the club was bought by William Wrigley, the ballpark's name was changed to Cubs Park starting with the 1919 season.

The Basis of Weeghman Park's Estimated Configurations and Dimensions

The 1914 dimensions listed in *Green Cathedrals* for the ballpark were LF: 345, 310, 327; CF: 440, and RF 356, 345.[27] These varying dimensions for LF and RF deserve further scrutiny. The source of the LF 310 and RF 345 dimensions was found in a pre-season story in the *Chicago Tribune*.[28] The actual distances in the story were "home plate-LF 310 yards, and home plate-RF 345 yards." The fact that the dimensions were expressed as yards and not feet makes one skeptical. In addition, the newspaper story was written while the ballpark was still under construction and the playing field was not yet laid out. Shortly after opening day, the team's management decided to move back the LF-CF fence. The LF dimension was increased by a reported 25 feet from 302 to 327.[29] This same newspaper story stated, "towards left-center is now 35 feet more and in left-center is nearly 50 feet more." The increased LF and LC dimensions meant that the LF fence now ran at more than 90 degrees to the LF foul line. The land added to the ballpark was an odd-shaped area with increasing depth towards CF. This odd shape resulted from the need to affect the changed configuration quickly because the residential buildings on the south side of Waveland Ave. could not be torn down until after the 1914 season. This alignment of the LF fence existed only from April 28 until the end of the 1914 season. A new LF fence was built for the 1915 season at 90 degrees to the foul line. This change was to permit the construction of a set of bleachers in LF before the 1915 season. Numerous photos of the 1915–1922 LF bleachers show them to have been rectangular.[30]

The variations in the listed 1914 RF dimensions are most interesting. As the RF wall was along Sheffield Ave. and could not be moved further from home plate, the only way to increase the RF dimension would have been to move home plate. After the 1922 season, the RF dimension was changed by doing just that. The club, now owned by William Wrigley, had the ballpark expanded and the park's configuration substantially altered. The principal change was implemented by jacking up the grandstand and third-base pavilion, placing them on rollers, and moving them 60 feet to the west.[31] This movement of the stands allowed for the move of home plate to the west and the construction of RF bleachers. This move increased the RF foul line distance from 298 to 318. These dimensions were confirmed by a 1923 Sanborn map.[32] The Sanborn map showed the location of the grandstand and pavilions but not the LF or RF bleachers. A park diagram was drawn on the Sanborn map such that the location and depth of the 1923 LF and RF bleachers and the extent of the playing field matched the listed 1923 dimensions.[33] Additional park diagrams were drawn on the Sanborn map for the earlier configurations. Also as part of the 1922–1923 expansion of the ballpark, the playing field was reoriented by about four degrees to the left such that the LF foul line now hit the LF fence at 86 degrees while the RF foul line now hit the RF fence at 94 degrees. The 1922–1923 revisions to the ballpark included a new set of RF bleachers, which were estimated to have been about 42 feet in depth. The home plate to RF distance, if at 90 degrees to the fence as in prior years, would have been 317 feet. As the 1922 RF distance was 299 and the stands and home plate were moved 60 feet away from RF, the resulting 1923 RF distance should have been 317 (299+60–42). The actual RF distance was 318 with the fence at 94 degrees to the RF foul line. This evidence shows that RF was always 298–299 from 1914 through 1922. Home run data for 1915–1919 (when LF was 327, and by the author's estimate RF was 298) show 108 OTF home runs (excluding bounce home runs and home runs for which the field is unknown). The distribution was LF/LC 33, CF 2, and RF/RC 73. Clearly, if nearly 70 percent of the OTF home runs were to RF and RC, then the RF distance must have been noticeably less than the LF distance.

The following tables show the dimensions, fence heights and average outfield distances for each configuration of Weeghman Park (1914–1918) and Cubs Park (1919).

DIMENSIONS (from ballpark diagrams)

Time Period	LF	SLF	LC	CF	RC	SRF	RF
April 1914 (a)	302	313	349	376*	298	308	298
May–September 1914	327	345	394	376**	307	308	298
1915–1919	327	338	377	422***	344	308	298

Backstop: 62
(a) Three home games, April 23–26
*CF corner left of dead center was 406
**CF corner left of dead center was 455
***Left of dead center at the scoreboard was 433

Average Outfield Distances

Time Period	LF	CF	RF
April 1914	318	357	307
May–September 1914	351	373	307
1915–1919	344	396	314

Fence Heights (estimated from photos and contemporary accounts)

Time Period	LF	CF	RF
April 1914	12–30	8–12	8–12
May–September 1914	12–30	8–12	8–12
1915–June 1916	8	8–12	12
July 1916–1919	8	8–22	22

Architect: Zachary Taylor Davis

Capacity: 14,000 (1914 Est.), 15,000 (1915–1919 Est.)

Park Size/Composite Average Outfield Distance: 327 (April 1914), 344 (May-September 1914), 351 (1915–1919)

Park Site Area: 5.9 acres (April 1914), 6.1 acres (May–September 1914), 6.7 acres (1915–1919)

Deadball Era Run Factor: 111 (Rank: NL 1)

The Impact of the Park's Configuration and Dimensions on Batting

Weeghman Park (1916–1919) was the second smallest and the best offensive ballpark in the NL during the Deadball Era with a run factor of 111. The ballpark was a great offensive park in 1916 (especially in the first half of the season) and a moderately good hitter's park in the 1917–1919 seasons. In the first half of the 1916 season (before the screen was added atop the RF wall), the park had park factors of 118 for slugging and 250 for home runs. The 118 park factor for slugging was higher than any full-season slugging park factor in the league during the Deadball Era. Weeghman Park, in each of its four Deadball seasons, had above average park factors for batting average, on-base, and slugging. The ballpark was great for doubles, and in 1916 it posted the highest single-season park factor in the NL Deadball Era (164). Not surprisingly for the second smallest ballpark in the NL in these years, it was a moderately poor park for triples.

The ballpark was always conducive to home runs, so much so that the park's configuration was twice changed (early in 1914 and again in mid-season 1916) to reduce home runs. Unlike the situation in other Deadball Era ballparks, IPHRs were not common at Weeghman Park. In the 1914–1919 time period, IPHR accounted for a mere 6.2 percent of the home runs hit at the ballpark, while bounce home runs amounted to an additional 7.2 percent. In the same six-year period, IPHR accounted for 24.6 percent of total home runs at all major league parks, while bounce home runs were 2.3 percent of the total.[34] No great importance should be attached to the larger-than-average proportion of bounce home runs at Weeghman Park. Unlike at other parks, such as Philadelphia's Baker Bowl, where bounce home runs simply bounced into the outfield bleachers' at Weeghman Park bounce home runs were typically flukes. For example, Felix Chouinard of Pittsburgh's Federal League club bounced the ball through the picket fence in RF on June 16, 1914. Fred Merkle of the Braves was credited with a home run on July 2, 1917, when the Cubs outfielder thoughtfully kicked the ball through the picket fence in LF. And as a real example of home park advantage, on June 8, 1919, Max Flack of the Cubs drove a ball to RF that hit the top of the RF wall and bounced *under* the RF screen that had been erected three seasons earlier to reduce home runs.

In 1914, Weeghman Park was a good park for home runs. In that season home runs at Weeghman Park amounted to 138 percent of the Federal League average per park. That season at the ballpark there were 51 home runs, none of which were IPHR and only one of which was a bounce home run. The distribution of the OTF home runs in the 1914 season is shown below.

1914 OTF Home Run by Field (excludes Bounce)

Category	Total	LF	CF	RF	Unknown
Season	50	10	0	36*	4
April 24–26	9	8	0	1	0
Rest of Season**	41	2	0	35	4

*Includes 19 home runs into or over the right-center field bleachers
**All games after April 26 with LF at 327

Recall that early in the 1914 season the LF distance had been increased to 327 and LC to about 390 after only three games, and that LC had the 30-foot-high scoreboard as an additional deterrent to OTF home runs to LF. By contrast, RF had no distance greater than 307 with a 12-foot wall in RF and a seven-to-eight-foot-high screen in front of the RC bleachers. As a result, the distribution of OTF home runs was sharply skewed towards RF. The zero home runs reported to CF is likely due to the reporting conventions of the day. The bleachers, actually located in RC-CF, were usually referred to as "the RF bleachers," and the wall from the RF foul pole to the junction with the CF corner was referred to as "the RF wall." Thus a home run over the right-hand portion of CF would usually be reported as a home run to RF or to RC. In the 1915 season with the RC bleachers having been removed, total home runs at Weeghman Park dropped (51 to 31), but the relative distribution of OTF home runs was similar to 1914.

1915 OTF Home Run by Field (excludes Bounce)

Category	Total	LF	CF	RF	Unknown
Season	28	3*	0	22*	3

*No home runs reported to left-center or right-center

The total number and distribution of home runs at Weeghman Park were greatly affected by the addition of the screen atop the RF wall in mid-season 1916. In the first half of the 1916 season, there were a total of 37 home runs in 39 games, a rate (0.95 per game) that was actually greater than the ML average (0.80/game) in the Lively Ball Era 1920s. Nor was the total number of home runs in the first half of 1916 substantially influenced by IPHR or bounce home runs. There were only three IPHR and no bounce home runs in the first half of the season (39 games). Why so many OTF home runs? The distribution of OTF home runs provides a clue. RF (at the foul pole) was only 298 feet. Until July 1916 (after 39 games), the wall was an estimated 12 feet in height. When the screen was added, the total height of the RF barrier became 22 feet. In the second half of the 1916 season (40 games) with the RF screen in place, there were far fewer OTF home runs (only 18) hit at Weeghman Park, of which three were bounce home runs. The distribution of OTF home runs hit at Weeghman Park in 1916 is shown below.

1916 OTF HOME RUN BY FIELD (EXCLUDES BOUNCE)

Time Period	Total	LF	CF	RF	Unknown
First Half	34	6*	1	26*	1
Second Half	15	7**	0	8**	0

*No home runs reported to LC, and two to RC
**No home runs reported to LC or RC

As shown in the above table, the number of OTF home runs to RF dropped from 25 to eight after the addition of the 10-foot screen to the RF wall. Since OTF home runs to LF and CF were unchanged (seven in both the first and second half of the season), the 10-foot increase in fence height appears to be the principal cause of the decline in OTF home runs. Other factors may have contributed to the drop in OTF home runs to RF. One which could be measured is the change in opportunities for the Cubs' left-handed batters. Of the 16 OTF home runs to RF hit by the Cubs in the first half, 14 were hit by left-handed batters. If the Cubs' left-handed batters had hit home runs in the second half of the season at the same rate (home runs per AB) as in the first half, the expected number of home runs would have been 9.9. In addition, the Cubs' left-handed batters in the second half of the season suffered a 20 percent decline in batting average. Adjusting for the 29 percent fewer at bats for left-handed batters and a 20 percent lower batting average in the second half, the expected number of Cubs OTF home runs to RF was eight compared to the five actually hit. The visitor's output of OTF home runs to RF in the second half dropped from ten to three. In total, the expected number of OTF home runs to RF in the second half was 17, and the actual total was eight. From this one can conclude the addition of a mere 10 feet in height to the screen reduced home runs to RF by more than 50 percent.

HOME RUNS BY TYPE AT WEEGHMAN/CUBS PARK

Time Period	Total	OTF	Bounce	IPHR
1st Half 1916	37	34	0	3
2nd Half 1916	19	18	3	1
1917–1919	57	50	9	7

OTF HOME RUN BY FIELD AT WEEGHMAN/CUBS PARK (EXCLUDES BOUNCE)

Years	Total	LF	CF	RF	Unknown
1916–1919	90	31	2	53	4

INSIDE-THE-PARK HOME RUN BY FIELD AT WEEGHMAN/CUBS PARK

Years	Total	LF	LC	CF	RC	RF	Unknown
1916–1919	11	0	0	7	2	0	2

BATTING PARK FACTORS AT WEEGHMAN/CUBS PARK

Time Period	BA	OBP	SLUG	2B*	3B*	HR*	BB**
1st Half 1916	109	108	118	164	71	250	116

Time Period	BA	OBP	SLUG	2B*	3B*	HR*	BB**
2nd Half 1916	110	106	113	165	68	145	94
1917–1919	102	102	100	129	62	85	100

*Per AB
**Per Total Plate Appearance (AB+BB+HP)

5

Cincinnati

Professional baseball started in Cincinnati in 1869 with the Red Stockings, the first avowedly professional team. The Cincinnati Red Stockings were a charter member in the NL in 1876 and continued in the NL through 1880. The NL returned to Cincinnati for the 1890 season and remained in the city to the present day. In the early 1890s the NL Cincinnati team, by then called the Reds, played in League Park I. This was the first of several ML Cincinnati ballparks located at Findlay St. and Western Ave. The all-wooden League Park I was used by the Reds for four seasons (1890–1893). Starting with the 1894 season, the Reds used League Park II. This ballpark was also a wooden structure and was built on the same site as League Park I, but with a different orientation. League Park I had home plate, the infield, and the grandstand in the southeast corner of the site, while League Park II had the grandstand and infield in the southwest corner. Interestingly, the grandstand of League Park I became the RF stands in League Park II.

There was a large fire on May 28, 1900, that destroyed the grandstand of League Park II. The Reds quickly moved home plate and the infield to the southeast corner of the park and made the RF grandstand into the main stands for the new configuration of League Park II. This configuration was exactly the same as what League Park I had been. The Reds finished the 1900 season with the reduced capacity of the ballpark. During the 1901 season, new bleachers were built in LF about where the third-base portion of the grandstand had stood before the May 1900 fire. This new configuration of League Park II lasted only until the end of the 1901 season.

After the 1901 season, the Reds had the wooden League Park II torn down and replaced on the same site with a new ballpark, Palace of the Fans. The new park had the same orientation as the original orientation of League Park II before the May 1900 fire. The Palace of the Fans was a partly steel-and-concrete ballpark with two grandstands—one between first base and third base (the steel-and-concrete one) and one on both wings of the RF corner. This curious arrangement was due to the wooden RF grandstand that was left over from League Park II. Despite the extensive use of steel-and-concrete construction in the foundation and superstructure of the main grandstand, Palace of the Fans is not considered as one of the Classic ballparks. Due to the limited capacity of Palace of the Fans after the 1911 season, the ballpark was replaced with a new Classic ballpark on the same site, Redland Field.

There were prohibitions on Sunday baseball in Cincinnati in the late 19th Century. The Reds, starting in the 1892 season, made it a practice to play on Sunday and then promptly pay the stipulated fine. This practice continued until 1897 when the local authorities relented as a result of developments in the playing Sunday games elsewhere in the state of Ohio that year.[1] In the first decade of the Deadball Era, not only were legal Sunday games being played in Cincinnati, but Sunday games were also played by the AL Cleveland team at neutral sites in nearby Dayton and Columbus. One consequence of Sunday baseball being legal in Cincinnati, but not in Pittsburgh, was the scheduling by the NL of several one-game road trips each season for the Pittsburgh Pirates to play on Sundays in Cincinnati.

League Park II

Cincinnati National League: 1901

There were two ML ballparks in Cincinnati called League Park. The first (League Park I) was used by the NL Cincinnati Reds for four seasons, 1890 to 1893. This wooden park was bordered by York St. on the north, Findlay St. on the south, and Western Ave. on the northeast. On the west, the park site was set back about 200 feet from McLean Ave. Note that Western Ave. ran northwest-southeast. The second park (League Park II) was in the same location and was built before the 1894 season, but with home plate and the grandstand located in the southwest corner of the site instead of the southeast corner. In this configuration, Western Ave. on the northeast limited the dimensions in both RC and CF, while the RF dimension could be very large. With the relocation of the infield back to the southeast corner of the park site (near the corner of Findlay St. and Western Ave.) after the fire of May 28, 1900, the RF dimension was limited, while the LF and CF distances could be very large.

When League Park II first opened in 1894, it had a new grandstand built of a combination of iron and wood. The Reds owner (John T. Brush, later owner of the New York Giants) chose to use both iron and wood in an effort to reduce the risk of fire.[2] This effort, while commendable, was not entirely successful; the park's main grandstand burned down on May 28, 1900. The Reds quickly moved home plate and the infield from the southwest corner to the southeast corner of the park site and made use of the un-burnt wooden stands in that corner of the field as the main grandstand of the park for the rest of the 1900 and the entirety of the 1901 seasons.

The ballpark, on Opening Day of the park's only Deadball Era season (1901), consisted of a covered grandstand in several sections located in the southeast corner of the park site. As a result, the RF line met the Western Ave. RF fence at an acute angle. At the start of the 1901 season, there were no seats in the fair portion of the outfield. The seating capacity of the park at that time was estimated to have been about 7,000. To increase capacity during the 1901 season, a new set of LF bleachers were built where the grandstand had stood before the fire of May 28, 1900.

The Basis of League Park II's Configuration and Dimensions

Dimensional data for this ballpark in *Green Cathedrals* are limited to LF 253 (in the original 1894 configuration) and were of no help in estimating the 1901 dimensions.[3] The basis of the park's 1901 configuration and dimensions was from two principal sources: an 1891 Sanborn fire insurance map of League Park I, and game accounts from the 1901 season.[4] The illustration in *Baseball Memories: 1900–1909* was used to position home plate in the southeast corner on the Sanborn map.[5] This location of home plate was used to develop a park diagram that was drawn on the Sanborn map. In the area of RF, the extent of the playing field of the park was limited by Western Ave. on the northeast and by York St. on the north. As shown on the Sanborn map, the LF, LC, and CF dimensions were not limited by the extent of the park site and could have been very large. The positioning and alignment of the LF and CF fences on the diagram were based on 1901 game accounts and home run data. All of the park's dimensions were derived from this diagram. The resulting estimated dimensions were LF 387, dead CF 414, and RF 340.

The first configuration change occurred during the 1901 season. Based on several 1901 game accounts, it was determined that there was a stone structure (referred to in the game accounts as the stone island) in deep LF.[6] During the 1901 season, new LF bleachers were built as an annex to that stone structure. It appears that the LF bleachers had to have been built in front of the LF fence as at least one IPHR was hit into a stack of lumber situated in LF for the new bleachers.[6] These LF bleachers were estimated to have extended from the LF corner to LC. The ballpark's capacity was increased to about 9,000 with the addition of the new bleachers. Like several other early Deadball Era ballparks, there was an embankment in front of the CF fence.[7]

In summary, the estimated dimensions of Cincinnati's League Park II contain a substantial amount of uncertainty. Only the home run data provide a confirmation of the park's overall large size.

Park data and dimensions for League Park II are shown below.

DIMENSIONS (from park diagram)

Year	LF	SLF	LC	CF	RC*	SRF	RF
1901	387	374	384	414	426	418	340

*Deepest point was to the right of RC (445).

AVERAGE OUTFIELD DISTANCES

Year	LF	CF	RF
1901	380	407	411

FENCE HEIGHTS (estimated from game accounts)

Year	LF	CF	RF
1901	8	10	10

CAPACITY: 7,000 (EARLY 1901 EST.), 9,000 (LATE 1901 EST.)

PARK SIZE/COMPOSITE AVERAGE OUTFIELD DISTANCE: 399

PARK SITE AREA: 6.4 ACRES

DEADBALL ERA RUN FACTOR: 97 (RANK: NL 12)

The Impact of the Park's Configuration and Dimensions on Batting

In the 1901 season, League Park II was the second-largest NL ballpark (only Exposition Park in Pittsburgh was larger). It appears that because of this large size, the batting park factors were noticeably below average (see table of League Park II Batting Park Factors below). Only for doubles, home runs, and walks were the park factors above 100. Why the large home run park factor of 156? For one thing, in the 1901 season, League Park II was the top home run park in the NL with 55 homers. The majority (47 of the 55) were IPHR, as there were only eight OTF home runs hit. More so than the typical Deadball Era ballpark, League Park II in its single Deadball season was very conducive to IPHR as shown by the home run data below. An even 85 percent of all home runs at the park were IPHR compared to 58 percent for the entire NL in the 1901 season. In fact, the 47 IPHR hit at League Park II in the 1901 season was the largest single season total for any ML ballpark in the Deadball Era (tied with Huntington Ave. Grounds-1903 Boston AL) or in any season since. The distribution of IPHR was quite widespread, as IPHR were hit to LF, CF, RF, and LC and RC. The largest number of IPHR were hit to CF, and most of the remainder were hit to LF and LC. The high number of IPHR is consistent with the large estimated dimensions of the ballpark. The OTF home run data is not very helpful. There were six non-bounce OTF home runs. Of these six, two were to LF, zero to CF, and one to RF (three were field unknown). It is likely the large number of IPHR and the below average park factors for triples were due to some would-be triples having been turned into IPHR by the ample outfield dimensions.

The home run data and batting park factors are shown below.

Home Runs by Type at League Park II

Year	Total	OTF	Bounce	IPHR
1901	55	8	2	47

OTF Home Runs by Field at League Park II (Excludes Bounce)

Year	Total	LF	CF	RF	Unknown
1901	6	2	0	1	3

Inside-the-Park Home Run by Field for League Park II

Year	Total	LF	LC	CF	RC	RF	Unknown
1901	47	7	5	22	2	3	8

Batting Park Factors at League Park II

Year	BA	OBP	SLUG	2B*	3B*	HR*	BB**
1901	95	97	101	123	87	156	106

*Per AB
**Per Total Plate Appearance (AB+BB+HP)

Palace of the Fans

Cincinnati National League: 1902–1911

The Palace of the Fans was a new ballpark built after the 1901 season at the same location (Findlay St. and Western Ave.) as the prior ballpark, League Park II.[8] Palace of the Fans was the second ML ballpark to use steel-and-concrete in its construction (Baker Bowl in Philadelphia was the first). The ballpark used steel-and-concrete for the foundation and superstructure of the new grandstand built before the 1902 season. Palace of the Fans was used by the Cincinnati Reds for 10 seasons, but the park proved to be too small and was replaced before the 1912 season by Redland (later Crosley) Field.

The main grandstand was architecturally distinctive with pillars and columns patterned after the 1893 Columbian Exposition in Chicago. When it opened for the 1902 season, the park consisted of a single-deck plus grandstand that extended from beyond third base to beyond first base. The single-deck plus designation is due to the boxes at ground level beneath the grandstand. The main grandstand was built of steel and concrete and had many ornate pillars and columns. A second wooden grandstand extended from about straightaway RF, wrapped around the RF corner, and ended at the right end of the main grandstand. This grandstand was called a pavilion and was retained from the 1901 configuration of the prior ballpark, League Park II. Down the LF foul line were bleachers that extended from the third-base end of the grandstand to nearly the LF corner. In addition, a small set of bleachers were located in RF that extended towards CF from the left end of the RF pavilion. There was a good-sized scoreboard set into the LF wall and located in the LC corner. The seating capacity of the ballpark in 1902 was 12,000. During the ten years the park was in use during the Deadball Era, no changes to either the stands or the playing field were made. While Palace of the Fans was an impressive-looking ballpark, it was limited in overall capacity and very limited in terms of box seats.

The Basis of Palace of the Fans' Configuration and Dimensions

The park's configuration and dimensions were based on three principal sources: a 1904 Sanborn fire insurance map, the dimensions in *Green Cathedrals*, and the journal of the Cincinnati Historical Society.[9] The 1904 Sanborn map of the ballpark can be seen in *Diamonds*.[10] The only dimensional data for this ballpark in *Green Cathedrals* is RF (450 in 1902), the deepest point in the ballpark. Home plate was located on the 1904 Sanborn map to fit the RF dimension of 450. Once home plate was located (about 60 feet from the backstop), a park diagram was drawn on the Sanborn map. All dimensions other than RF were calculated from this park diagram. The configuration of the Palace of the Fans had the unusual characteristic of RF being the deepest part of the park. LF was 360 and CF was 400. Because the location of Western Ave. limited the size of RC and CF, the low RF fence (the front of the RF pavilion and bleachers) intersected the RF foul line at an angle of only 60 degrees. As a result, the ballpark's dimensions decreased rapidly as one moved away from the RF line (450) to straightaway RF (404) and RC (375). The LF foul line intersected the LF fence at 96 degrees; therefore, the LF dimensions increased noticeably as one moved away from the foul line to straightaway LF (385) and towards LC (418). The LF and RF fences met at an angle of more than 90 degrees at a point slightly to the left of LC. At this sort of LC corner the distance was 430 feet from home plate.

Park data and dimensions for Palace of the Fans are shown below.

DIMENSIONS (calculated from park diagram)

Years	LF	SLF	LC	CF	RC	SRF	RF
1902–1911	360	385	418	400	375	404	450

AVERAGE OUTFIELD DISTANCES

Years	LF	CF	RF
1902–1911	391	398	405

FENCE HEIGHTS (from photos)

Years	LF	CF	RF
1902–1911	10–20	20	4

ARCHITECT: JOHN G. THURTLE

Palace of the Fans, April 14, 1905. A view from the left-field corner of Palace of the Fans from Opening Day, 1905, Pittsburgh vs. Cincinnati. The grandstand was then only three years old. Note that while the crowd in right field has flowed onto the grounds in front of the bleaders and grandstand, the left-field bleachers are partially empty. Total attendance at the game was 18,287 in a ballpark with a seating capacity of 12,000. (Photograph by the George R. Lawrence Co., Panoramic Photographs Collection [No. 5274-A], Library of Congress.)

5. Cincinnati

CAPACITY: 12,000

PARK SIZE/COMPOSITE AVERAGE OUTFIELD DISTANCE: 398

PARK SITE AREA: 6.4 ACRES

DEADBALL ERA RUN FACTOR: 108 (RANK: NL 2)

The Impact of the Park's Configuration and Dimensions on Batting

Overall, Palace of the Fans must be considered one of the best hitter's parks in the NL during its ten Deadball seasons (see table of Batting Park Factors below). Except for home runs, doubles, and walks, the park posted batting park factors noticeably above average. The Cincinnati Reds posted impressive team home batting averages of .296 in 1902 and .304 in 1903. In the 1906 season, Palace of the Fans had the highest-ever NL Deadball Era park factor for batting average of 112. Surprisingly, neither the Reds nor their opponents that season posted impressive averages. In the 1906 season, the Reds hit a pedestrian .258 at home vs. a terrible mark of .219 on the road, while their opponents hit .260 at Palace of the Fans vs. .239 at home. The overall NL batting average that year was .244. The high park factor of 112 for batting average in 1906 reflected the relatively good batting performance at Palace of the Fans in a context of extremely low level of hitting in the NL that season. During the ten Deadball seasons Palace of the Fans was in use (1902–1911), the ballpark's park factor for batting average amounted to 105. This meant that the batting averages at the ballpark were five percent (12–13 points) more than they would have been at the average NL ballpark in the same time frame.

For home runs, the generous dimensions in RF, LC, and CF limited OTF home runs to just five in ten full seasons. More so than the typical Deadball Era ballpark, Palace of the Fans was a park conducive to IPHR. In fact, 90 percent of all home runs at the park were IPHR, compared to 52 percent for the entire NL in the first decade of the Deadball Era. The distribution of IPHR was quite uneven: 65 percent of the IPHR were hit to RF (that was the deepest part of the ballpark), a few were hit to RC, and an additional 17 percent were hit to CF. Despite all of the IPHR, the ballpark's home run park factor ranged from 26 to 162 and averaged 61 over 10 seasons. By contrast, Palace of the Fans was a premier park for triples. The ballpark's triples park factor ranged from 133 to 213 and averaged 155 over the park's 10 seasons of use. The extreme range of the home run park factors is best understood when one realizes the absolute number of home runs in any given season at the ballpark was in the range of 10–15. In 1907, the triples park factor for Palace of the Fans was an impressive 213. This was the highest single-season park factor for triples of any NL ballpark in the 19 seasons of the Deadball Era. The high park factor for triples and the below average park factor for home runs is likely due to the not very large dimensions in LC (385) and RC (375). These distances were generally sufficient for triples but not IPHR on balls hit in between the outfielders. The large average outfield distances for all fields reduced the number of doubles as many balls hit past the outfielders went for triples rather than doubles.

The home run and batting park factor data for Palace of the Fans are shown below in four tables.

HOME RUNS BY TYPE AT PALACE OF THE FANS

Years	Total	OTF	Bounce	IPHR
1902–1911	145	15	10	130

OTF HOME RUN DISTRIBUTION BY FIELD
AT PALACE OF THE FANS (EXCLUDES BOUNCE)

Years	Total	LF	CF	RF	Unknown
1902–1911	5	3	1	0	1

INSIDE-THE-PARK HOME RUN BY FIELD AT PALACE OF THE FANS

Years	Total	LF	LC	CF	RC	RF	Unknown
1902–1911	130	8	9	22	3	85	3

BATTING PARK FACTORS FOR PALACE OF THE FANS

Years	BA	OBP	SLUG	2B*	3B*	HR*	BB**
1902–1911	105	103	105	87	155	61	98

*Per AB
**Per Total Plate Appearance (AB+BB+HP)

Redland Field

Cincinnati National League: 1912–1919

Redland Field was a completely new ballpark built after the 1911 season at the same location (Findlay St. and Western Ave.) as the Palace of the Fans. One of the first Classic ML ballparks built largely of steel and concrete, Redland Field, like its predecessor Palace of the Fans, had home plate, the infield, and the grandstand located in the southwest corner of the site. When it opened for the 1912 season, Redland Field consisted of a double-deck grandstand that extended from beyond third base to beyond first base, pavilions down each foul line, and a large set of bleachers in fair RF that extended in reduced depth to RC. There was a modest-sized scoreboard in RC set above the left end of the RF bleachers. A unique feature of this Classic ballpark was the four-foot-high terrace in LF. In the 1930s, the terrace was extended into CF and RF to serve as a warning track. The seating capacity of Redland Field in 1912 was 25,000. During the eight years the park was in use during the Deadball Era, no changes to either the stands or the playing field were made. Redland Field was renamed Crosley Field in 1934 (after the team's new owner Powel Crosley) and was used by the Cincinnati Reds for nearly 60 seasons until the Reds moved to Riverfront Stadium during the 1970 season. Redland Field was torn down in 1972.

The Basis of Redland Field's Configuration and Dimensions

Redland Field had the largest playing area of any ML ballpark when it opened in 1912. It remained the largest ML ballpark until Braves Field opened in August 1915. For the remainder of the Deadball Era, Redland Field was the second largest ballpark in the ML. The configuration and dimensions of the ballpark were based on three principal sources: a 1950 Sanborn fire insurance map of Crosley Field, the dimensions listed in *Green Cathedrals*, and articles from the journal of the Cincinnati Historical Society.[11] The 1950 Sanborn map of Crosley/Redland Field was modified as follows: the field boxes added after the 1926 season in front of the grandstand were deleted, the diagonal alignment of the RF and LF pavilions as shown in photos were added, and the RF foul line was aligned such that it intersected the RF bleachers at the front edge of the high wall that formed the boundary of the park site (in the same place as it had in photos of the 1919 World Series). The dimensional data for this ballpark in *Green Cathedrals* are LF 360, LC 380, CF 420, and RF 360.[12] Home plate was located on the modified 1950 Sanborn map to fit the RF dimension of 400. Once home plate was located (about 60 feet from the backstop), a park diagram was drawn on the Sanborn map. All dimensions other than RF were calculated from this park diagram. LF was 352 and CF was 420. This LF dimension is close to the 360 in *Green Cathedrals,* and the two CF dimensions are exactly the same. Because the location of Western Ave. limited the size of RC and CF, the RF fence (the front of the RF bleachers) intersected the RF foul line at an angle of 83 degrees. As a result, the ballpark's dimensions actually decreased as one moved away from the RF line (400) to straightaway RF (397). The LF foul line intersected the high concrete LF wall at 97 degrees, and the LF dimensions increased noticeably as one moved away from the foul line to straightaway LF (373) and LC (427). The LF and RF walls met at an angle of more than 90 degrees at a point slightly to the right of LC. At this junction in a sort of LC corner, the distance was 438 feet from home plate, the deepest point in the ballpark.

Park data and dimensions for Redland Field are shown below.

DIMENSIONS (calculated from park diagram)

Years	LF	SLF	LC	CF	RC	SRF	RF
1912–1919	352	373	427	420	431	397	400

AVERAGE OUTFIELD DISTANCES

Years	LF	CF	RF
1912–1919	378	428	403

FENCE HEIGHTS (from photos)

Years	LF	CF	RF
1912–1919	20	20	4

ARCHITECT: HARRY HAKE OF HAKE AND HAKE

CAPACITY: 25,000

PARK SIZE-COMPOSITE AVERAGE OUTFIELD DISTANCE: 401

PARK SITE AREA: 6.4 ACRES

DEADBALL ERA RUN FACTOR: 100 (RANK: NL 8)

The Impact of the Park's Configuration and Dimensions on Batting

Overall, Redland Field in the Deadball Era must be considered an average NL ballpark for batting. Measured by the runs scored, the ballpark was truly average with a runs park factor of exactly 100. Redland Field posted batting park factors that were very typical of the NL for batting average, on-base, and slugging. The park was about average for the total of extra-base-hits, but varied for the individual categories of doubles, triples and home runs (see table of Batting Park Factors below). The ballpark was below average for doubles and home runs, but the best park in the NL for triples.

Redland Field was one of the toughest NL ballparks for home runs. In the 1912 season, the Reds' opponents hit just two home runs at Redland Field vs. 26 at their respective home parks. The home run park factors for Redland Field ranged from 25 to 75 and averaged 48 over the ballpark's eight Deadball seasons. The generous dimensions to all fields limited the number of OTF home runs to just 1.1 per season. An important fact to note: all of these OTF home runs were bounce home runs. In the Deadball Era, no home runs were hit over any of Redland Field's outfield fences on the fly! Not until 1921, with the lively ball in use, was the first fly ball OTF home run hit at Redland Field (the Reds Pat Duncan was the first to hit a home run over the LF wall; the first home runs over the CF and RF fences were hit in an exhibition game that same season by Babe Ruth). Much more so than the typical Deadball Era ballpark, Redland Field was conducive to IPHR. In fact, 92 percent of all home runs at the park were IPHR, compared to 35 percent for the entire NL in the second decade of the Deadball Era. The distribution of IPHR was noticeably uneven; 85 percent of the IPHR were hit to CF, RC, or RF. By contrast, Redland Field was a premier park for triples. The park factors for triples ranged from 126 to 160 and averaged 147 over the park's eight Deadball Era seasons. The large average outfield distances for all fields curbed doubles, and many balls hit past the outfielders went for triples rather than doubles. A case in point was a game in 1913 where Fred Merkle of the Giants accomplished the unheard of feat of hitting the LF wall on the fly. For his unprecedented efforts, he was credited with a triple, but was out at home trying for an IPHR.[13] Another factor which contributed to triples and curbed both doubles and home runs at Redland Field was the ground rule in place at the ballpark when there were overflow crowds in the outfield. Any ball hit into the crowd confined behind the ropes in the outfield was a ground-rule triple (unlike the ground rule at most other parks where such hits were doubles). In the frequent games at Redland Field during the Deadball Era when there were overflow crowds, doubles and IPHR (92 percent of total home runs were IPHR) were curtailed, while the chances for triples were greatly enhanced.

The home run and batting park factor data for Redland Field are shown below.

HOME RUNS BY TYPE AT REDLAND FIELD

Years	Total	OTF	Bounce	IPHR
1912–1919	115	9	9	106

OTF HOME RUN DISTRIBUTION BY FIELD AT REDLAND FIELD (EXCLUDES BOUNCE)

Years	Total	LF	CF	RF	Unknown
1912–1919	0				

INSIDE-THE-PARK HOME RUN BY FIELD AT REDLAND FIELD

Years	Total	LF	LC	CF	RC	RF	Unknown
1912–1919	106	2	12	37	18	31	6

BATTING PARK FACTORS FOR REDLAND FIELD

Years	BA	OBP	SLUG	2B*	3B*	HR*	BB**
1912–1919	100	101	100	90	147	45	102

*Per AB
**Per Total Plate Appearance (AB+BB+HP)

6

Cleveland

The NL had a franchise in Cleveland from 1879 to 1899. In the 1890s, the Cleveland NL team, then called the Spiders, played in National League Park (also called League Park III). In 1899, syndicate baseball was in vogue, allowing an owner to control more than one team. The owner of the Cleveland NL franchise also owned the NL St. Louis franchise. A series of very one-sided trades moved the better players from Cleveland to St. Louis. As a result, the Cleveland Spiders were not very good and came to a sad end. After 42 home games in the first half of the 1899 season, the team was so bad (their season's record was 20–134, and they finished 84 games out of first place) and their home attendance was so sparse that the team went on a road trip and never returned, playing all their remaining games on the road. Being exclusively a road team for the rest of the season did not improve the team's fortunes. The hapless Spiders managed to lose 90 percent of their road games (11–101). The 101 losses on the road that season is one baseball record that is truly unbreakable! One small consolation was that this arrangement spared the Cleveland fans from having to watch the woebegone Spiders. Not surprisingly, Cleveland was one of the four teams eliminated after the 1899 season when the NL contracted from 12 to eight reams.

For the 1900 season, the AL moved one of its existing franchises to Cleveland, and the team took over the former NL ballpark (League Park III). The AL team, known as the Bluebirds in the 1901 season and as the Broncos in the 1902 season, became the Naps (after their star player-manager Napoleon Lajoie) starting with the 1903 season and continuing through the 1914 season. Beginning with the 1915 season, the team was called the Indians, a name that remains in use today.

After the 1909 season, the Cleveland team had the wooden League Park III torn down and replaced on the same site with a new Classic ballpark, League Park IV. The new park was much larger and was built of steel and concrete with a double-deck grandstand and bleachers in LF.

There were prohibitions on Sunday baseball in Cleveland both in the late 19th Century and in the early years of the twentieth century. As a result, Cleveland played some Sunday home games at a variety of not-very-nearby neutral sites. The neutral sites for Sunday games in 1902 included one in Canton, OH, one in Columbus, OH; one in Dayton, OH, and two in Fort Wayne, IN. The neutral site Sunday games in 1903 included one in Columbus, OH, and two in Canton, OH. Another consequence of the prohibition on Sunday baseball in Cleveland was a number of one-day road trips to play a Sunday game in cities where Sunday baseball was permitted. The players did not like these out-and-back one-game road trips, but the railroads did! The AL cities where Cleveland journeyed to play Sunday baseball were Milwaukee (1901), Chicago (1901–1910), St. Louis (1902–1910) and Detroit (in 1901–1902 at Burns

Park outside Detroit, and at Bennett Park 1908–1910). Not until the 1911 season was Sunday baseball legal in Cleveland.

League Park III

Cleveland American League: 1901–1909

There were four ballpark in Cleveland called League Park. The first (League Park I) was used by the NL Cleveland Spiders 1879–1884. This park was located at Silby (later Carnegie) St., Kennard (later East 46th) St., and Cedar St. The second park (League Park II) was used by the American Association Cleveland Spiders 1887–1888 and the NL Cleveland Spiders 1889–1890. This second park in Cleveland to be called League Park was at a different location (39th St., East 35th St., Euclid Ave., and Payne Ave.). League Park III was at a third location (in downtown Cleveland at East 70th St., Linwood Ave., Dunham [later East 66th] St., and Lexington Ave. Northeast).[1] League Park III was used by the NL Cleveland Spiders for the 1891–1899 seasons and was the first Cleveland ballpark used by the AL, starting as a minor league park in 1900.

At League Park III, home plate and the grandstand were located in the northwest corner of the park site. Dimensional data for this ballpark in *Green Cathedrals* are limited to RF (290) and the height of the RF fence (20 feet).

The park, on Opening Day 1901 when it was first used by the AL as a ML park, consisted of a covered wooden grandstand in several sections from well beyond first base to well beyond third base. In addition, small bleachers were located far down the LF and RF foul lines. In 1901–1902, there were no seats in the fair portion of the outfield. The seating capacity of the park in 1901 was about 9,000. The ballpark's dimensions were constrained by the inability of the club to purchase a saloon on Lexington Ave., in what would have been the RF corner. Except for this aspect, the park site for 1901–1907 was rectangular. The playing field was angled such that the RF foul line just missed the corner of the saloon property. As a result, the RF line met the RF fence at more than 90 degrees, and the LF foul line therefore had to intersect the LF fence at less than 90 degrees. The LF and RF fences met in the CF corner (to the right of dead CF) at a right angle.

The Basis of League Park III's Configurations and Dimensions

The knowledge of the park's configuration and dimensions was based on an 1896 Sanborn fire insurance map and a 1909 panoramic photo of the park from the *Cleveland Leader*. The known RF dimension (290) was used to position home plate (at 75 feet from the backstop) on the Sanborn map.[2] Using this location of home plate, a park diagram was drawn on the Sanborn map. All other dimensions were derived from this diagram. The resulting LF dimension was 353, and dead CF was 409. The CF corner, at the junction of the LF and RF fences, was about halfway between dead CF and RC and was a substantial 445-foot distance from home plate. The first configuration change occurred before the 1903 season. Capacity was increased with the building of bleachers in RF in front of the high RF wall. These bleachers were largely in RF and extended from CF to within about 50 feet of the RF foul line. These bleachers, whose depth was estimated, reduced the straightaway RF distance from 323 to about 290. The seating capacity of the park was again increased for the 1908 season by the

An afternoon game at Cleveland's League Park III. View from left field in League Park III. Note the screen above the grandstand roof to keep foul balls in the park. This photograph (undated) is known to be from the time period 1901–09, and is most likely from 1908 or 1909, the only seasons when there were left-field bleachers at the ballpark (and from where the photograph was likely taken). (American Memory Collection, Library of Congress.)

construction of a second set of bleachers behind the LC portion of the LF fence. The addition of these new bleachers increased the area of the park site by about 4,500 square feet. These bleachers, as shown in the 1909 photo from the *Cleveland Leader*, extended from about LC all the way to the CF corner.[3] Early in the 1908 season, a game account in the *Cleveland Plain Dealer* referred to a home run to CF by Hickman as the first Cleveland home run on the enlarged grounds.[4] This meant that the CF portion of the RF bleachers had been removed, most likely to unblock the sight lines from the new CF bleachers. Additional evidence suggesting that the old CF bleachers were removed is that IPHRs to CF increased from 1.8 per season (1903–1907) to six in 1908. The main portion of the RF bleachers remained in use for another season (1908) after which they were removed as shown by the 1909 photo in the *Cleveland Leader*.[5]

Park data and dimensions for League Park III are shown below.

DIMENSIONS (derived from park diagrams)

Years	LF	SLF	LC	CF*	RC	SRF	RF
1901–1902	353	347	362	409	390	323	290
1903–1908	353	347	362	409	352	286	290
1909	353	347	362	409	390	323	290

*Deepest point was the CF corner (445)

AVERAGE OUTFIELD DISTANCES

Years	LF	CF	RF
1901–1902	351	402	328
1903–1907	351	390	303
1908	351	397	303
1909	351	402	328

FENCE HEIGHTS (from *Green Cathedrals* and estimated from photos)

Years	LF	CF	RF
1901–1902	10	10–20	20
1903–1907	10	10–20	6–20
1908	10	6–20	6–20
1909	10	6–20	20

CAPACITY: 9,000 (1901), 11,200 (1903–1907 Est.), 12,200 (1908 Est.), 11,200 (1909 Est.)

PARK SIZE/COMPOSITE AVERAGE OUTFIELD DISTANCE: 360 (1901–1902), 348 (1903–1907), 350 (1908), 360 (1909)

PARK SITE AREA: 3.9 ACRES (1901–1907), 4.0 ACRES (1908–1909)

DEADBALL ERA RUN FACTOR: 96 (RANK: AL 14)

The Impact of the Park's Configurations and Dimensions on Batting

For the 1901–1902 seasons, League Park was the second smallest AL ballpark. Despite this small size, the batting park factors were unexceptional; in fact, they were downright average (see table of League Park III Batting Park Factors below). Only for doubles was the park factor above 100. In the 1901 season, the Cleveland Bluebirds set an unbreakable record for the fewest home runs at home — zero. Apparently that was not entirely due to the ballpark, as the visitors managed an even dozen home runs at League Park that season. With those numbers in mind, one concludes that unlike many of today's ballparks, League Park's original AL configuration was not designed to suit the home team's sluggers. In the next season, things turned out a lot better for the Cleveland team, now called the Broncos, as the Broncos hit 15 home runs to the visitors' five in the 60 games played at League Park, while at the same time compiling a .310 team batting average (the highest in the AL).[6]

The reconfiguration of the park for the 1903 season significantly reduced the size of the already smaller-than-average RF. However, this change appears to have had virtually no impact on batting at the ballpark, except for home runs. The League Park batting park factors for 1901–1902 vs. 1903–1907 were virtually unchanged, except for a small increase in doubles and a small decrease in triples (see Batting Park Factors at League Park III below). It is interesting to note that the short RF fence at League Park in 1903 resulted in only six OTF home runs to RF, while in that same season the short LF fence at Washington's American League Park resulted in 30 OTF home runs to LF. It would appear that the AL in general and the Cleveland team in particular did not have many power-hitting left-handed batters. In the six seasons (1903–1908) when the RF bleachers were in place, there were on average only five OTF home runs hit to RF per season. In the same six seasons in this configuration of the ballpark, League Park was a very average hitter's park, being slightly above average for doubles and slightly below average for triples and home runs.

The removal of the RF bleachers before the 1909 season had a negligible impact on batting, except for triples (the park factor increased 35 percent) and home runs. The number of home runs fell from 15 in the 1908 season to only three in the 1909 season, while the park's home run park factor dropped from 81 to 20. Unlike many Deadball Era ballparks, League Park III was not a park conducive to IPHR, as shown by the home-run data below. The installation of the RF bleachers for the 1903 season led to a drop in IPHR from 5.0 per season for 1901–1902 to 1.8 per season for the next five seasons. During the five seasons (1903–1907) with the RF-CF bleachers in place, IPHR accounted for just 13 percent of the total home runs hit at League Park III. In the 1908 season with the removal of the CF portion of the RF-CF bleachers, IPHR accounted for 60 percent of total home runs at the park. In 1909, after the removal of the remaining RF bleachers, all three home runs hit were IPHR.

The home-run data and batting park factors for League Park III are shown below.

HOME RUNS BY TYPE AT LEAGUE PARK III

Years	Total	OTF	Bounce	IPHR
1901–1902	32	22	0	10
1903–1907	71	62	4	9
1908	15	6	0	9
1909	3	0	0	3

OTF HOME RUNS BY FIELD AT LEAGUE PARK III (EXCLUDES BOUNCE)

Years	Total	LF	CF	RF	Unknown
1901–1902	21	13	1	3	4
1903–1907	58	29	4	24	1
1908	6	0	0	6	0
1909	0				

INSIDE-THE-PARK HOME RUN BY FIELD AT LEAGUE PARK III

Years	Total	LF	LC	CF	RC	RF	Unknown
1901–1902	11	1	0	5	1	2	2
1903–1907	9	3	1	3	1	1	0
1908	9	2	1	6	0	0	0
1909	3	0	0	3	0	0	0

Batting Park Factors for League Park III

Years	BA	OBP	SLUG	2B*	3B*	HR*	BB**
1901–1902	100	99	100	118	83	69	91
1903–1907	99	99	98	105	87	75	92
1908	103	101	102	111	84	81	94
1909	102	100	102	112	113	20	88

*Per AB
**Per Total Plate Appearance (AB+BB+HP)

League Park IV

Cleveland American League: 1910–1919

League Park IV was built at the same location as League Park III. Both parks were located in downtown Cleveland at East 70th St., Linwood Ave., Dunham (later East 66th) St., and Lexington Ave. Northeast.[7] League Park IV was a steel-and-concrete Classic ballpark built between the 1909 and 1910 seasons. The park was used by the AL Cleveland Indians until mid-season 1932 and for most home games from 1934 to 1946.

Like its predecessor League Park III, the park had home plate, the infield, and the grandstand located in the northwest corner of the site. The 1910 dimensional data for this ballpark in *Green Cathedrals* are LF (385), CF (420), CF corner (505), RF (290), backstop (76), and the height of the RF wall and screen (45).[8] The RF wall extended to the CF corner as did the 25-foot-high steel columns and supporting wires on top of the wall. Over the life of the ballpark (1910–1946) the length of the RF screen varied. Which is to say, in some seasons the screen ended in RC, and in other seasons the screen extended all the way to dead CF.

The park, when it opened for the 1910 season, consisted of a double-deck grandstand that extended from the RF wall to almost the LF corner. In addition, a moderate-sized set of deep concrete bleachers extended around the LF corner and into fair LF. At the straightaway LF point, a set of wooden bleachers began and extended until abutting the diagonal CF scoreboard. The wooden bleachers in LF were set forward a few feet from the front edge of the concrete bleachers. The seating capacity of the park in 1910 was 21,400. Unlike League Park III, this ballpark's dimensions were not affected by the saloon property on Lexington Ave. This saloon property and others on Lexington Ave., that had constrained the orientation of the field at League Park III were acquired and added to the ballpark site. This site expansion allowed the RF fence to be close to 90 degrees to the foul line. The RF wall, 20 feet in height, was topped by a 25-foot in-play wire screen, making a home run barrier with a total height of 45 feet. Home runs over the RF wall and screen ended up on Lexington Ave. During the ten years the park was in use during the Deadball Era, no changes to either the stands or the playing field were made.

The Basis of League Park IV's Configuration and Dimensions

The park's configuration and dimensions were based on three principal sources: a 1911 Sanborn fire insurance map, the dimensions in *Green Cathedrals*, and an aerial photo of the park from *Lost Ballparks*.[9] Earlier research by the author and others into League Park IV had treated the playing field as essentially rectangular, with the LF and RF fences perpendicular to the foul lines. This research was based on aerial photos in which the LF foul line appeared to be perpendicular to the LF fence. SABR member Bob Boynton unearthed the original plans for the park.[10] According to the plans, the angle of the foul line and the RF wall was about 94 degrees. The listed dimensions in *Green Cathedrals* (RF 290 and CF 420) are not consistent with the foul line-RF wall angle being either 90 or 94 degrees. If the angle were 90 degrees, CF would be 410, and if the angle were 94 degrees, it would be 438. Using the CF dimension as 420, by geometry the RF wall angle works out to be 92 degrees. Using 92 degrees as the angle of the RF wall and foul line has the useful property of making RC (at 30 degrees) 340, which is what was marked on the wall at the estimated RC location in the 1930s. The 1911 Sanborn map also has the angle of the RF wall at about 92 degrees to the RF foul line, and 88 degrees for the angle of the LF fence and foul line. The LF distance on the Sanborn map was 375. The LF and RF fences met in the CF corner (to the left of dead CF) at a right angle. The CF corner was a huge distance from home plate (a distance estimated at 498 on the Sanborn map, which is quite close to the 505 dimension for the 1910 CF corner listed in *Green Cathedrals*). However, note that the location of the large diagonal CF scoreboard, as shown on the 1911 Sanborn map, meant the scoreboard masked the CF corner, making the largest actual dimension in the ballpark 460 feet to the left of dead CF. It is possible that the CF scoreboard was not in place on Opening Day 1910 and the CF corner then would have been in play until the scoreboard was installed.

Park data and dimensions for Cleveland's League Park IV are shown below.

DIMENSIONS (CALCULATED FROM PARK DIAGRAM)

Years	LF	SLF	LC	CF*	RC	SRF	RF
1910–1919	375	383	413	420	340	304	290

*Deepest point (460) was the CF scoreboard that was to the left of dead CF

AVERAGE OUTFIELD DISTANCES

Years	LF	CF	RF
1910–1919	384	409	308

FENCE HEIGHTS (from *Green Cathedrals*)

Years	LF	CF	RF
1910–1919	5	10–20	45

ARCHITECT: OSBORN ENGINEERING

CAPACITY: 21,400

PARK SIZE/COMPOSITE AVERAGE OUTFIELD DISTANCE: 367

PARK SITE AREA: 5.4 ACRES

DEADBALL ERA RUN FACTOR: 110 (RANK: AL 4)

The Impact of the Park's Configuration and Dimensions on Batting

Overall, League Park IV must be considered the best regular-use hitter's park in the AL during its ten Deadball seasons (see table of Batting Park Factors below). Except for home runs and walks, the park posted batting park factors noticeably above average. The Cleveland Indians posted impressive team home batting averages of .300 in 1911 and .292 in 1919. In the 1917 season, League Park posted the highest-ever Deadball Era AL batting average park factor of 116.2 (for regular-use ballparks). This park factor meant that batting at League Park produced batting averages that were 40 points better than at the average AL ballpark that season. The overall AL batting average that year was .248. Surprisingly, neither the Indians nor their opponents posted impressive averages: the Indians hit a pedestrian .265 at home vs. a lowly .221 on the road, while their opponents hit .270 at League Park vs. .223 at home. Over the ten Deadball seasons League Park IV was in use, its batting average park factors averaged 109, nine percent better than the average AL ballpark.

For home runs, the combination of generous dimensions in LF and CF and the 45-foot height of the RF wall/screen limited OTF home runs to just 4.4 per season. When the park opened in 1910, the Cleveland management boasted that Detroit slugger Sam Crawford would never be able to clear the 45-foot-high RF wall/screen. In fact, it took Crawford only half a season to do so (on July 1, 1910, and he was the first to accomplish the feat). The close and high RF wall/screen did have a major impact on doubles. The ballpark was always a very good park for doubles. Left-handed-hitting Tris Speaker, who played 11 seasons of his Hall of Fame career in League Park IV, still holds the ML record for career doubles with 792. Speaker led the AL in doubles six times in the 11 seasons he played his home games in League Park.

More so than the typical Deadball Era ballpark, League Park IV was conducive to IPHR, as shown by the home run data below. In fact, 60 percent of all home runs at the park were IPHR, compared to 32 percent for the AL in the years 1911–1919. The disparity between the LF dimension (375) and the RF dimension (290) was reflected in the distribution of OTF home runs — all but one was hit to RF. The distribution of IPHR was quite different; none were hit to RF or RC, the majority were hit to CF, and the remainder went to LF and LC (one to an unknown field).

There was a curious effect of the RF wall and screen. As noted above, in some seasons the RF screen ended in RC. With this configuration, balls hit to the CF side of the screen were home runs, except if batters were unlucky enough to hit one of the screen supports or wires in an area where there was no screen. An example of this occurred in a game (June 27, 1921) when George Sisler of the visiting St. Louis Browns hit a ball high and deep to RC. The ball was going for a home run until it hit one of the wires strung between two of the steel columns. The ball dropped down into CF, and Sisler had to settle for a double.

The home run and batting park factor data for League Park IV are shown below in four tables.

HOME RUNS BY TYPE AT LEAGUE PARK IV

Years	Total	OTF	Bounce	IPHR
1910–1919	110	44	10	66

OTF HOME RUN BY FIELD AT LEAGUE PARK IV (EXCLUDES BOUNCE)

Years	Total	LF	CF	RF	Unknown
1910–1919	34	1	0	33	0

INSIDE-THE-PARK HOME RUN BY FIELD AT LEAGUE PARK IV

Years	Total	LF	LC	CF	RC	RF	Unknown
1910–1919	66	15	7	43	0	0	1

Batting Park Factors for League Park IV

Years	BA	OBP	SLUG	2B*	3B*	HR*	BB**
1910–1919	109	105	109	126	102	61	96

*Per AB
**Per Total Plate Appearance (AB+BB+HP)

7

Detroit

The NL had a team called the Wolverines in Detroit from 1881 to 1888 that played at Recreation Park. In the 1890s, Detroit was a minor league city with a team in the Western League, the forerunner of the AL. The Western League team (called both the Wolverines and the Tigers in those years) played at Bennett Park starting with the 1896 season.

In 1900, the Western League changed its name to the AL, and Detroit was one of the eight original AL franchises. The team (now called the Tigers) expanded the existing Western League ballpark (Bennett Park), where it stayed until the end of the 1911 season. That ballpark was then torn down and a new steel-and-concrete Classic ballpark was built on the site. This ballpark was named Navin Field, later it was renamed Briggs Stadium before finally acquiring the name by which it is best known, Tiger Stadium.

As a result of prohibitions on Sunday baseball, Detroit played all of their Sunday home games at Burns Park in 1900–1902 (the park was in located in Springwells Township, conveniently outside the Detroit city limits). Pressured by the AL to stop using Burns Park because of its rowdy reputation, the Tigers played a few Sunday games at a variety of neutral sites in the 1903 and 1905 seasons. In 1903, two games were played at Armory Park in Toledo, OH, and one at Ramona Park in Grand Rapids, MI. There were two neutral site 1905 games played at Neil Park II in Columbus, OH. Legal AL Sunday baseball in the city of Detroit did not begin until the 1908 season.

Bennett Park

Detroit American League: 1901–1911

Bennett Park was named for Charlie Bennett, a popular catcher with Detroit's NL team for eight seasons (1881–1888), who lost both legs in a railway accident in 1894. The ballpark, which came to be called Charlie Bennett's Park, or simply Bennett Park, opened in 1896. It was the home field of the Western League Detroit Wolverines (also known as the Tigers) for a span of four seasons: 1896–1899. In 1900, the Western League was renamed the American League, and the league continued to use Bennett Park for the only minor league season played by the AL. Major league baseball returned to Detroit in 1901 with the debut of the now major league AL. On Opening Day, the Tigers sent the overflow crowd home happy with a memorable ten-run rally in the bottom of the 9th inning to defeat Milwaukee 14–13. Led by Ty Cobb and Sam Crawford, the Tigers won three consecutive pennants, 1907–1909, and Bennett Park hosted the World Series in those years. Bennett Park was built of wood, but unlike many of the other contemporary wooden ballparks, it never burned. The park was demolished after the 1911 season to make way for Navin Field

Bennett Park was located at the northwest corner of Michigan and Trumbull Avenues, not far from downtown Detroit. When Bennett Park was built in 1896, the area was not highly developed, as Detroit in the late-nineteenth century was not yet a major U.S. city. The park site was in a semi-rural area and was not large, consisting of 4.2 acres. By comparison, other wooden AL and NL ballparks occupied sites ranging from 3.9 acres (League Park III in Cleveland) to 9.6 acres (Hilltop Park in New York). When it opened in 1896, Bennett Park had a seating capacity of around 5,000. With the return of ML baseball to Detroit, the ballpark's capacity was expanded to accommodate 8,500 fans for the 1901 season. All capacity figures refer to permanent seating; temporary outfield bleachers were added for each of the 1907–1909 World Series. The park's stands were modified and seating expanded a number of times after 1901. RF bleachers were added for the 1908 season, the main grandstand was expanded, and both foul line bleachers were extended to about the foul poles. Additional bleachers were built for the 1910 season in LF, and after this last expansion, the park's capacity reached 14,000.

On Opening Day of the ballpark's first ML season (1901), the grandstand was not yet complete. The roof had not been added to the first base-home plate section of the grandstand. When completed later that season, the park consisted of a covered grandstand, which extended past third base and about as far as first base, and uncovered bleachers that extended part way down both the LF and RF foul lines. Home plate was in the southeast corner of the site with the LF line running about west to east so that left-handed batters faced the afternoon sun. In the 1901–1907 seasons, a wooden clubhouse, a scoreboard, and a groundskeeper's shed all stood in LC near the corner where the LF and RF fences met. The scoreboard and both buildings were in play, but were rarely reached by a batted ball.

Before the 1908 season, the Tigers purchased the property behind RF (previously used as a lumberyard) and thus extended the ballpark's northern boundary to Cherry St. This addition increased the size of the park site to 5.5 acres. Home plate was shifted about 40 feet towards the outfield to allow additional rows of seats in front of the existing grandstand. The additional room in RF allowed for the construction of the first permanent outfield bleachers. The new RF bleachers added about 2,000 seats to the park's capacity and extended from RC to within about 50 feet of the RF foul line. During this expansion of the ballpark, a clubhouse was built beneath the grandstand. This allowed the removal of the CF clubhouse, as well as the nearby groundskeeper's shed, and they were replaced with an interior CF fence.

There were other bleachers from which to view games at Bennett Park; however, they were outside the park. The "wildcat bleachers" were built on the roofs of homes or barns on National Ave. behind the low LF fence. Not until the 1910 season were there inside-the-park bleachers in LF. The new bleachers were built in front of the 1909 LF fence, and the bleachers had the useful property (from the viewpoint of the Tiger's management) of blocking the view from the wildcat bleachers. The Bennett Park LF bleachers were relatively shallow in depth and extended from about the LF line almost to LC. With this and the prior additions, seating capacity was increased from 8,500 in 1901 to 14,000 by 1910. These capacity figures were exclusive of as many standees as could be squeezed into the outfield and foul areas for big games. The popularity of the park as an advertising venue may be judged from the double-billboards making up the fence in CF in the last two years of the park's existence.

In its early years of use as an AL ballpark, compared to the other pre–Classic wooden ballparks, Bennett Park had a smaller playing field, while it was about average in seating capacity. After the LF bleachers were installed in 1910, Bennett Park now possessed the smallest LF in the AL, while by contrast RF was much above average in size.

A crowded Bennett Park during the 1907 World Series. A view of Bennett Park during the 1907 World Series (Detroit Tigers vs. the Chicago Cubs). Note not only the rings of standees in the outfield, but the fans sitting on the top of a single-story wooden structure in the left foreground. This structure was the clubhouse and was in the field of play. (Photograph by the George R. Lawrence Co., American Memory Collection, Library of Congress.)

The Basis of Bennett Park's Configurations and Dimensions

No listed dimensions for Bennett Park were found in any of the usual ballpark reference books.[1] The 1901 dimensions (LF 345, CF 432, RF 370) were derived entirely from an 1897 Sanborn Fire Insurance Co. map and ballpark photos.[2] A diagram of the park and the dimensions of the park's land plat were also derived from the 1897 Sanborn map. The only known dimension for Bennett Park was LF in 1910 (295) from the Opening Day article in the *Detroit Free Press*. The artists' renditions of the park in *Diamonds* and *Baseball Memories: 1900–1909* were used to position the 1901 and later grandstands/bleachers and the playing field on the park diagram.[3] Because the shape of the land plat was a trapezoid and not a rectangle, the outfield fences were aligned at more than 90 degrees to the foul line in LF and less than 90 degrees in RF.

The description of the 1901 configuration of the ballpark was taken from Benson's *Ballparks of North America*.[4] In its original configuration, Bennett Park had a small scoreboard in LC to the left of the back of the CF clubhouse (Okkonen 10). A small tool shed was to the right of the clubhouse in front of the LC-CF fence. Behind the RC-CF fence (on the northern boundary of the ballpark) was a lumberyard. The first reported change in the park's configuration (Benson 49) was before the start of the 1908 season. This substantial expansion consisted of the acquisition of the adjacent lumberyard property and the movement of the RF-CF fence back a considerable distance; the construction of additional rows of grandstand seating in front of the old infield grandstand; and the erection of permanent bleachers in fair RF territory. Because of the additional rows of seats in front of the grandstand, home plate was moved about 40 feet towards the outfield.[5] There is also photographic evidence of some RF bleachers in a 1907 World Series photo of Bennett Park.[6] In this photo (Bak and Vincent 158–59, Okkonen 51), low temporary bleachers are visible in RC next to the other larger and higher bleachers in RF. It is believed that both sets of bleachers were temporary seating constructed for the 1907 World Series. If the larger and higher RF bleachers had existed during the regular season, the distance to straightaway RF would have been reduced to about 325–335. At that distance, a goodly number of bounce and OTF home runs into the RF bleachers should have occurred. A review of all home runs hit at Bennett Park for the 1907 season showed no home runs hit into any outfield bleachers.[7]

The same photo reveals the RC-CF fence to be aligned with the back of the RF bleachers. This same configuration is shown in a 1911 photo (Bak, Vincent, and the *Detroit Free Press* 215). These bleachers were built about 40 feet in front of the perimeter fence, in part of the area that was added to the ballpark before the 1908 season. Thus the area of the ballpark's land plat was significantly increased for the 1908 season. In CF, there was a new short diagonal fence adjacent to a new and larger scoreboard, which was situated slightly to the left of dead CF. The enlarged land plat was drawn on the Sanborn map and was used to estimate the RF dimensions for the 1908 and subsequent seasons. The next reported change consisted of the addition of two small sections of seats to the grandstand in 1910 (Benson). In Benson, there is no report of bleachers in LF. The photo of temporary LF bleachers built for the 1909 World Series (Okkonen 53) confirms that as late as the end of the 1909 regular season there were no permanent bleachers in left field. For the final two seasons of its existence, the park's seating capacity was increased by the construction of shallow permanent bleachers in LF. There is a report of "permanent bleachers in RF and LF" (Bak and Vincent 215) at the start of the 1911 season. However, research into the newspaper accounts of home runs in the 1910 season showed the LF bleachers were actually in place and in use during the 1910 season. Additional newspaper research found a description of the LF bleachers in use on Opening Day

A panoramic photograph of Bennett Park during the 1909 World Series. A wide angle view of Bennett Park during the 1909 World Series taken from the left-field corner. The higher bleachers in right field (those further in the background) were a permanent fixture of the ballpark built before the 1908 season. The lower bleachers in the left foreground of the photograph were temporary seats for the World Series. (Photograph by the Peninsular Engraving Co. of Detroit, Panoramic Photographs Collection [PAN Sports No. 14], Library of Congress.)

1910.[8] This same Opening Day story gave the new LF distance as 295. Another photo, this one included in a video on Classic ballparks, shows both the depth and width of the LF bleachers.[9] Visible are 14 rows of seats, which were the basis of the estimated depth of the LF bleachers. The estimated depth of the LF bleachers in combination with the known LF dimension for 1910 (295) was the basis of the 1908–1909 LF dimension (330). In addition, in this part of the video the scoreboard is visible as part of the CF diagonal fence; only in this photo the scoreboard is among the upper tier of billboards. As this photo shows the LF bleachers, it must be from either 1910 or 1911.

In summary, most of the Bennett Park dimensions were estimated from the 1897 Sanborn map and contain a moderate amount of uncertainty. All dimensions were checked against, and are consistent with, the available photographic evidence and the home-run data.

Park data and dimensions for Bennett Park are shown below.

DIMENSIONS (largely estimated)

Years	LF	SLF	LC	CF	RC	SRF	RF
1901–1907	345	384	456	432*	384	374	370
1908–1909	330	368	440	490	386	374	440
1910–1911	295	330	420	490	386	374	440

*Deepest point was 480 to the right of LC

FENCE HEIGHTS (from 1897 Sanborn and estimated from photos)

Years	LF	CF	RF
1901–1907	10	10	10
1908–1909	12	12	6–12
1910–1911	8	6–16	6–12

AVERAGE OUTFIELD DISTANCES

Years	LF	CF	RF
1901–1907	392	430	380
1908–1909	373	457	385
1910–1911	337	456	385

CAPACITY: 8,500 (1901–1907), 10,500 (1908–1909), 14,000 (1910–1911)

PARK SIZE/COMPOSITE AVERAGE OUTFIELD DISTANCE:
401 (1901–1907), 405 (1908–1909), 393 (1910–1911)

PARK SITE AREA: 4.2 ACRES (1901–1907), 5.5 ACRES (1908–1911)

DEADBALL ERA RUN FACTOR: 107 (RANK: AL 6)

The Impact of the Park's Configurations and Dimensions on Batting

For all 11 seasons of its ML use, Bennett Park was one of the largest ballparks in the AL, with a park size 20–30 feet larger than the average AL ballpark. There were three different configurations during Bennett Park's ML years: 1901–1907, 1908–1909, and 1910–1911. The two changes in configuration had a measurable and impressive effect on home runs. The two configuration changes had a far more modest impact on doubles and (for one configuration change) slugging but virtually no impact on batting average, on-base, triples, or walks (see table of Batting Park Factors below). Only in the 1911 season did the Tigers post a home batting average above .300. The Tigers hit .305, the best in the AL that season, while the visitors hit .287. As 1911 was the first full season with the use of the cork-center ball, batting averages increased throughout the AL. The combined batting mark at Bennett Park of Detroit and their opponents of .296 was only four percent better than the average of AL parks that season. Over the full range of 11 ML seasons, Bennett Park was very near to average for doubles, triples, and walks; the respective park factors fell within a range of 98 to 104.

Not surprisingly, the park's generous dimensions made it a good park for IPHR. In the original 1901–1907 configuration, IPHR accounted for 86 percent of total home runs, and with the expansion of the park for the 1908–09 seasons, IPHR were a remarkable 91 percent of total home runs. Only with the installation of the LF bleachers before the 1910 season did the proportion of IPHR fall to 55 percent. The increase in park size for the 1908–1909 seasons was accompanied by a 65 percent increase in total home runs per season vs. 1901–1907. In the Deadball Era, there was no simple negative relationship between park size and home runs.

A specific comparison of the number and type of home runs at Bennett Park was made for the 1910–1911 seasons vs. the 1908–1909 seasons. The comparison shows that home runs per season more than doubled after the LF bleachers were built. The apparent effect of the introduction of the LF bleachers is exaggerated because the cork-center ball was used for part of the 1910 AL season and all of the 1911 season. Total ML home runs increased 42 percent during the first full season with the cork-center ball. All of the 11 OTF home runs (excluding bounce home runs) hit in 1910 at Bennett Park were hit into the LF bleachers. In 1911, 86 percent of the OTF home runs were to LF: 12 home runs were into or over the LF bleachers and two were to RF. With the low screen at the front of the LF and RF bleachers, there were nine bounce home runs in the two seasons. IPHR were concentrated in the deeper areas of the park (LC and CF), and these two fields accounted for 65 percent of the IPHR during the life of the park.

The Tigers used the park-specific ground rules to increase their home-park advantage. After the expansion of the park before the 1908 season, overflow crowds were allowed behind ropes only in RF. The Tigers manager Hugh Jennings then set a ground rule that any ball hit into the overflow crowd in RF was a three-base hit.[10] In that era, the Tigers had four left-handed batters, two of whom were future members of the Hall of Fame. Ty Cobb and Sam Crawford made good use of that ground rule. In 1909, the AL established a new rule. Previously ground rules were established by the home team. Now, ground rules were to be set by the agreement of the two team's captains. If the two captains could not reach an agreement, then the umpire would set the ground rules.[11]

HOME RUNS BY TYPE AT BENNETT PARK

Years	Total	OTF	Bounce	IPHR
1901–1907	69	10	3	59
1908–1909	33	3	0	30
1910–1911	75	34	9	41

OTF Home Runs by Field at Bennett Park (excludes Bounce)

Years	Total	LF	CF	RF	Unknown
1901–1907	7	5	1	1	0
1908–1909	3	3	0	0	0
1910–1911	25	23	0	2	0

Inside-the-Park Home Runs by Field at Bennett Park

Years	Total	LF	LC	CF	RC	RF	Unknown
1901–1907	59	6	19	22	0	7	5
1908–1909	30	5	6	10	0	6	3
1910–1911	41	5	4	15	2	13	2

Batting Park Factors at Bennett Park

Years	BA	OBP	SLUG	2B*	3B*	HR*	BB**
1901–1907	102	101	100	90	107	64	98
1908–1909	103	102	103	103	104	98	98
1910–1911	103	102	103	86	98	155	99

*Per AB
**Per Total Plate Appearance (AB+BB+HP)

Burns Park

Detroit American League: 1901–1902

No photos of this ballpark could be found. According to *The Corner* and Detroit ballpark author Richard Bak, there are none to be found.

Burns Park was the ballpark used by the Detroit Tigers for Sunday games in the 1901 and 1902 seasons. Located west of the city limits in the Michigan township of Springwells, the wooden ballpark was on Dix St., a street that in 2006 runs at an angle mostly east-west, between Waterman St., and Livernois Ave., both of which run north-south.[12] The problem with this described location is that in 2006 Waterman St. and Livernois Ave. were four blocks apart. In 2006, this location was in the southwest portion of the city of Detroit.

The ballpark was built before the 1900 season for the purpose of playing Sunday baseball games, which was prohibited in the city of Detroit until 1907. Burns Park was built on land owned by the then (1900–1901) owner of the Tigers, James D. Burns, who named the park after himself. A quickly constructed all-wooden ballpark, the structural strength of the facility can be judged from an incident early in the 1901 season. On April 20, 1901, a wind blew the roof of the grandstand onto the field.

The park was opened on May 6, 1900, when it was first used by the AL Detroit Tigers. On Opening Day 1900, the park consisted of a grandstand with a seating capacity of about 3,000. On Opening Day and at several other Sunday games that season, there were unruly overflow crowds. During the 1900 season, the grandstand was expanded. Opening Day in 1901 drew over 10,000 fans, including an overflow crowd in the outfield. As the 1900 expansion of the grandstand had proved inadequate, a set of bleachers 160 feet long were built in May 1901 down the RF line. This expansion eliminated most overflow crowds. In 1901, with the AL now a self-proclaimed ML circuit, the Tigers played 13 Sunday games at Burns Park.

During the 1902 season, additional bleachers were built that permitted the outfield, for at least that game, to be clear of spectators.[13] The Tigers played an additional 10 Sunday games at Burns Park in the 1902 season to avoid the prohibition of Sunday baseball in Detroit. The Sunday games at Burns Park were a popular success; attendance in 1901 averaged 5,208 per game vs. 3,364 for non–Sunday games at the regular Detroit home park, Bennett Park. Likewise, in 1902, attendance averaged 4,473 per game at Burns Park vs. 2,539 for games at Bennett Park. However, the park suffered from being in an unsavory area; both stockyards and numerous saloons were nearby. After forcing a sale of the club after the 1901 season, the AL (which at that time meant AL President Ban Johnson) put pressure on the new Tigers ownership to cease the use of Burns Park as the AL sought to improve the image of the league and baseball in general. While the moral reputation of the park was none too good, AL hitters certainly thought highly of the place; Burns Park posted run park factors of 137 and 172 in its two seasons of ML baseball.

The Basis of Burns Park's Configuration and Dimensions

As noted above, the author has not been able to find any photos of this ballpark. In addition, the Sanborn Map Co. did not cover Springwells Township in their maps from 1900–1902; thus, there were no Sanborn maps available to use to estimate either the size of the park site or the dimensions of the playing field.

There is also no available dimensional data for this ballpark. A 1902 game account refers to a home run over the scoreboard and inside of the LF foul pole.[13] This established that there was a scoreboard in LF not far from the LF corner. Based on the batting data, and in particular the home-run data, LF was most likely small, while CF and RF were more moderate sized. Estimates of the average outfield distances are LF 305–315, CF 380–390, RF 355–365. The CF and RF estimates are merely guesses. The LF dimensions are based on comparisons of the Burns Park home run data to the home run data for other 1901–1902 AL parks. Thus the park size is unknown, but inferred from the batting data as most likely small. The less-than-specific location of this park, the total absence of park photos, and the lack of any Sanborn map makes the park's dimensions and the overall park size simply informed estimates.

From comparisons of home-run data, the LF fence was rather close, most likely about the same as the short LF fence at the 1901–1903 Washington Senators home park (AL Park I), that had a LF foul line distance of about 290 and an average LF distance of 319. Home-run data for Washington's AL Park I in 1901–1902 show 88 OTF home runs to LF in 136 games, a rate of 0.65/game. At Burns Park, the rate of OTF home runs/game to LF were at a minimum 0.74/game (17 home runs known in 23 games). This home-run data suggests the average LF distance at Burns Park was roughly the same as at AL Park I (about 310–320). Logically, the average distances for CF and RF must have been greater than for LF. There were no IPHR at Burns Park in either 1901 or 1902. By comparison, at Washington's AL Park I that had similar LF dimensions, IPHR accounted for 20 percent of total home runs in the same two seasons. The Burns Park assumed configuration is with the LF and RF fences at 90 degrees to the foul lines, and a CF diagonal fence. Based on this assumed configuration and dimensions of LF 295, CF 390, and RF 340, a park diagram was developed. All of the ballpark's estimated dimensions were derived from this diagram.

Park data and dimensions for Burns Park are shown below.

7. Detroit

DIMENSIONS (estimated from park diagram)

Years	LF	SLF	LC	CF	RC	SRF	RF
1901–1902	295	305	340	390	392	352	290

AVERAGE OUTFIELD DISTANCES

Years	LF	CF	RF
1901–1902	310	380	358

PARK SIZE/COMPOSITE AVERAGE OUTFIELD DISTANCE: 349

CAPACITY: 3,000 (1900), 6,000 (1901 EST.), 6,500 (MAY–SEPTEMBER 1902 EST.)

PARK SITE AREA: 3–4 ACRES (EST.)

DEADBALL ERA RUN FACTOR: 154 (RANK: AL 1)

The Impact of the Park's Configuration and Dimensions on Batting

Burns Park was overwhelmingly the best hitter's park in the Deadball Era (see following table of Burns Park batting data). No other Deadball Era ballpark had batting park factors to compare with it (see second table of Batting Park Factors). Burns Park was, in a manner of speaking, the Coors Field of the Deadball Era. For example, the Tigers at Burns Park had a batting average of .354 in 1901 and .322 in 1902. In the same two seasons, the AL as a whole posted batting averages of .277 and .275. The .354 average in 1901 at Burns Park was the highest ML home park team batting average since 1900. The exceptional Burns Park batting averages posted by the Tigers in these two seasons were helped by two other environmental factors. First, the AL had not yet adopted the foul-strike rule for the 1901 and 1902 seasons. Thus, in the AL (but not in the NL) foul batted balls were not strikes. A comparison of batting averages before and after the AL adoption of the foul-strike rule (starting with the 1903 season) indicates that the deferred adoption of this rule increased averages in the AL in these two seasons by 15–20 points. Second, the AL as a whole in 1901–1904 had very high levels of home park advantage, as the league batting average that season was 24 points higher (nearly 10 percent more) in home games vs. road games. To correct for this second factor, the author has included the batting data for the Tiger's opponents. Even with the inclusion of the visitor's batting data, the impression of Burns Park as a hitter's delight is still striking.

In the 23 games played at Burns Park in its two seasons of Sunday-only baseball, 19 home runs were hit, amounting to a rate of 11.2 home runs per 100 at bats, or more than three times the rate of home runs at Bennett Park. Of these 19, 18 are known to have been OTF home runs. One home run could not be confirmed as OTF. That home run was hit by a right-handed batter and was likely also an OTF home run to LF. Of the total of 18 known OTF home runs, one was hit over the CF fence, and all of the other 17 home runs were hit over the LF fence.

Burns Park was a very good park for average, on-base, slugging, doubles, and home runs, but a below average park for triples. The high park factors for doubles and home runs along with the low park factor for triples are consistent with the estimated dimensions and average outfield distances shown in the above tables. Compared to Bennett Park, the main Detroit ballpark, Burns Park was a far better offensive ballpark, as shown below by the table of batting park factors.

Home Runs by Type at Burns Park

Years	Total	OTF	Bounce	IPHR
1901	12	12	0	0
1902	7	7	0	0

OTF Home Runs by Field at Burns Park (excludes Bounce)

Years	Total	LF	CF	RF	Unknown
1901	12	10	1	0	1
1902	7	7	0	0	0

Inside-the-Park Home Runs by Field at Burns Park

Years	Total	LF	LC	CF	RC	RF	Unknown
1901	0						
1902	0						

Batting Park Factors (average of 1901 and 1902)

Category	Burns Park	Bennett Park
BA	116	103
OBP	113	103
SLUG	123	100
2B/AB	178	90
3B/AB	65	105
HR/AB	188	76
BB/TPA	98	97

Navin Field

Detroit American League: 1912–1919

The Detroit ballpark best known as Tiger Stadium started life as Navin Field, one of the earliest, long-lived, and best-loved of the Classic ballparks. Navin Field, a mostly steel-and-concrete ballpark, was built after the 1911 season on the site of the previous ballpark, Bennett Park. The park opened the same day as Fenway Park in Boston (April 20, 1912) and remained the home park of the Tigers for 88 seasons. During its long life there were two name changes, becoming Briggs Stadium in the 1930s before ending up as Tiger Stadium. Navin Field was located at the northwest corner of Michigan and Trumbull Avenues. When Navin Field was built after the 1911 season, the park site was larger than the size of the prior park site because the Tigers had acquired the properties along National Blvd. where the outside-the-park "wildcat bleachers" of Bennett Park had been located. The Navin Field park site now included the entirety of the city block bounded by Michigan, Trumbull, National and Cherry, and was thus larger in size (6.7 acres), than the 5.5 acres of Bennett Park in its final seasons. The Navin Field park site was typical of the size of the park sites for the Classic ballparks.

Home plate in Navin Field was in the southwest corner of the site, and although the shape of the land plat was a trapezoid and not a rectangle, the outfield fences were oriented at 90 degrees in LF and RF. The extra area in the trapezoid-shaped site (in the southeast portion of the site near the corner of Michigan and Trumbull) was used for a main entrance and ticket offices. In the ballpark's first season (1912), the seating consisted of a covered single-deck grandstand, which extended past first and third bases, covered pavilions down both foul lines, and outfield bleachers. The distinctive look of later Tiger Stadium — double-decked all around — was absent as the first double-deck portion of the grandstand was not built until 1923. In front of the majority of the RF fence, a single set of bleachers extended from about straightaway RF to nearly the CF corner. These bleachers had a capacity of about 2,000. In addition, the park included a large scoreboard in LF and a flag pole located at the left end of the RF-CF bleachers. The 1912 Opening Day attendance was 24,383, a total that included outfield standees. The total seating capacity of Navin Field in 1912–1919 was 23,000.

The Basis of Navin Field's Configurations and Dimensions

No Deadball Era dimensions for Navin Field were found in any of the usual ballpark reference books.[14] The only dimensions for 1912 Navin Field were found in *A Place for Summer* (LF 340, CF 400, and RF 365).[15] The values for LF and RF were certainly likely; however, CF was always much greater than 400 feet. A park diagram was developed based on the 1897 Sanborn map of Bennett Park that included the entirety of the city block that later became the Navin Field park site.[16] The dimensions of the park site were derived from the scale used on the Sanborn map. The configuration of the park was based on a 1912 Opening Day photo from *A Place for Summer*. In addition, the artist's rendition of the park in *Diamonds* and the Opening Day photo were used to position the 1912 grandstand, pavilions, and bleachers on the park diagram.[17] When these facilities were added to the park diagram, the resulting LF and RF dimensions were the same as the 1921 dimensions listed in *Green Cathedrals* (LF 345 and RF 370).[18] The CF distance at 469 and the CF corner distance at 479 were then determined from the park diagram. It appears there was no change to any of the Navin Field dimensions from Opening Day 1912 until 1921.

All of the Navin Field dimensions were checked against, and are consistent with, the available photographic evidence and the home-run data.

Park data and dimensions for Navin Field are shown below.

DIMENSIONS (largely estimated)

Years	LF	SLF	LC	CF*	RC	SRF	RF
1912–1919	345	357	398	469	385	346	370

*Deepest point was the CF corner at 479

FENCE HEIGHTS (estimated from photos)

Years	LF	CF	RF
1912–1919	12–25*	6–12**	6–20**

*The scoreboard was 25-feet high
**The 6 foot height was the screen at the front of the bleachers

AVERAGE OUTFIELD DISTANCES

Years	LF	CF	RF
1912–1919	363	430	366

ARCHITECT: OSBORN ENGINEERING

CAPACITY: 23,000 (1912–1919)

PARK SIZE/COMPOSITE AVERAGE OUTFIELD DISTANCE: 386

PARK SITE AREA: 6.7 ACRES

DEADBALL ERA RUN FACTOR: 102 (RANK: AL 8)

The Impact of the Park's Configuration and Dimensions on Batting

Navin Field had only a single configuration in the park's eight Deadball seasons. The park was slightly larger than the average AL ballpark, with a park size that was only six feet greater than the AL average. Navin Field was very near the league average for batting average, on-base, slugging, doubles, and walks in the Deadball Era, as the respective batting park factors were within a range of 100 to 102. Only the park factors for triples (19 percent above average) and home runs (25 percent below average) were outside the average range (see table of Batting Park Factors below).

Not surprisingly, the park's nearly average dimensions made it a typical park for IPHR. In 1912–1919, IPHR at Navin Field accounted for 34 percent of total home runs, compared with 29 percent for the AL as a whole in the same time period.

Despite only a six-foot-high screen at the front of the RF bleachers, there were only six bounce home runs in eight seasons. IPHR at Navin Field were not numerous—about five per season—and CF accounted for 60 percent of those. Batting park data and home-run data are shown below for Navin Field in four tables.

HOME RUNS AT NAVIN FIELD 1912–1919

Time Period	Total	OTF	Bounce	IPHR
1912–1919	123	81	6	42

OTF HOME RUNS BY FIELD AT NAVIN FIELD (EXCLUDES BOUNCE)

Years	Total	LF	CF	RF	Unknown
1912–1919	75	38	6	26	5

INSIDE-THE-PARK HOME RUNS BY FIELD AT NAVIN FIELD

Years	Total	LF	LC	CF	RC	RF	Unknown
1912–1919	42	3	2	25	4	8	0

BATTING PARK FACTORS AT NAVIN FIELD

Years	BA	OBP	SLUG	2B*	3B*	HR*	BB**
1912–1919	100	100	101	102	117	75	98

*Per AB
**Per total plate appearance (AB+BB+HP)

8

Milwaukee

The NL had a franchise in Milwaukee for one of the early seasons of the league's existence. The Milwaukee Cream Cities were a NL team for the 1878 season. The other nineteenth century ML teams in Milwaukee were the Union Association Milwaukee Grays in 1884 and the American Association Milwaukee Brewers for the latter part of the 1891 season. For most of the 1890s, Milwaukee had been a top minor league city with a team in the Western League from 1894 to 1899 and the AL in 1900. Milwaukee was one of the original AL cities in the 1900 season, and the team (called the Brewers) used Lloyd Street Grounds as their home park. As the AL was already in Milwaukee, they continued to use the Lloyd Street Grounds ballpark for the 1901 AL season.

After only a single season, the Milwaukee franchise was transferred to St. Louis for the 1902 season, where they became the St. Louis Browns. Milwaukee did not again have ML baseball until the Boston Braves moved to Milwaukee shortly before the start of the 1952 season. AL baseball did not return to Milwaukee until 1969 when the one-year-old expansion franchise in Seattle (the Pilots) moved to Milwaukee.

In the Deadball Era, playing Sunday baseball in Milwaukee had been legal as far back as 1884.[1] In fact, Milwaukee was the site of many AL Sunday games in 1901, as the East Coast teams (Baltimore, Boston, Philadelphia, and Washington) could only play Sunday games on the road.

Lloyd Street Grounds

Milwaukee American League: 1901

Lloyd Street Grounds was an all-wooden ballpark, built in 1894, and used as a minor league park for seven seasons. As a minor league park, Lloyd Street Grounds was used by the Western League in 1894–1899, and by the AL in 1900.

The ballpark was located at the corner of 16th St., and Lloyd St. near downtown Milwaukee in 1901. The park was configured in a manner similar to the Polo Grounds in New York. The park site was quite narrow, and as a result the right and left field fences, located on the eastern and western boundaries of the park, were parallel to each other. The CF fence was perpendicular to the home plate-CF axis and extended from almost straightaway LF to almost straightaway RF. Like the Polo Grounds, the foul lines intersected the right and left field fences at about 135 degrees. There were two 90 degree corners in the park: one each where the LF and RF fences met the CF fence.

The seating capacity was about 10,000 and consisted of a covered grandstand in three sections between first and third base, and bleachers down both the LF and RF lines. There was no seating in the fair portion of the outfield.

The Basis of Lloyd Street Grounds' Configuration and Dimensions

The basis of the park's configuration and dimensions (that are certainly less than definitive) were an 1894 Sanborn fire insurance map of the city block in which the ballpark was later sited and photos of the park from *Baseball Memories: 1900–1909*.[2] The 1894 Sanborn map showed the width of the park site (425 feet) to have been a bit more than half of the width of that city block. The eastern boundary was 16th St., and the parcel shown on the 1894 Sanborn map that included the park was quite deep (855 feet). From the photos of the ballpark, it is clear that the park site was not actually 855 feet deep. The only clue to the actual depth of the park was a photo taken from behind the CF fence. This photo from a 1901 game shows the centerfielder playing relatively close to the CF fence. This suggests the park's CF dimension was probably a fair amount less than 400 feet. Another photo from *Baseball Memories: 1900–1909* shows a substantial amount of foul territory adjacent to both first base and third base, and suggests the home plate-backstop distance was about 65–75 feet. In addition, this photo shows the RF fence meeting the foul line at much more than 90 degrees. The artist's depiction of the park's configuration in *Baseball Memories: 1900–1909* shows home plate and the infield centered between the eastern and western boundaries of the park site. Given this location of home plate, the LF and RF dimensions would have been equal, and they were calculated on the Sanborn map. This estimated location of home plate and the alignment of the CF fence being parallel to the park's southern boundary (Lloyd St.) made the entire playing field perfectly symmetrical. As there were no known OTF home runs to CF, the CF dimension could not have been too short, and it was estimated to have been about 380.

A study of home runs hit at Lloyd Street Grounds during the 1901 season showed more than half of the total home runs (17 of 29) were of the OTF type. This OTF proportion (59 percent) of the total home runs at Lloyd Street Grounds was more than the ML average (47 percent) for the first decade of the Deadball Era. This fact suggests that the outfield distances, most likely in LC, CF, and RC, were less than the average AL ballpark in the first decade of the Deadball Era. The distribution of OTF home runs provides little more insight into the park's configuration. Of the 17 OTF home runs hit in 1901, eight were to LF, none to CF, two to RF, with a discouraging large number (seven) to an unknown field. Thus the scanty OTF home run data cannot confirm the park's estimated symmetrical configuration. The known distribution of IPHR is interesting. There were three to LF, two to LC, six to CF, none to RC or RF, and one to an unknown field. If, as has been described above, the ballpark was symmetrical with straightaway LF and RF at 413, then it is surprising there were no IPHR to RC or RF. The reporting conventions of the Deadball Era may have affected that data. In the Deadball Era, many home runs were reported as being to LF or RF when further study revealed they were actually more to LC or RC.

Park data and dimensions for Lloyd Street Grounds are shown below.

DIMENSIONS (estimated)

Year	LF	SLF	LC	CF	RC	SRF	RF
1901	295	413	384	380	384	413	295

8. Milwaukee

FENCE HEIGHTS (estimated)

Year	LF	CF	RF
1901	20	10	10

AVERAGE OUTFIELD DISTANCES (Est.)

Year	LF	CF	RF
1901	368	382	368

CAPACITY: 10,000 (EST.)

PARK SIZE/COMPOSITE AVERAGE OUTFIELD DISTANCE: 373

PARK SITE AREA: 4.7 ACRES (EST.)

DEADBALL ERA RUN FACTOR: 92 (RANK: AL 19)

The Impact of the Park's Configuration and Dimensions on Batting

Home-road AL batting data and the runs park factor for the 1901 season showed Lloyd Street Grounds to have been a below-average to slightly-below-average hitter's park. The only exception was for triples, where the park was one percent above average. As shown in the Team Batting tables below, the Milwaukee team batting average was better at home than on the road (.269/.253). This 16 point home-road differential was not that good for the early years in the AL. Milwaukee opponents hit .257 in games at Lloyd Street Grounds, compared with a sparkling .311 mark at their home parks. This suggests both that the park was an overall poor hitter's park and/or there was a strong factor in home park advantage in the 1901 AL. The opponents other batting data (on-base and slugging) also show large differences between games at Milwaukee and in the opponents' home parks. At the overall park level (team and opponents), Lloyd Street Grounds had the second lowest 1901 park factor (94) for batting average — only Chicago's South Side Park was worse. Park factors are shown below for a total of seven offensive categories. For all categories of extra-base hits, the park factors range from 90 to 101, all unremarkable values. For base on balls, Lloyd Street Grounds was a modest four percent below average with a park factor of 96. All in all, this ballpark was a downright below-average hitter's park. As the AL use of Lloyd Street Grounds lasted only a single season, definitive judgments about the impact of the ballpark on batting are difficult.

Home-run data, team batting data, and batting park factors for Lloyd Street Grounds are shown below.

HOME RUNS BY TYPE AT LLOYD STREET GROUNDS

Year	Total	OTF	Bounce	IPHR
1901	29	17	0	12

OTF HOME RUNS BY FIELD AT LLOYD STREET GROUNDS (EXCLUDES BOUNCE)

Year	Total	LF	CF	RF	Unknown
1901	17	8	0	2	7

Inside-the-Park Home Runs by Field at Lloyd Street Grounds

Years	Total	LF	LC	CF	RC	RF	Unknown
1901	12	3	2	6	0	0	1

Team Batting 1901 Milwaukee

	G	AB	H	2B	3B	HR	BB	HP	BA	OBP	SLUG
HOME	70	2409	647	101	39	15	178	25	.269	.322	.362
ROAD	69	2386	603	91	27	14	159	24	.253	.306	.327

Team Batting 1901 Milwaukee Opponents

	G	AB	H	2B	3B	HR	BB	HP	BA	OBP	SLUG
HOME	70	2511	646	85	49	14	190	39	.257	.319	.347
ROAD	69	2371	737	111	57	18	203	23	.311	.371	.429

Lloyd Street Grounds Batting Park Factors

Years	BA	OBP	SLUG	2B*	3B*	HR*	BB**
1901	94	95	94	90	101	97	96

*Per AB
**Per total plate appearance (AB+BB+HP)

9

New York

New York City had a NL franchise from 1883 to 1957, and again with the Mets starting in 1962 until the present day. The New York NL team in the nineteenth century was first called the Gothams and then the Giants, starting with the 1884 season. In addition, there was a New York entry in the 1890 Players League that was also called the New York Giants. That meant there were two ML teams called the New York Giants in New York that season. The NL used four New York City ballparks in the nineteenth century: Polo Grounds I and II (same site with two different diamonds) 1883–1888, Polo Grounds III 1889–1890, and Polo Grounds IV 1891–1910. Polo Grounds I and II were located in midtown Manhattan, while Polo Grounds III and IV were at the far north end of Manhattan very close to the Harlem River. Before about 1900 when sportswriters referred to New York City, they excluded Brooklyn, because until 1898 Brooklyn was a separate city (one of the largest in the country) and was not part of the city of New York. When Brooklyn was absorbed into New York City in 1898, Brooklyn became one of five boroughs of the city.

The NL Giants after the 1890 season (and the demise of the Players League) took over the adjacent and better built ballpark used by the Players League Giants. Polo Grounds IV was used by the NL until the park was largely destroyed by fire early in the 1911 season. After the fire, the Polo Grounds were rebuilt with a steel-and-concrete double-deck grandstand. This ballpark (Polo Grounds V) was one of the earlier Classic ballparks and is the ballpark most associated with the name Polo Grounds, In the second decade of the Deadball Era, the ballpark was officially renamed Brush Stadium (after the owner of the Giants John T. Brush). However, the name change never stuck, and the ballpark was still referred to as the Polo Grounds. The ballpark remained in continuous use by the NL until the Giants moved to San Francisco after the 1957 season. The ballpark had two more season of ML usage, when the NL expansion Mets played there in 1962–1963 while Shea Stadium was being built.

There were prohibitions on Sunday baseball in all of the state of New York until early in the 1919 season. After 1915, the Brooklyn Dodgers considered playing Sunday home games at Harrison Field in Newark, New Jersey, some 10–15 miles away, but such plans never materialized. One reason was the International League's Newark team had the territorial rights. During the 1907–1914 period, there were two law-bending professional Sunday baseball games played in New York City. One (July 4, 1909) was a charity function to aid newsboys at the Dodgers' Washington Park III, and the other at the Polo Grounds was to aid survivors of the sinking of the *Titanic* (April 21, 1912). Both games skirted the existing prohibitions on Sunday baseball by charging no admission. Instead fans were asked to buy a program at the usual admission price. Early in 1919, the New York state legislature passed a bill legalizing Sunday baseball, and the bill was signed by the governor on April 19, 1919.[1] The first completely legal

ML Sunday baseball games in New York City were played on May 4, 1919. The response to Sunday baseball in New York City was tremendous! The Brooklyn Dodgers hosted the Boston Braves at Ebbets Field before 22,000 baseball fans, while 35,000 watched the Giants play the Phillies at the Polo Grounds.[2] These crowds were the largest regular-season attendance marks at both ballparks to that date.

Polo Grounds IV

New York National League: 1891–1911

The first ML ballpark in New York called the Polo Grounds (Polo Grounds I) was a field originally used to play polo that was located close to the northeast corner of Central Park. This park site was in midtown Manhattan at 110th Street. A confusing aspect of the original Polo Grounds site was the existence of two separate baseball diamonds on the site. These two diamonds on the site have been designated as Polo Grounds I and Polo Grounds II.[3]

The next ballpark to be called the Polo Grounds (number III) was officially named Manhattan Field and was located at 155th St. on the north end of Manhattan. The Giants decided to move in 1889 because the city of New York had extended 111th St. through the original Polo Grounds site, which seriously interfered with playing baseball! The Giants called the new site the New Polo Grounds so their fans would know it was the new venue for baseball. Later, the "New" portion of the park's name was dropped. The field was both narrow and pear-shaped.

In 1890, the short-lived Players League built a ballpark (called Brotherhood Park) on the parcel of land immediately north of Manhattan Field. This ballpark was located at Eighth Ave., West 159th St., Bridge Park, and West 157th St. in the northern part of Coogan's Hollow below Coogan's Bluff and was adjacent to and north of Polo Grounds III. The field of Brotherhood Park/Polo Grounds IV had severe drainage problems, perhaps related to the location having been shown on an 1874 map as under the Hudson River! The park site had been filled in with dirt in the late 1870s. The Players League New York Giants and the games played at Brotherhood Park proved to be far more popular than the NL games played next door at Polo Grounds III. Brotherhood Park was, by the standards of the day, of an almost normal size and shape.

While the Players League was a success in New York City (the Player's League outdrew the NL in New York by better than 3 to 1), the league as a whole agreed to a treaty of sorts with the NL after the 1890 season and ended its operation. The NL New York Giants, after the end of the 1890 season, moved their operation some 400 feet north to Brotherhood Park (from Manhattan Field) when the Players League ended operations. With not even a trace of originality, the Giants renamed the park the Polo Grounds. This park (Polo Grounds IV) and the subsequent ballpark on this site (Polo Grounds V) were the parks usually associated with the name Polo Grounds. One should note that contrary to the name, polo was never played on this site. During the 1890 season, even before the NL Giants moved in, the ballpark had been modified and the foul line distances were substantially reduced (335 to 277 for LF and 335 to 258 for RF). As a result, the park acquired its later-to-be famous horseshoe configuration before it ever became the home of the NL New York Giants.

The park in 1901 consisted of a double-deck wooden grandstand that extended from beyond first base to beyond third base and bleachers down both the LF and RF foul lines. Both the first base and third base bleachers extended about 50 feet into fair territory. From the end of the LF bleachers to about straight-away RF, the outfield boundary consisted of ropes strung between three-foot posts. This made the CF dimension 500 feet. Behind these roped off areas, carriages were allowed to park, and the occupants of the carriages could watch the game. Before the 1907 season new RF bleachers were built. In addition, between the end of the 1905 season and the start of the 1908 season additional bleacher sections were built in LF that extended the seating to about straight-away LF. Before the 1909 season, CF bleachers were built, such that the field was now completely encircled with fences and bleachers. As a consequence of the installation of the CF bleachers, the dead CF dimension was reduced by about 70 feet. Before the 1910 season, the double-deck wooden grandstand was extended into fair RF, replacing a portion of the prior RF bleachers.

Like all of its predecessors, Polo Grounds IV was built of wood. As Boy Scouts already know and baseball owners of that era were slow to learn, wooden structures burn. Only two games into the 1911 season, disaster struck early in the morning of April 14, 1911. A fire broke out which destroyed the entire wooden grandstand and a small portion of the wooden RF bleachers near the RF end of the grandstand. In addition to nearly all of the RF bleachers, all of the LF bleachers, all of the CF bleachers, and the clubhouse/office building survived. These structures were separated by gaps from the rest of the burning grandstand. The Giants moved in with their nearby neighbors, the AL New York Yankees, and played two months of the 1911 season at the AL's Hilltop Park.

The fire-damaged Polo Grounds IV was rebuilt in far more fireproof steel and concrete during the 1911 season. The superstructure of the grandstand was finished by mid-season, and the Giants moved back to the Polo Grounds for their home games on June 28, 1911. When the ballpark was finished by the start of the 1911 World Series (played that year at the Polo Grounds and Shibe Park in Philadelphia), the ballpark had become the Classic ballpark we know today as Polo Grounds V.

The Basis of the Polo Grounds IV's Configurations and Dimensions

During the Deadball Era, the configuration of the stands at Polo Grounds IV changed a number of times. From photos of the ballpark, it was determined that the wooden double-deck grandstand was extended at least twice. In 1904, the grandstand extended only as far as the infield. From other photos, the grandstand reached to about the LF and RF corners by the 1908 season. The fair territory LF bleachers were in place by at least the 1904 season and most likely before. The RF bleachers were expanded for the 1907 season.[4] Before the 1909 season, additional sections of bleachers were added to completely encircle the outfield. The installation of these additional sections of bleachers reduced the previously generous dimensions in CF. Before the 1910 season, the portion of the RF bleachers adjacent to the RF corner were dismantled and replaced by an extension of the double-deck grandstand into fair RF.

The dimensions of the playing field were based on *Green Cathedrals*, a 1909 Sanborn Fire Insurance Co. map of the park, and game accounts.[5] The listed dimensions in *Green Cathedrals* for Polo Grounds IV are LF 277, CF 500, and RF 258 as of July 1890. These dimensions remained unchanged until 1909 when the building of CF bleachers reduced the CF dimension to 433. These dimensions and estimates from photos of the ballpark were used with the 1909 Sanborn map of the ballpark to derive a Polo Grounds IV park diagram for 1901–1908. The dimensions derived from the scale used on the Sanborn map were consistent with the 1909 listed dimensions in *Green Cathedrals*. The Sanborn map was then used to produce a ballpark diagram for 1909–1910. All subsequent ballpark dimensions for 1909–1910

Overflow crowd at the Polo Grounds: Cincinnati vs. New York, 1904. This panoramic photograph of Polo Grounds IV on August 13, 1904, was taken from the center-field clubhouse/office building. The free standing clubhouse/office building of Polo Grounds IV was set back behind right center. Note that the double-deck grandstand ended just past the infield. Beyond the grandstand, bleachers down both foul lines extend into the fair portions of both left field and right field. In 1904, Polo Grounds IV had rather limited seating in both the left-field and right-field bleachers, and no stands of any kind in right center, left center or center field. This restricted capacity of the ballpark led to overflow crowds for many games. For big games, the Giants and the City of New York allowed the overflow crowds to stand in the majority of the outfield. Fire safety laws in the Deadball Era were remarkably lax by today's standards. In this photograph, the standees in the outfield block the view of the center-field "fence." That fence extended from the end of the left-field bleachers to dead center field and all the way around to the end of the right-field bleachers. The "fence" consisted of nothing more than ropes strung between three-foot posts. (Photograph by the George R. Lawrence Co., the Panoramic Photographs Collection [PAN Sports No. 85], Library of Congress.)

Capacity crowd at the Polo Grounds 1910. A panoramic photograph of Polo Grounds IV in 1910 taken from the upper deck of the grandstand a little to the right of home plate. The right-field foul line was not really curved as it appears in this photograph. Note that in this 1910 photograph the double-deck wooden grandstand extended on the third-base side to just before the left-field corner, while on the first-base side it extended into fair right field. This photograph is dated October 13, 1910, in the Library of Congress collection. This date was at first a mystery. This photograph is definitely from 1910, as that was the only season the double-deck grandstand extended into fair right field. However, the New York Giants did not play in the 1910 World Series (the Chicago Cubs won the NL pennant that year), and the last regular season game at the Polo Grounds was on October 11 that year. Additional research found that the October 13, 1910, game shown in this photograph was one of the games of the New York City Series played that year between the Giants and Yankees after the end of the regular season. (Photograph by the Pictorial News Co. of New York, Panoramic Photographs Collection [PAN 6a 29227], Library of Congress.)

were derived from this diagram. The game accounts and park photos were used to determine the extent of the rope-on-post CF fence and when it was removed to permit the construction of bleachers. From research into home runs hit at the Polo Grounds, it was learned that the first home run into the LF bleachers came in 1905, and there were home runs hit through or under the ropes in the outfield in every season from 1901 to 1908.[6]

DIMENSIONS (calculated from park diagrams)

Years	LF	SLF	LC	CF	RC	SRF	RF
1901–1908	277	381	446	500	450	359	258
1909–1910*	277	377	446	433	404	348	258

*In addition, the ballpark was used for only two 1911 regular season games before a fire destroyed the majority of the park on April 14, 1911

FENCE HEIGHTS (LF/RF from *Green Cathedrals*, CF from photos)

Years	LF	CF	RF
1901–1908	0–25*	0*	0–15*
1909–1910	10	8	10

*The zero-foot heights were outfield sections with the ropes

AVERAGE OUTFIELD DISTANCES

Years	LF	CF	RF
1901–1908	370	474	359
1909–1910	370	429	356

CAPACITY: 16,000 (1901–1905), 18,000 (1906–1908 EST.), 27,000 (1909 EST.), 30,000 (1910)

PARK SIZE/COMPOSITE AVERAGE OUTFIELD DISTANCE: 401 (1901–1908), 385 (1909–1910)

PARK SITE AREA: 7.4 ACRES

DEADBALL ERA RUN FACTOR: 100 (RANK: NL 8)

The Impact of the Park's Configurations and Dimensions on Batting

Polo Grounds IV was one of the largest ballparks in the NL, but it had the shortest LF and RF dimensions. All in all, it was a uniquely shaped ballpark. How did this unique shape affect batting? The batting average, on-base, and slugging park factors reveal Polo Grounds IV to have been average (compared to other NL ballparks in the same years) except for extra-base hits in both 1901–1908 and 1909–1910. The ballpark was very close to average for doubles in 1901–1908 and slightly below average in 1909–1910. Despite the huge distances in LC and RC (both more than 440 feet in 1901–1908), the Polo Grounds was a below average park for triples, as shown by the range of triples park factors (82–89). The park's original 1901–1908 configuration with the ropes-on-posts fence in most of the outfield had a substantial impact on home runs and on triples as well. Balls hit between or past the outfielders often rolled under the ropes and were therefore bounce home runs, not IPHR or triples. In addition, because the park had such short dimensions in both the LF and RF corners, teams played their corner outfielders more towards CF, which cut down on triples and IPHR. Overall, the Polo Grounds (1901–1908) was more than 70 percent better than the average NL ballpark for home runs. The Polo Grounds had a substantially greater proportion of OTF home runs than the typical early Deadball Era ballpark. At Polo Grounds IV, 61 percent of home runs were of the OTF type in 1901–1908, compared to 46 percent in the entire NL. What was remarkable was that there were 73 bounce home runs at all NL ballparks in those eight seasons. Of that number, 42 (58 percent of the total NL) were hit at the Polo Grounds. Clearly the unique rope fence in the outfield led to this large total of bounce home runs. Because of the numerous bounce home runs, there were fewer IPHR. The large majority of the IPHR were hit to CF, RC, and RF. There were only 3.0 IPHR per season hit to LF/LC. The scarcity of IPHR to LF/LC at the Polo Grounds (only 30 in ten seasons) is difficult to understand. The average LF distance was greater than the average RF distance at the park and there were more right-handed batters than left-handed batters, yet IPHR were slightly more numerous to RF/RC than to LF/LC.

The data on home runs and batting park factors for Polo Grounds IV are shown below in four tables.

Home Runs by Type at Polo Grounds IV

Years	Total	OTF	Bounce	IPHR
1901–1908	230	143	49	85
1909–1910	79	37	2	42

OTF Home Runs by Field at Polo Grounds IV (excludes Bounce)

Years	Total	LF	CF	RF	Unknown
1901–1908	98	16	0	54	28
1909–1910	35	14	0	16	5

Inside-the-Park Home Runs by Field at Polo Grounds IV

Years	Total	LF	LC	CF	RC	RF	Unknown
1901–1908	90	8	6	41	6	21	8
1909–1910	42	4	12	15	8	1	2

Batting Park Factors at Polo Grounds IV

Years	BA	OBP	SLUG	2B*	3B*	HR*	BB**
1901–1908	101	101	102	102	82	172	96
1909–1910	100	99	99	87	89	135	95

*Per AB
**Per total plate appearance (AB+BB+HP

Hilltop Park

New York American League: 1903–1912

The first ballpark used by the AL in New York City was Hilltop Park. The park got its name because it was situated on the top of a hill in northern Manhattan overlooking the

Hilltop Park, Washington vs. New York, 1910. This panoramic photograph shows Hilltop Park on Memorial Day 1910. Note the overflow crowd of standees not only in the outfield but along both of the foul lines, and the double fence in left field. The apparent curvature of the left-field foul line in this photograph is due to the process used in producing panoramic photographs. (Photograph by the Pictorial News Co. of New York and obtained from the Panoramic Photographs Collection [PAN No. 94], Library of Congress.)

Hudson River. The ballpark was built for the recently relocated AL franchise that had spent its first two seasons in Baltimore as the Orioles. The park opened on April 30, 1903, as the home park of the then New York Highlanders, later known as the Yankees. The location of Hilltop Park was at the southwest corner of Broadway and 168th St. on the northwest portion of the island (and borough) of Manhattan. During its ten seasons of use by the AL (1903–1912), the ballpark was usually called American League Park or referred to indirectly as Hilltop Park, as in "games at the Hilltop." In later years, the name Hilltop Park came to be used to identify the ballpark, and that is the name by which we know the park today.

The ballpark site was quite large for its time (9.6 acres or about 60 percent larger than the average pre–Classic ML ballpark site), and the southern portion of the park site was used for the parking of first carriages and later automobiles. The shape of the land plat was not rectangular, as only the site's northeast and southeast corners were right angles.[7] The LF foul line ran mostly north to south and was parallel to Fort Washington Road that was the western boundary of the park. The LF foul line would, if extended about 20 additional feet, have intersected 168th St. at less than 90 degrees. The RF foul line would, if extended, have intersected Broadway (the eastern boundary of the park) at more than 90 degrees. The ballpark site was thus trapezoidal in shape and large for the Deadball Era.

The park was built entirely of wood, and when it opened it had a seating capacity of 15,000. Capacity in the Deadball Era was a flexible concept. In accordance with the practices of the day, overflow crowds were allowed to stand in the outfield. For really big games, additional standees were allowed down the foul lines, and even between home plate and the backstop. Including standees, the effective overall capacity of the park was near 25,000. The original 1903 construction of Hilltop Park cost about $300,000, more than two-thirds of which was spent for rock blasting and excavations. The groundskeeper for the Highlanders, Phil Schenck, laid out the playing field.[8] In 1903, the ballpark consisted of three sections of covered grandstand, although it was not actually roofed until June 1, 1903. Two sections of the grandstand were parallel to the foul lines, and the third section was a short intermediate diagonal, which formed the backstop. The grandstand extended a short way past both first and third bases, and a clubhouse was located behind the CF fence. Bleachers extended down both foul lines and reached from the grandstand almost to the fences. The third-base bleachers were not finished until June 1903. These first-base and third-base bleachers angled towards the foul lines, reducing the foul area at the fences to about 15 feet. A modest-sized scoreboard was part of the LF fence and was in fair territory near the LF foul line. The main entrance to the ballpark was on Broadway, and a ramp led up to the top of the first-base side of the grandstand. Unlike many other Deadball Era wooden ballparks, this one never burned.

The park's original listed dimensions of LF 365, CF 542, and RF 400 were taken from *Green Cathedrals* and *Lost Ballparks*.[9] Based upon these dimensions, the deepest part of the park would have been located at the junction of the LF fence and the RF fence, and would have been considerably to the right of dead CF. For Opening Day and the following five games of the first homestand, RF had a large roped-off hollow, and balls hit into that area were ground-rule doubles. The first change to the park's configuration occurred after the first homestand (all of six games) of the 1903 season. When the Highlanders returned home on June 1 after a four-week road trip for the start of their second homestand, a new temporary RF fence had been built to put the RF hollow out of play. Balls hit over this short and batter-friendly fence were home runs. This move reduced the RF distance to about 290. At this same time, a short diagonal CF fence section was added and reduced dead CF to about 390. For 1904, the RF fence was moved again, this time back to about a 385 distance (at the foul line), and at this same time the diagonal CF fence section was relocated. These moves increased both dead CF (390 to about 420) and near RC (390 to an estimated 432).

Before the 1911 season, a roof was added over a portion of the bleachers down the LF foul line. At this same time in an effort to increase capacity, CF bleachers were added in front of the 1910 CF fence. The Yankees (as the team was now known) shared the park with the New York Giants for the first two months of the 1911 season while the fire-damaged Polo Grounds were being rebuilt. After the 1912 season, the Giants return the favor and allowed the Yankees to share the Polo Grounds with them for the next ten seasons.

Hilltop Park was demolished in 1914, and the site has been occupied since the 1920s by Columbia-Presbyterian Medical Center.

The Basis of Hilltop Park's Configurations and Dimensions

The Hilltop Park configurations and dimensions shown below are in part estimates, but they represent the best possible estimates that take into account all known data, and they are internally consistent. Where possible, ballpark photos have been used to confirm or disprove reported dimensions. Only the LF dimension (365 for all years) is the same in all sources, is consistent with all other measurements, and is known with high confidence.

The original 1903 dimensions (LF 365, CF 542, and RF 400, and home plate backstop 91) were taken from *Green Cathedrals* and *Lost Ballparks*.[10] The dimensions of the park site were taken from a 1903 *New York Times* article.[11] Given the known dimensions of the park site, it was possible to confirm the scale shown on the Sanborn map. These land plat dimensions were used with a 1909 Sanborn map of the ballpark site to derive a ballpark diagram.[12] All subsequent ballpark dimensions, other than the LF dimension, were derived from this diagram, in conformance with available photos, data from the SABR Home Run Log, and home run data by field (LF, CF, RF) from Larry Zuckerman's and the author's extensive research.[13]

The evidence supporting the original 1903 listed RF distance as having been 400 feet is limited to a single photo (*Ritter* 93). This photo shows a fence located about 40–50 feet in from (to the west of) Broadway, which on the Sanborn map would make the fence about 400 feet from home plate. As the photo in question is undated, the fence may have been built later than 1903 and may not have been used as an outfield fence. Thus the 400-foot RF distance, and the associated 542 somewhere in CF distance, for Opening Day 1903 might never have existed. While the Sanborn map does establish that the RF dimension of 400 and the CF dimension of 542 were possible, no IPHR were hit in the games when this configuration of the ballpark might have existed. The question of whether the RF distance was ever 400 feet, while both interesting and still unproven, is not terribly important, as only six games were played when the ballpark could have been in this configuration. The dimensional data shown below assumed the RF dimension was never 400 feet.

The 1903 LF distance (listed as 365 in both of the previously noted ballpark books) was confirmed to be correct, and the LF interior fence was estimated to have been at 79 degrees to the LF foul line. This estimate was based on 1907 photos which show both the RF and LF foul lines and both fences to be very near to the end of the first-base and third-base bleachers, and the location on the Sanborn map of the third-base bleachers close to the park's northern perimeter (168th Street). Given this orientation of the foul lines, the placement of home plate at the listed 91-foot distance from the backstop makes the LF distance about 365. This also places the interior LF fence and scoreboard about 15–20 feet in front of a second exterior LF fence (the perimeter fence along 168th Street). The RF distance, in use for all but six games of the 1903 season, was estimated to have been about 290 feet. The estimate was based on an analysis of the number and distribution of OTF home runs hit during June-September 1903 (the only time the new closer RF fence was in use).[13] This temporary RF fence would likely have been low in height, to avoid obstructing the fan's view from the last sections of the first-base bleachers. It is unclear if this temporary RF fence ran all the way to the LF fence, cut back in RC to the original CF fence, or intersected a CF diagonal fence. The fact that no IPHR was hit to CF (the only IPHR that season was to LF) in the entire 1903 season suggests that the RF fence did extend to a CF diagonal, as such a configuration would make the CF distance about 380, which would have made IPHR unlikely. The estimated June-September 1903 CF distance shown in the dimensions was based on the configuration with a diagonal CF fence. Based on recent additional research on 1901–1908 AL home runs and average outfield distances, the RF foul line distance at 1903 Sportsman's Park (St. Louis AL) was 300 feet.[14] Sportsman's Park had an average RF distance fence of 336. Based on New York newspaper accounts and photos, the Hilltop RF fence was at 90 degrees to the foul line. In that same 1903 season, OTF home runs to RF at Sportsman's Park amounted to seven. By comparison, there were 12 OTF home runs hit to RF at Hilltop in the 1903 season. From this comparison it was estimated that the Hilltop average RF distance must have been less than the 336 average RF distance at Sportsman's Park, and the RF dimension could have been about 290 feet. The dimensions which follow used 290 feet for the June-September 1903 RF distance. The April-May 1903 CF and RF dimensions were assumed to have been the same as in 1904–1906.

For 1904–1906, the RF distance (about 385) was estimated with somewhat greater accuracy based on the ballpark descriptions from Opening Day 1904. The Opening Day account of the game *(New York Times,* April 15, 1904) noted that nearly 100 feet of RF had been filled in. This meant that the temporary RF fence in place at the end of the 1903 season (estimated at 290 feet from home plate) was replaced with a RF fence that was about 380–390 feet from home plate for the 1904 season. The dimensions which follow used 385 feet for the 1904–1906 RF distance. That same game account referred to an IPHR by Buck Freeman as being hit to the stone fence in RF. All photos dated 1907 and later of RF at Hilltop show wooden RF fences. A 1904–1906 RF distance of 380–390 is consistent with 1907–1910 photos of RF at Hilltop. A 1909 photo shows a second fence in RF about 20 feet behind the interior RF fence with billboards visible above the interior fence.[15] The location of the second fence is about where the 1904–1906 RF fence would have been with a RF distance of 385. In addition, the estimated RF distance of 385 (and the corresponding RC distance of 422) is generally consistent with the 1904–1906 home run data. There were 45 IPHR in 1904 vs. one the prior season. Of the IPHR in 1904, all but two were to RF, RC, or CF.[16] For the three seasons (1904–1906), there were on average 31.0 IPHR at Hilltop, nearly all to CF, RC, or RF. By comparison, the other seven AL parks averaged slightly more than eight IPHR per season in these years.

The 1907 RF dimension was determined from the 1907 photo (Ritter 90–91) that shows the RF fence to be at the end of the RF foul line bleachers. From the Sanborn map, which shows the location and extent of those bleachers, the RF fence was estimated to be 365 from home plate. From photos of the RF fence or fences in later years, it was estimated that the RF fence ran at 90 degrees to the foul line. The estimated RF distance of 365 (and the corresponding RC distance of 412) is generally consistent with the 1907–1910 HR data. The IPHR data support the configuration with RF at 385 for 1904–1906. For the 1904–1906 seasons at Hilltop, IPHR averaged 31.0 per season (nearly all to RF, RC, or CF). For the 1907–1910 seasons, and with no change to LF, IPHR fell to 19.8 per season. This suggested a closer RF fence in 1907–1910. Over nearly the entire life of the ballpark (1904–1910), there were no instances of OTF home runs to RF or CF.[17]

One can note that in this instance the substantial increase in the RF dimension at Hilltop Park between 1903 and 1904 was associated with a 194 percent *increase* in home runs. The low number of OTF home runs to LF and the low level of IPHR to LF support the known LF distance of 365 and the estimated LC distance of 378 for the entire life of the park.[18] Lesser distances to LF and LC would likely have been the cause of more OTF home runs (as was true at Sportsman's Park in this same time period), and greater distances should have produced more IPHR (in the entire life of the park there were only a few IPHR to LF).

Ballpark photos for 1909 (*Lost Ballparks* and *Green Cathedrals*) show a second higher fence behind the 1907–1910 interior RF and RC fence. Like the inner fence, the outer fence was covered with many billboards advertising the products of the day. Additional billboards were mounted on the western and southern sides of the CF clubhouse. The RF to CF fence, which existed for 1907–1910, most likely consisted of two sections, with a kink in RC as shown in a photo (Ritter 94). Incorporating this kinky feature into the park diagram produced a CF distance of 409 for 1907–1910, which is consistent with the data from the home run research.

With the construction of a new trapezoid-shaped section of CF bleachers for the 1911 season, the dead CF distance was noticeably reduced. These CF bleachers were built in front of the prior (1910) CF diagonal fence and ran from a point to the right of LC over to a point to the right of RC. With the construction of the CF bleachers, the dark batter's background was lost, and the large Bull Durham sign was moved from CF to RF. Using a photo from *Green Cathedrals,* it was possible to estimate the location, width, and depth of the CF bleachers, and therefore the location of a new low CF fence that made up the front of these bleachers.[19] Dead CF was now only an estimated 370 feet from home plate. Thus, 1911–1912 Hilltop Park had probably the shortest CF dimension of any major league park then or since.

Park data and dimensions for Hilltop Park are shown below.

DIMENSIONS (calculated from park diagrams)

Time Period	LF	SLF	LC	CF	RC	SRF	RF
April–May 1903	365	365	378	420	424	398	385
June–September 1903	365	365	378	380	335	300	290
1904–1906	365	365	378	420	424	398	385
1907–1910	365	365	378	409	412	378	365
1911–1912	365	365	378	370	372*	378	365

*In the notch at the right end of the CF bleachers (to the right of RC at 27 degrees) the distance was 405. Home Plate-to-Backstop: 91.

FENCE HEIGHTS (estimated from photos)

Time Period	LF*	CF	RF
April–May 1903	8	12	12
June–September 1903	8	12	3
1904–1906	8	12	12
1907–1908	8	12–16**	12
1909–1910	16	16	12
1911–1912	12–16	3	12–16***

*LF 16 foot height was the scoreboard 20–25 feet wide near the foul line
**CF 16 foot height for 1907–1910 was the Bull Durham sign and the batter's background
***RF 16 foot height for 1911–1912 was the Bull Durham sign

Average Outfield Distances

Time Period	LF	CF	RF
April–May 1903	367	412	404
June–September 1903	367	373	305
1904–1906	367	412	404
1907–1910	367	407	383
1911–1912	367	372	379

CAPACITY: 15,000 (1903–1910), 17,000 (1911–1912 Est.)

PARK SIZE/COMPOSITE AVERAGE OUTFIELD DISTANCE:
387 (April–May 1903), 348 (June–September 1903),
394 (1904–1906), 386 (1907–1910), 373 (1911–1912)

PARK SITE AREA: 9.4 ACRES

DEADBALL ERA RUN FACTOR: 116 (RANK AL 2)

The Impact of the Park's Configurations and Dimensions on Batting

Hilltop Park had five configurations in the park's ten Deadball Era seasons. The first configuration, where RF was roped off and balls hit into the roped-off area were ground-rule doubles, was in use for only six games. This unusual configuration appears to have little impact on the games played here, as doubles in these first six games were hit at a rate of 5.7 per game compared with a rate of 5.9 for the entire 1903 season. The first configuration change consisted of the erection of a temporary fence in short RF, on June 1, 1903. This short RF fence led to an upsurge in OTF home runs for the rest of the 1903 season (three to LF and 12 to RF), but may have reduced overall home runs at the park by making IPHR to RF impossible.[20] This tentative conclusion is supported by the fact that the 1903 Hilltop Park, even with a short RF, was a poorer-than-average park for home runs, as the park's 1903 home run factor was 81. The next configuration change moved the RF fence back nearly 100 feet before the 1904 season. As a result, the number of OTF home runs to RF, which had been 12 in the 1903 season, dropped to zero in 1904.[21] However, total home runs at Hilltop Park increased from 16 in 1903 to 47 in the 1904 season (incredibly, 45 IPHR). In the 1904–1906 and 1907–1910 configurations, Hilltop Park had batting park factors for batting average, on-base, slugging, triples, and home runs well above 100, despite being one of the larger ballparks in the AL. For doubles the park was nine percent below average, for triples 47 percent above average, and for home runs the park factors were 201 (1904–1906) and 141 (1907–1910). In these two configurations, Hilltop Park was larger than the average AL ballpark and was a great ballpark for IPHR, as in the seven seasons between 1904 and 1910, IPHR made up an astounding 95 percent of total home runs, compared with 61 percent for the AL as a whole in the same time period.

The final configuration of the park was the result of the building of CF bleachers before the 1911 season, which increased the park factors for batting average, on-base, slugging, and doubles. As expected with a substantially shorter CF dimension, the park factor for triples decreased about 10 percent. The new CF bleachers had a substantial impact on the type of home runs at the park. With the CF distance reduced to 370 and with 1911 also being the first full season to use the cork-center ball, OTF home runs to CF became both possible and, by Deadball Era standards, numerous. In the four prior configurations (1903–1910), there was only one OTF home run to CF. In the 1911–1912 seasons, with this revised CF configuration, OTF home runs to CF became the predominant type of home run at Hilltop Park.[22] One cause was the low fence in front of the CF bleachers that allowed many bounce home runs. In 1911, there were 19 OTF home runs, 17 were to CF, and 12 of these were bounce home runs. For 1912, there were 17 OTF home runs, all of which were to CF, and seven of these were bounce home runs.[23] For the 1911–1912 seasons the CF bleachers at Hilltop accounted for 39 percent of all bounce home runs at AL ballparks. Over its ten seasons, Hilltop Park had the highest run factor in the Deadball Era (116) of any full-season ML ballpark (a category of ballparks that excludes Burns Park in Detroit).

The home run and batting park factor data are shown below.

HOME RUNS BY TYPE AT HILLTOP PARK

Time Period	Total	OTF	Bounce	IPHR
1903	16	15	0	1
1904–1906	100	5	0	95
1907–1910	84	5	3	79
1911–1912	61	36	20	25

OTF HOME RUNS BY FIELD AT HILLTOP PARK (EXCLUDES BOUNCE)

Years	Total	LF	CF	RF	Unknown
1903	15	3	0	12	0
1904–1906	5	5	0	0	0
1907–1910	2	1	1	0	0
1911–1912	16	2	14	0	0

INSIDE-THE-PARK HOME RUNS BY FIELD AT HILLTOP PARK

Years	Total	LF	LC	CF	RC	RF	Unknown
1903	1	1	0	0	0	0	0
1904–1906	95	6	2	35	6	28	18
1907–1910	79	4	2	20	8	37	8
1911–1912	25	2	0	2	6	15	0

BATTING PARK FACTORS AT HILLTOP PARK

Years	BA	OBP	SLUG	2B*	3B*	HR*	BB**
1903	98	99	100	126	88	81	98
1904–1906	105	104	110	91	147	201	101
1907–1910	103	102	106	94	142	141	101
1911–1912	106	104	109	104	126	138	96

*Per AB
**Per Total Plate Appearance (AB+BB+HP)

Polo Grounds V

New York American League: 1913–1919, National League: 1911–1919

Polo Grounds V was the ballpark built in 1911 to replace the fire damaged Polo Grounds IV (see Polo Grounds IV above for information on the earlier Polo Grounds I–IV). After a fire destroyed the entire grandstand and the portion of the RF bleachers near the RF corner in April 1911, the Giants shared Hilltop Park with the Yankees until late June, playing 28 games there. The new Polo Grounds had a steel-and-concrete double-deck grandstand built on a foundation that included piles driven 20–40 feet below the surface to bedrock.[24] The new grandstand extended from the LF foul pole to beyond the RF foul pole about 50–60 feet into fair RF. Between the RF end of the grandstand and the RF bleachers there was an in-play gap of 15–20 feet. This new grandstand, unlike the grandstand extension into LF built before the 1923 season, had no second-deck overhang. By June 28, 1911, the lower deck of the new double-deck grandstand was completed and allowed the Giants to return to the Polo Grounds. Capacity at this time was 16,000 seats in the lower-deck of the grandstand plus the undamaged and rebuilt bleachers for a total capacity of about 26,000. Construction continued for the rest of the season on the upper-deck portion of the grandstand with additional seating being added in stages, such that by the start of the 1911 World Series capacity had reached 34,000. In addition, capacity in the CF bleachers was increased in 1917 by the removal of the green canvas screens that had been used as batter's backgrounds.[25] Seating capacity was now about 36,000. The Yankees used the Polo Grounds for three games in 1912 and moved permanently from Hilltop Park to the Polo Grounds at the start of the 1913 season, where they stayed as tenants of the Giants for ten years.

The Polo Grounds did not reach its final configuration until after the end of the Deadball Era. The park was expanded after the 1922 season, and work continued into the 1923 season. Both the north and south-side double-deck grandstands were extended towards CF, and new concrete bleachers were constructed in the now far-distant CF area. This produced the famous bathtub shape, which in combination with the CF alcove, were the park's most distinctive features. The new clubhouse was located at the far end of the CF alcove and was reached via the field, which was also the post-game exit route for many of the fans.

The Basis of the Polo Grounds V's Configuration and Dimensions

During the Deadball Era, the configuration of the playing field at Polo Grounds V did not change. When the ballpark was rebuilt after the April 14, 1911, fire as Polo Grounds V, the principal dimensions (LF 277, CF 433, and RF 258) of the prior ballpark (Polo Grounds IV) remained the same. The only change was to a portion of RF where the grandstand ended and the RF bleachers began. These dimensions were used with the 1909 Sanborn map of the ballpark site to derive a Polo Grounds V ballpark diagram.[26] All subsequent ballpark dimensions were derived from this diagram.

DIMENSIONS (calculated from park diagram)

Years	LF	SLF	LC	CF	RC	SRF	RF
1911–1919	277	377	447	433	443	367	258

Polo Grounds V during the 1913 World Series — a photograph taken from the back of the right-field bleachers with a view of right field, the infield, and most of the double-deck grandstand. Note the large buildings behind and above the grandstand. Polo Grounds IV and V were built in a hollow and were situated below Coogan's Bluff. The buildings in the photograph are on Coogan's Bluff. (George Grantham Bain Collection, Library of Congress.)

FENCE HEIGHTS (LF/RF from *Green Cathedrals*, CF from photos)

Years	LF	CF	RF
1911–1919	10–16	10–20*	11–12

*20-foot height was the canvas batter's background until May 1917

AVERAGE OUTFIELD DISTANCES

Years	LF	CF	RF
1911–1919	370	437	356

CAPACITY: 30,000 (APRIL 1911), 26,000 (JUNE 28, 1911 EST.), 34,000 (OCTOBER 1911), 36,000 (MAY 1917–1919 EST.)

PARK SIZE/COMPOSITE AVERAGE OUTFIELD DISTANCE: 388

PARK SITE AREA: 7.4 ACRES

DEADBALL ERA RUN FACTOR—AL: 101 (RANK: 10); NL: 93 (RANK: 14)

The Impact of the Park's Configuration and Dimensions on Batting

The AL and NL batting park factors were nearly identical, except for home runs (see last table below). The batting average, on-base, and slugging park factors reveal the Polo Grounds to have been average compared to other AL ballparks and slightly below average vs. other NL parks. It is interesting to compare the AL and NL home run data at Polo Grounds V. The AL averaged 42.7 home runs per season vs. 39.3 per season for the NL. For both the AL and the NL, substantially more OTF home runs were hit to RF than to LF, likely due to the RF dimension being 19 feet less than for LF. The proportions of IPHR at the park were nearly identical: 22 percent for the AL and 23 percent for the NL. The distribution of IPHR by field was also quite similar: for the AL, 85 percent to CF, RC, and RF; while the corresponding figure for the NL was 80 percent. What is surprising is the difference in the home run park factors between the AL and NL. For both leagues, the Polo Grounds was clearly an above-average home run park. However, for the AL, the Polo Grounds was more than twice as favorable for home runs as the average AL ballpark. With the NL, the park was 38 percent better than the average NL ballpark. Since the AL and NL had virtually the same rate of home runs at the Polo Grounds (AL: 0.86/100 AB, NL: 0.84/100 AB), the other AL ballparks must have been much worse for home runs than the other NL ballparks.

Despite the huge distances in LC and RC (both more than 440 feet), the Polo Grounds V was a poor park for triples, as shown by both the AL and NL triples park factors (AL 73, NL 77). Because the park had such short dimensions in both the LF and RF corners, teams played their corner outfielders more towards CF, which cut down on triples and IPHR. The scarcity of IPHR to LF and LC at the Polo Grounds for both the AL and NL (only 18 in sixteen seasons) is difficult to understand. The average LF distance was greater than the average RF distance at the park, yet IPHR were slightly more numerous to RF/RC than to LF/LC. One curious aspect of the park's configuration was the in-play gap between the RF bleachers and the RF end of the grandstand. This opening in RF, which was not included in the computation of the average RF distance, made any ball going into the gap a virtually certain IPHR, as the right-fielder had to run down the ball in the out-of-sight gap and await help from a teammate before he could return the ball to the normal field of play. Ty Cobb got such an IPHR in 1915 by hitting the ball over the end of the RF grandstand into this gap. Cobb's home run was described as the "longest wallop ever made inside the grounds."[27]

The data on home runs and batting park factors for Polo Grounds V are shown below in four tables.

Home Runs by Type at Polo Grounds V

Years	Total	OTF	Bounce	IPHR
1913–1919 (AL)	300*	235*	1	65
1911–1919 (NL)	354	273	4	81

*Includes one home run in three 1912 games

OTF Home Runs by Field at Polo Grounds V (Excludes Bounce)

Years	Total	LF	CF	RF	Unknown
1913–1919 (AL)	234*	85	0	145*	5
1911–1919 (NL)	269	104	0	170	5

*Includes one home run in 1912

Inside-the-Park Home Runs by Field at Polo Grounds V

Years	Total	LF	LC	CF	RC	RF	Unknown
1913–1919 (AL)	65	2	5	20	16	19	3
1911–1919 (NL)	81	2	9	19	31	15	5

Batting Park Factors at Polo Grounds V

Years	BA	OBP	SLUG	2B*	3B*	HR*	BB**
1913–1919 (AL)	99	99	100	90	73	209	102
1911–1919 (NL)	97	98	97	90	77	138	100

*Per AB
**Per Total Plate Appearance (AB+BB+HP)

10

Philadelphia

Philadelphia was one of the original NL franchises, but that lasted for only one season–1876. The NL did not return to Philadelphia until the 1883 season. This time, the NL stayed in Philadelphia, and the franchise has remained there until the present day. In the time period 1883–1900, the NL team, called the Quakers until 1890 and thereafter the Phillies, played in a total of three ballparks. The first, Recreation Park, was used from 1883 to 1886. The second ballpark, aptly named Philadelphia Baseball Grounds, was used for 1887–1894. This ballpark was located at Huntingdon St. and 15th St., and as a result the ballpark was also known as Huntingdon Grounds. The Phillies' use of this park ended when the ballpark burned down on August 6, 1894. The third and final NL ballpark in this time period was Baker Bowl, built in 1895 on the smoldering site of Huntingdon Grounds. Baker Bowl was used by the Phillies for more than 40 years until mid-season 1938 when they moved to share Shibe Park with the AL Athletics. Baker Bowl was notable as the first ballpark to use steel and concrete for the construction of the double-deck grandstand. However, the other stands were built of wood.

In 1901, the AL moved one of its eight franchises to Philadelphia and the team built a new ballpark (Columbia Park II) about two miles from the NL's Baker Bowl. The new AL team, the Athletics, played at Columbia Park II for eight seasons (1901–1908). In 1909, the Athletics left Columbia Park and moved into the newly constructed Classic ballpark, Shibe Park, where they stayed until the franchise (including the ballpark) was sold and the club moved to Kansas City after the 1954 season.

In the AL, the Athletics were one of the most successful franchises in the Deadball Era with pennant-winning seasons in 1902, 1905, 1910, 1911, 1913, and 1914. After the 1914 season, the emergence of a third ML (the Federal League) led the Athletics to breakup their championship team of the prior years as they sold off star players and did not compete with the Federal League to retain top players. The Athletics were doormats for about a decade thereafter. It is interesting to note that Athletics manager Connie Mack was not fired after his 1916 club set a ML record for the lowest winning percentage in the 20th Century (.235). In addition to being the manager, he was also the largest minority owner of the ball club! In the NL, while the Phillies were not as successful as the AL Athletics, they were occasionally contenders in the Deadball Era and actually won the pennant in 1915. After the end of the Deadball Era, the Phillies' decline was captured in a very colorful story about Baker Bowl. For many years, the RF wall at the ballpark had a large advertising sign that proclaimed the Phillies used Lifebuoy, a deodorant soap. One night, some unknown wag snuck into the park and added at the bottom of the sign, "But the Phillies Still Stink."

Sunday baseball was illegal everywhere in the state of Pennsylvania until 1934.[1] This long-lasting prohibition on Sunday baseball adversely affected the economic performance of both Philadelphia franchises, because Sunday games in other AL and NL cities drew far and away the largest attendance of any day of the week. One other negative impact was higher travel costs as both the Athletics and Phillies had to make a number of one-day road trips to cities where Sunday baseball was legal. The Phillies made large numbers of one-day road trips to New York (starting in 1919 to play either the Giants or the Dodgers), while the Athletics made trips to Washington starting in 1918 when Sunday baseball became legal in the nation's capitol.

Baker Bowl

Philadelphia National League: 1895–1919

Baker Bowl was a one-of-a-kind ballpark. Very modern and technically advanced when it was built in 1895, it suffered in its later years with a bad reputation. The ballpark is not considered to have been one of the Classic ballparks. The park's official name was National League Park, and in its early years it was commonly called Huntingdon Street Grounds. The ballpark acquired the name Baker Bowl in the Deadball Era from Phillies owner William F. Baker (1913–1930), and Baker Bowl is the name by which the ballpark is remembered today.

When Baker Bowl opened in 1895, it boasted of a fireproof steel, brick, and concrete double-deck grandstand. In addition, Baker Bowl was the first ballpark in the country to use a cantilever design that eliminated many view-obstructing posts. In the early years of the 20th Century, when all other ML ballparks were built of wood and nearly all (except the Polo Grounds in New York) had only single-deck grandstands, Baker Bowl was ahead of its time and considered the standard of excellence in ballparks.

The ballpark was located on a rectangular lot that consisted of one entire city block in North Philadelphia, not far from downtown. The park was bounded by on the north by West Lehigh Ave., on the south by West Huntingdon St., on the west by North 15th St., and on the east by North Broad St. The grandstand and home plate were located in the southwest corner of the site. The 4.9 acre park site was not large: 540 feet (north-south) by 392 feet (east-west). By comparison, other pre–Classic ballparks in the Deadball Era occupied sites ranging from 3.9 acres (League Park III in Cleveland) to 9.4 acres (Hilltop Park in New York). The 392 foot (east-west) dimension, along Huntingdon St. on the south and Lehigh Ave. on the north, always limited the park's RF dimensions. One unique feature of Baker Bowl was the existence of the Philadelphia and Reading Railroad tunnel under CF. This railroad tunnel caused there to be a hump in CF that made that portion of CF about ten feet above the level of home plate.

When it opened in 1895, the ballpark consisted of the double-deck grandstand that extended on both sides a short way beyond first base and third base. In addition, bleachers were located down both foul lines. Only the grandstand was built of steel and concrete, as the bleachers were built of wood, an arrangement that was to have tragic consequences later. Unlike many later ML ballparks, the original first-base and third-base bleachers did not converge with the foul lines. This alignment, while not appreciated by the fans seated far down the foul lines, did allow the bullpens in Baker Bowl to be located in foul territory relatively close to the infield. There was no seating in the fair portion of the outfield. A large (for the times) multi-story clubhouse was located in CF diagonally between the LF and RF walls and

Baker Bowl during the 1915 World Series. This photograph shows the third base bleachers and a portion of the left-field bleachers, built before the 1910 season. Just to the right of the man in the white coat the two set of bleaders meet at a crease in the fence. Before the 1925 season the field was rotated two degrees to the right, such that the left-field foul line intersected the stands at the crease. (George Grantham Bain Collection, Library of Congress.)

thus faced home plate. The RF wall was 40 feet high and built of brick and included a manually operated scoreboard built onto the wall about ten feet above the level of the playing field. In the early years of the ballpark, the RF wall had ornamental terraces or shallow balconies. These were referred to as the "Hanging Gardens." Between 1904 and 1912, the RF wall was redone with the removal of the balconies and the addition of a tin (actually thin steel sheeting) facing that, in turn, was covered with a number of large advertising signs. The entire outfield had a 15-foot-wide banked bicycle track that doubled as a warning track for the outfielders.

Before the 1910 season, the ballpark's capacity was significantly increased by building additional bleachers in front of the LF perimeter wall. This new set of bleachers extended from the LF corner to the left edge of the CF clubhouse. The old third-base bleachers were rebuilt and now angled toward the new LF bleachers. The seats in the old third-base bleachers now faced towards the pitcher's mound, and the seats in this area were now called field seats to differentiate them from the new LF bleachers. At about the same time, the double-deck grandstand was extended on the first-base side down to the RF corner. Capacity now amounted to about 17,000. Additional seating was added on the roof of the clubhouse before 1914. These not-very-safe seats were removed in the early 1920s after they were condemned by the city. Before the 1914 season, the bleachers in LF were expanded and now extended from the LF corner to LC and across CF all the way to the junction with the RF wall. These additional sections of bleachers were thus located in front of the CF clubhouse and had the effect of both reducing the CF dimension as well as obstructing the players' access to the clubhouse. Most of these sections of CF bleachers were removed after the 1917 season. The ballpark's total seating capacity after the addition of the CF bleachers was 18,800. Attendance in the second and fifth games of the 1915 World Series played at Baker Bowl was 20,306; this total included standees in the outfield and fans in the temporary CF bleachers erected for the World Series.

In the second decade of the Deadball Era, Baker Bowl began to acquire a reputation as a bandbox. Visiting team's baseball writers made derisive comments about the park and many references to cheap home runs over the close RF wall. Contributing to the ballpark's negative image was a deadly catastrophe that occurred during the 1903 season. On August 8, 1903, during the second game of a doubleheader against the Boston Braves, a tragic incident occurred. Two drunks walking down North 15th St. (just at the back of the third-base bleachers) were being teased by a group of girls. One of the drunks grabbed one of the girls and fell on top of her. The resulting screams and shouts attracted the attention of fans in the top rows of the third-base bleachers. These fans moved to the overhanging balcony at the top of the bleachers to see what the commotion was about. Other fans in the lower rows of the bleachers then crowded onto this overhanging balcony to join the first group of fans. Suddenly, the wooden balcony collapsed and crashed 30 feet to the concrete sidewalk below. In total, 12 people were killed and 232 injured. The subsequent investigation determined that the wooden timbers supporting that portion of the third-base bleachers and the overhanging balcony were rotten and the weight of nearly 400 people caused the collapse.[2] As a result of this calamity, the Phillies had to transfer several home games to the AL's Shibe Park.

The Phillies continued to use Baker Bowl until mid-season 1938 when they moved to Shibe Park and became tenants of the Athletics. After the Phillies left, the ballpark was used for high school football games and later midget auto races. The remains of the park were demolished in 1950.

The Basis of Baker Bowl's Configurations and Dimensions

The park's Opening Day 1901 dimensions of LF 390, CF 408, and RF 272 were derived from *Green Cathedrals* and a 1921 Sanborn Fire Insurance Co. map of the ballpark.[3] The CF and RF dimensions listed in *Green Cathedrals* were found consistent with the dimensions derived from the Sanborn map. The 1921 Sanborn map confirmed the dimensions of the park site, and provided the location and extent of the grandstand, bleachers, and perimeter fences. A diagram of the park was drawn on the Sanborn map. Home plate was located to fit the RF and CF dimensions of 272 and 408 respectively; then the LF dimension (390) was determined by calculating the distance from home plate to the LF perimeter wall. This resulted in an estimated distance of 53 feet from home plate to the backstop that was the diagonal section of the grandstand. Given the location of home plate, all of the other outfield dimensions were then calculated from this park diagram. Because the shape of the park's land plat was a rectangle and the foul lines were not quite parallel with 15th St. and Huntingdon St., the LF foul line hit the LF wall at slightly less than 90 degrees, and the RF foul line hit the RF wall at slightly more than 90 degrees.

The alignment of the foul lines to the LF and RF walls changed during the life of the park. Photos from the 1910s showed dead CF to have been at the junction of the clubhouse and the RF wall.[4] In the 1920s, other photos showed dead CF to have been about 15–20 feet to the right of the junction of the clubhouse and the RF wall.[5] Thus, the playing field must have been reoriented two or three degrees toward right field. A number of photos from the 1910–1921 time period confirm that the LF foul line intersected the third-base bleachers (now called field seats) before reaching the LF corner. Photos from the mid-and-late 1920s showed the LF foul line to now meet the LF bleachers exactly in the LF corner. In addition, in 1922 home plate was moved away from RF by seven feet in an attempt to increase the RF dimension.[6] For the LF foul line to avoid hitting the third-base field seats, it was necessary to rotate the foul lines a couple of degrees to the right. It could be argued that the foul lines had been at 90 degrees to the LF and RF walls before the 1922 field reorientation and that the intersection of the foul lines with the wall was more than 90 degrees in LF and less than 90 degrees in RF thereafter. However, an aerial photo of the ballpark in 1928 indicated the intersection angles of the foul lines with the LF and RF walls to have been 90 degrees.

Before the 1910 season, a number of alterations were made to Baker Bowl. The first-base side of the grandstand was extended to the RF perimeter wall.[7] This extension was parallel with the RF foul line, and a substantial amount of foul territory remained to the right of the foul pole. New bleachers were built in LF in front of the LF perimeter wall. The third-base bleachers were rebuilt (still built of wood) and now curved to meet the new LF field seats. The depth of these LF bleachers and the reduced LF dimension of 335 were obtained from the park diagram drawn on the Sanborn map.

In summary, all of the Baker Bowl's dimensions were calculated from the Sanborn map and resulting park diagram. As neither the foul lines nor the home plate locations were shown on the map, these dimensions contain a small amount of uncertainty. All dimensions were checked against, and are consistent with, the available photographic evidence and the home run data.

Park data and dimensions for Baker Bowl are shown below.

DIMENSIONS (calculated from park diagrams)

Years	LF	SLF	LC	CF	RC	SRF	RF
1901–1909	390	400	410*	408	325	288	272
1910–1913	335	356	379	408	325	288	272
1914–1917	335	356	379	388	325	288	272
1918–1919	335	356	379	408	325	288	272

*Deepest point was left of LC at 427

FENCE HEIGHTS (from *Green Cathedrals* and estimated from photos)

Years	LF	CF	RF
1901–1909	12	35	40
1910–1913	3*	35–47	40
1914–1917	3*	3–47*	40
1918–1919	3*	3–47*	40

*The three-foot heights were the front of the LF and CF bleachers

Average Outfield Distances

Years	LF	CF	RF
1901–1909	403	382	292
1910–1913	360	382	292
1914–1917	360	373	292
1918–1919	360	382	292

ARCHITECT: JOHN D. ALLEN

CAPACITY: 14,000 (1895–1909 EST.), 17,000 (1910–1913 EST.), 18,800 (1914–1917), 18,300 (1918–1919 EST.)

PARK SIZE/COMPOSITE AVERAGE OUTFIELD DISTANCE: 359 (1901–1909), 345 (1910–1913), 342 (1914–1917), 345 (1918–1919)

PARK SITE AREA: 4.9 ACRES

DEADBALL ERA RUN FACTOR: 106 (RANK: NL 4)

The Impact of the Park's Configurations and Dimensions on Batting

Baker Bowl in its original configuration (1895–1909), despite being the smallest ballpark in the NL by about 20 feet, had the second-largest LF (only Robison Field in St. Louis was larger). Over the park's first nine Deadball Era seasons, Baker Bowl was *not* a hitter's park. The batting park factors for batting average, on-base, and slugging were quite average (100, 100, 98 respectively). In 1901–1909, Baker Bowl was moderately above average for doubles and moderately below average for triples, with park factors of 117 for doubles and 79 for triples. The park's unique configuration, with RC only 300 feet from home plate, made the usual triples alley in RC too close for very many triples. Of course, any configuration that curbed triples made doubles more common. In addition and in sharp contrast to the park's reputation in the next decade as a bandbox, Baker Bowl was 39 percent worse than the average NL park for home runs. As the smallest NL ballpark in the NL, it is not surprising that the Baker Bowl was not a good park for triples or IPHR. There were only 3.6 IPHR per season (1901–1909) at the ballpark, while the average NL ballpark averaged nearly three times that number per year. The embankments located in front of all of the outfield fences are the likely explanation why Baker Bowl, despite an ample-sized LF, had so few IPHR. These embankments curtailed IPHR, as balls that were potential IPHR rolled back to the outfielders. The majority of IPHR were to CF. During the Deadball Era, there were never any home runs hit completely out of the park over the LF perimeter wall. The first player to accomplish this feat was Cliff Lee of the Phillies in 1922. By contrast, there were 52 home runs hit over the much-closer RF perimeter wall and out into Broad St. in the nine seasons between 1901–1909.

Before the 1910 season, LF was made substantially smaller with the building of the LF bleachers. This alteration of the ballpark, in combination with the introduction of the cork-center ball in the 1911 season, led Baker Bowl to becoming the hitter's ballpark we know it as today. The 1910–1919 Baker Bowl batting park factors averaged 105, 103, and 107 for batting average, on-base, and slugging respectively. With the shorter distances in LF and CF, the doubles park factor increased (117 to 130) and the triples park factor decreased (79 to 53). Thus it can be said that Baker Bowl was never a good park for triples. The impact of the LF bleachers (and the use of the cork-center ball) on home runs was quite dramatic. After the LF bleachers were in place starting with the 1910 season, total home runs per season increased by an amazing 490 percent (1910–1919 over 1901–1909). Even more striking was the increase in bounce home runs. This little-known type of home run increased tenfold from 0.6 per season to 6.6 per season. As the ballpark was made smaller, the number of IPHR declined from 3.6 to 2.2 per season. The overall home run park factor for Baker Bowl's ten Deadball seasons with the LF bleachers (1910–1919) was an impressive 183–83 percent better than the average NL ballpark. This result occurred because OTF home runs were possible to all fields. As shown in one of the above tables, the average CF distances in the second decade of the Deadball Era were modest, ranging from 373 to 382, while both LF and RF were noticeably closer. An additional contributing factor was the low fence (only three-feet high) at the front of the reachable LF bleachers (straightaway LF was only 356) that resulted in several bounce home runs per year.

Baker Bowl was an asymmetrical ballpark, even after the installation of the LF bleachers made LF considerably smaller. The average LF distance (1910–1919) was 360 vs. 292 for RF. The question arises as to what was the impact of this very asymmetrical ballpark on left vs. right-handed batters. For this ten-year time period home-road batting splits were compiled for Philadelphia's left-handed and right-handed batters. The results are shown in the following table.

1910–1919 Philadelphia NL

Left-Handed Batters*	BA	OBP	SLUG	HR/AB
Home	.281	.347	.404	.0185
Road	.252	.317	.349	.0090
Right-Handed Batters*	BA	OBP	SLUG	HR/AB
Home	.265	.324	.370	.0128
Road	.243	.305	.320	.0038

*Excludes switch hitters

Home-Road Ratio	BA	OBP	SLUG	HR/AB
PHL Left-Handed	1.116	1.097	1.157	2.048
PHL Right-Handed	1.090	1.062	1.156	3.366
Total NL	1.045	1.045	1.062	1.294
Gavvy Cravath**	BA	OBP	Slug	HR/AB
Home	.306	.397	.563	.0541
Road	.277	.366	.423	.0128

**Cravath was a right-handed batter

The above data show that left-handed batters benefited more than right-handed batters in the categories of batting average, on-base, and slugging. However, the advantage in slugging was minuscule (1.157 vs. 1.156) because at Baker Bowl the home-park advantage for home runs (adjusted for the number of at bats) was substantially greater for right-handed batters than for left-handed batters. What can explain this anomalous result? The answer is Gavvy Cravath. This Deadball Era slugger led the NL in home runs six times in his eight Deadball seasons with Philadelphia (1912–1919). Cravath playing in Baker Bowl was a potent combination as he hit 92 of his 116 home runs (not quite 80 percent) at home in those years. When adjusted for more at bats in road games, the comparison is even more striking-Cravath had a home-road ratio of home runs per at bat of 4.23.[8] His overall batting measures (batting average, on-base, and slugging) had home-road ratios of 1.105, 1.085, and 1.331 respectively. As the average home-road ratios in the NL in this time period were 1.045 (batting average and on-base), 1.062 (slugging), and 1.294 (home runs), Cravath's record displayed a generous amount of home-park advantage. An interesting aspect of the Cravath record in Baker Bowl is that despite being a right-handed batter, his home runs (excluding eight bounce home runs) were hit to all fields: 26 to LF, 20 to CF, two to RC, and 35 to RF (one was to an unknown field).

The home-run data and park factors and for Baker Bowl are shown in four tables below.

Home Runs by Type at Baker Bowl

Years	Total	OTF	Bounce	IPHR
1901–1909	98	66	5	32
1910–1913	229	208	32	21
1914–1917	176	175	26	1
1918–1919	85	85	8	0

OTF Home Runs by Field at Baker Bowl (Excludes Bounce)

Years	Total	LF	CF	RF	Unknown
1901–1909	61	0	3	52	6
1910–1913	171	78	15	73	5
1914–1917	183	70	29	80	4
1918–1919	77	32	8	33	4

Inside-the-Park Home Runs by Field at Baker Bowl

Years	Total	LF	LC	CF	RC	RF	Unknown
1901–1909	32	4	4	22	0	0	2
1910–1913	21	2	0	13	1	4	1
1914–1917	1	0	0	0	0	1	0
1918–1919	0						

Batting Park Factors at Baker Bowl

Years	BA	OBP	SLUG	2B*	3B*	HR*	BB**
1901–1909	100	100	98	117	79	61	101
1910–1919	105	103	107	130	53	183	97

*Per AB
**Per Total Plate Appearance (AB+BB+HP)

Columbia Park II

Philadelphia American League: 1901–1908

Columbia Park II was the second ML ballpark in Philadelphia with that name. The original Columbia ballpark (denoted as Columbia Park I and at a different location) was used by the National Association Philadelphia Centennials for only two months in 1875. Columbia Park II opened for baseball on April 26, 1901, as the first home park of the AL Philadelphia Athletics. The ballpark had been quickly built before the start of the 1901 season on a vacant lot that had been leased for 10 years by the A's manager and part-owner Connie Mack. Columbia Park was built almost entirely of wood; only the front or street side of the main entrance was brick. Unlike many of the other Deadball Era wooden ballparks, this one never burned.

On a rectangular lot in North Philadelphia, the park was bounded by on the north by Columbia Ave., on the south by Oxford St., on the west by 30th St., and on the east by 29th St. The location of the ballpark was not far from downtown Philadelphia. The grandstand and home plate were located in the southwest corner of the site. The park site was not large — 400 by 455 feet — and amounted to 4.2 acres. The 400 foot (east-west) dimension, along Oxford St. on the south and Columbia Ave. on the north, limited the park's RF dimension.

For Opening Day 1901, the park's seating consisted of a single-deck covered grandstand that extended from first base to third base, and bleachers down both foul lines. There was a short diagonal section of the grandstand that formed the backstop. On the roof of the grandstand were both a small press box and a wire screen on each side of the press box to keep foul balls in the park. There were gaps between the grandstand and both sets of bleachers. Both the LF and RF bleachers ran parallel to the foul lines. The first-base bleachers reached nearly to the RF corner, and the third-base bleachers extended all the way to the LF perimeter fence on Columbia Ave. and then hooked around as far as the LF foul line to face home plate. There was a wire screen erected on top of the RF perimeter wall that was intended to keep home runs and foul ball from hitting vehicles and possible pedestrians on 29th St. As home plate was in the southwest corner of the site, the LF line ran due north-south, and RF was the sun field. There was a modest-sized scoreboard near RC that was set into the RF-CF fence. There was one clubhouse (for the use by the home team only), but no dugouts; the players sat on benches in front of the grandstand. On Opening Day 1901, Columbia Park had seating for 4,000 in the grandstand and 4,500 in the bleachers for a total of 9,500. Capacity was expanded by a small amount in 1903 by adding seats to the foul-area first-base bleachers.[9] Additional unspecified foul-area expansion raised the seating capacity to 13,600 for the 1905 season. The park's all-time record attendance was far in excess of the park's seating capacity. This was demonstrated when 25,187 were in attendance for a crucial game against the White Sox late in the 1905 season. The A's won two AL pennants playing at Columbia Park, but hosted only one World Series (1905), when they lost to the New York Giants. The A's other pennant was in 1902 when there was no World Series. In addition to the A's, the park was used by the Phillies for 16 games in 1903 when the Phillies' home park (Baker Bowl) was temporarily closed after a tragic collapse of a portion of the stands. Columbia Park was abandoned after the 1908 season when the A's moved into the first of the Classic ballparks, Shibe Park. After the A's left Columbia Park, it was used for a circus and for other events for a couple of years before being demolished. The site is now a mixed commercial and residential area.

The Basis of Columbia Park's Configuration and Dimensions

No listed dimensions for Columbia Park were found in any of the usual ballpark reference books.[10] The 1901 dimensions of LF 340, CF 396, and RF 280 were derived entirely from a finely detailed 1907 Philadelphia City Atlas.[11] This atlas provided the size of the park site, and the location and extent of the grandstand and bleachers. A diagram of the park and the dimensions of the park site were copied from the 1907 atlas. The details copied from the atlas included the location of the grandstand, bleachers, and the main entrance to the ballpark (located at the corner of 30th St. and Oxford St.). The location of home plate was based on photos of the park; it was estimated to have been 72 feet from the diagonal section of the grandstand that formed the backstop. Given the location of home plate, all of the outfield dimensions were then calculated from the park diagram. Because the shape of the land plat was a rectangle and the foul lines were parallel with 29th St. and 30th St., the outfield fences were aligned at 90 degrees to the foul line in both LF and RF. Based on research into home runs at Columbia Park, it was found that there had been home runs hit over an interior fence in RF and RC.[12] From the Opening Day photo in the *Philadelphia Inquirer*, this interior fence was quite close to the exterior RF wall and screen and included a modest-sized scoreboard in RC.[13] The RF screen was a chicken-wire screen estimated to have been 25 feet in height and mounted on top of the exterior RF wall. This screen, as it was erected on the exterior wall, was out-of-play and extended all the way to the CF corner.

In summary, all of the Columbia Park dimensions were estimated from the 1907 Philadelphia City Atlas. As neither the foul lines nor the home plate locations were shown in the atlas, these dimensions contain a small amount of uncertainty. All dimensions were checked against, and are consistent with, the available photographic evidence and the home-run data.

Park data and dimensions for Columbia Park are shown below.

DIMENSIONS (calculated from park diagram)

Years	LF	SLF	LC	CF	RC	SRF	RF
1901–1908	340	352	392	396*	323	290	280

*Deepest point was 440 at the CF corner to the left of dead CF

FENCE HEIGHTS (estimated from photos)

Years	LF	CF	RF
1901–1908	8	8–11*	8

*The 11-foot height was only the scoreboard in RC

AVERAGE OUTFIELD DISTANCES

Years	LF	CF	RF
1901–1908	358	385	295

CAPACITY: 9,500 (1901–1902), 10,000 (1903–1904 EST.), 13,600 (1905–1908)

PARK SIZE/COMPOSITE AVERAGE OUTFIELD DISTANCE: 346

PARK SITE AREA: 4.2 ACRES

DEADBALL ERA RUN FACTOR: 108 (RANK: AL 5)

The Impact of the Park's Configuration and Dimensions on Batting

In its limited lifetime, Columbia Park was the smallest ballpark in the AL, with a park size about 30 feet smaller than the AL average. Over the park's eight ML seasons, Columbia Park was above average for batting average, on-base, slugging, and doubles (see table below of Batting Park Factors). In the 1902 season, the A's compiled a .322 team batting average (the highest in the AL that season) at Columbia Park, while hitting a lowly .249 on the road. This 73-point difference was the largest single season home-road differential in batting average for any team in the Deadball Era. As the smallest AL ballpark, it was a poor park for triples and IPHR. There were only 4.2 IPHR per season at Columbia Park, while the average AL ballpark averaged more than twice that number per year in 1901–1908. At Columbia Park, the large majority of IPHR were to CF, as that was the only deep part of the ballpark. The home run park factor for the eight-year life of Columbia Park was only 107, a surprisingly modest value for the smallest park in the AL and one with a composite average outfield distance of 346. This result occurred because while OTF home runs were relatively numerous, there were not many IPHR. In the Deadball Era generally, and especially in the first decade of the Deadball Era before the introduction of the cork-center ball, there was no simple negative relationship between park size and home runs.

Home Runs by Type at Columbia Park

Years	Total	OTF	Bounce	IPHR
1901–1908	197*	163	5	34

*Includes four NL home runs in 1903

OTF Home Runs by Field at Columbia Park (Excludes Bounce)

Years	Total	LF	CF	RF	Unknown
1901–1908	158	46	18	79	15

Inside-the-Park Home Runs by Field at Columbia Park

Years	Total	LF	LC	CF	RC	RF	Unknown
1901–1908	34	2	3	26	2	1	0

Batting Park Factors at Columbia Park

Years	BA	OBP	SLUG	2B*	3B*	HR*	BB**
1901–1908	104	104	104	125	76	107	104

*Per AB
**Per Total Plate Appearance (AB+BB+HP)

Shibe Park

Philadelphia American League: 1909–1919

Shibe Park was the first of the Classic ballparks when it opened on April 12, 1909. Named for Ben Shibe, the principal owner of the Philadelphia Athletics, the ballpark had been built before the start of the 1909 season on a city block that had previously been used for a city dog pound and a brickyard. Shibe Park was built almost entirely of steel and concrete; only a portion of the upper deck of the grandstand was built of wood on steel girders. The park was located on a rectangular lot that consisted of one entire city block in North Philadelphia. Shibe Park was bounded on the north by Somerset St., on the west by North 21st St., on the south by West Lehigh Ave., and on the east by North 20th St. The park site was not large (with dimensions of 481 and 520 feet) and amounted to 5.7 acres. Shibe Park was the second-smallest Classic ballpark in terms of the size of the park site — only League Park IV in

Shibe Park during the 1913 World Series. The above photograph (dated October 8, 1913) shows the left-field bleachers and the third-base pavilion. Note the left-field bleachers, built before the 1913 season, extend from the far right of the photograph in center field almost to the left-field foul line, and the low fence at the front of the left-field bleachers that led to numerous bounce home runs in the Deadball Era. The left-field foul line in this configuration of Shibe Park ran all the way to the perimeter left-field fence, just as it had in the earlier 1909–1912 configuration. This photograph illustrates how, while the area in left field was substantially reduced with the addition of the left-field bleachers, the left-field dimension was unchanged. (George Grantham Bain Collection, Library of Congress.)

Cleveland was smaller. By comparison, other Classic ballparks in the Deadball Era occupied sites ranging from 6.1 acres (Griffith Stadium in Washington) to 10.5 acres (Braves Field in Boston). The 481-foot (east-west) dimension that was along Somerset St. on the north and Lehigh Ave. on the south limited the park's RF dimension. The cost of the land was $142,000, and the cost of the park's construction was $315,000.[14] Sod was transplanted to the park from the A's prior ballpark, Columbia Park. A French Renaissance church-like dome was on the exterior side of the roof behind home plate and provided an office for minority owner and long-time manager Connie Mack.

For Opening Day 1909, the park's seating areas consisted of a double-deck covered grandstand that extended from beyond first base to beyond third base, and bleachers down both foul lines.[15] A short diagonal section of the grandstand formed the backstop. An in-play raised scoreboard was located about 18–20 feet in front of the LF wall. A ladder in front of the scoreboard went all the way to the top. There were gaps between the grandstand and both sets of bleachers. The first-base bleachers reached nearly to the RF corner, and the LF bleachers extended all the way to the LF perimeter fence on Somerset St. Both bleachers were angled towards the foul lines as they approached the corners. Home plate was in the southwest corner of the park site, with the LF line running due north-south, and RF was the sun field. On Opening Day 1909, Shibe Park had seating for 10,000 in the grandstand and 13,000 in the bleachers for a total of 23,000. There were slopes in front of the outfield fences in the early years that proved useful for the over-flow crowds that filled up the outer reaches of the outfield for big games.

A major expansion occurred before the 1913 season. The first-base and third-base bleachers were roofed (and henceforth called pavilions), and a new set of bleachers were built in LF. The new LF bleachers extended at their front from about 15 feet to the right of the LF line to nearly the CF corner. At this time, the previously in-play LF scoreboard was relocated to the right side of CF and enlarged. The new LF bleachers increased the total capacity of the park by about 3,000.

The Basis of Shibe Park's Configurations and Dimensions

The park's Opening Day 1909 dimensions (LF 378, CF 509, RF 340) were derived from *Green Cathedrals* and a Sanborn Fire Insurance map.[16] The April 1909 dimensions listed in *Green Cathedrals* (LF and RF 360) are impossible given the Sanborn map and the dimensions of the park site. More recent ballpark books have in whole or in part corrected this error.[17] Photographic evidence shows the LF dimension on Opening Day to be the same as listed in *Green Cathedrals* for late 1909. The Sanborn map confirmed the dimensions of the park site and provided the location and extent of the grandstand, bleachers, and perimeter fences. A diagram of the park was drawn on the Sanborn map. Home plate was located to fit a LF dimension of 378 and a RF dimension of 340 (the LF and RF dimensions taken from *Green Cathedrals* for late 1909). This resulted in an estimated distance of 75 feet from home plate to the backstop that was the diagonal section of the grandstand. Given the location of home plate, all of the other outfield dimensions were then calculated from the park diagram. Because the shape of the park's land plat was a rectangle and the foul lines were parallel with 20th St. and Lehigh Ave., the outfield fences were aligned at 90 degrees to the foul line in both LF and RF.

Before the 1912 season, the ground rules concerning the raised LF scoreboard must have been changed. During the 1909–1911 seasons, the scoreboard was in play, and balls hit through the supports of the scoreboard were also in play. During the 1912 season, home run research found two examples of balls hit through the supports of the scoreboard having been ruled home runs.[18] For this to be the case, the area behind the scoreboard in LF must have been out of play. This effectively reduced the LF dimension to 360.

Before the 1913 season, two major alterations were made to Shibe Park. The first-base and third-base bleachers were roofed, and new bleachers were built in LF in front of the 12-foot-high concrete LF perimeter wall. The LF dimension was unchanged at 378, but merely 15 feet to the right of the foul line it was 334. The resulting notch down the LF line is visible in the above 1917 photo.[19] The depth of these new bleachers was obtained from the Sanborn map that also determined the 334 dimension about 15 feet to the right of the LF foul line.

In summary, all of the Shibe Park dimensions were calculated from the Sanborn map and resulting park diagram. As neither the foul lines nor the home plate locations were shown on the map, these dimensions contain a small amount of uncertainty. All dimensions were checked against, and are consistent with, the available photographic evidence and the home-run data.

Park data and dimensions for Shibe Park are shown below.

DIMENSIONS (calculated from park diagrams)

Years	LF	SLF	LC	CF	RC	SRF	RF
1909–1911	378	391	436	481*	392	352	340
1912	360	391	436	481*	392	352	340
1913–1919	378	346	384	481*	392	352	340

*Deepest point was 509 at the CF corner to the left of dead CF

FENCE HEIGHTS (from *Green Cathedrals* and estimated from photos)

Years	LF	CF	RF
1909–1912	12	12	12
1913–1919	4–12*	4–12*	12

*The four-foot heights were at the front of the LF-CF bleachers

AVERAGE OUTFIELD DISTANCES

Years	LF	CF	RF
1909–1911	391	454	358
1912	380	454	358
1913–1919	352	431	358

ARCHITECT: WILLIAM STEELE AND SONS CO. (ALSO THE BUILDERS)

CAPACITY: 23,000 (1909–1912), 26,000 (1913–1919 EST.)

PARK SIZE/COMPOSITE AVERAGE OUTFIELD DISTANCE:
401 (1909–1911), 397 (1912), 380 (1913–1919)

PARK SITE AREA: 5.7 ACRES

DEADBALL ERA RUN FACTOR: 100 (RANK: AL 11)

The Impact of the Park's Configurations and Dimensions on Batting

In its early years (1909–1912), Shibe Park was one of the largest ballparks in the AL, with a park size about 20 feet larger than the AL average. Over the park's 11 ML seasons, Shibe Park was almost exactly average for batting average, on-base, and slugging (see table below of Batting Park Factors). As one of the largest AL ballparks, the ballpark was a good park for triples but not IPHR. There were only 6.0 IPHR per season at Shibe Park (1909–1912), while the average AL ballpark averaged more than twice that number per year. The existence of slopes in front of the outfield fences likely explains so few IPHR. These slopes curtailed IPHR as potential IPHR rolled back to the outfielders and often resulted in triples. In the 1909–1912 seasons, the park factor for triples was 128. At Shibe Park, the majority of IPHR were to CF, as that was the deepest part of the ballpark. During the Deadball Era, there were never any home runs hit completely out of the park over the LF or CF perimeter fences. By contrast, there were 26 home runs hit over the RF fence in the four seasons from 1909 to 1912. After the LF bleachers were in place for the 1913 season, total home runs per season increased by 140 percent. In particular, bounce home runs increased from 1.25 per season to 5.0 per season. The home run park factor for Shibe Park's seven Deadball seasons with the LF bleachers (1913–1919) was an impressive 186, a surprising value for what was by then merely an average-sized AL ballpark. This result occurred because OTF home runs, including bounce home runs into the reachable LF bleachers (straightaway LF was only 346), were relatively numerous. In the 1919 season, Shibe Park had a run factor of 125, as the associated batting park factor was a modest 104 for batting average, but 240 for home runs and 112 for walks. In the park's first configuration (1909–1912), home runs were much more difficult for right-handed hitters than left-handed hitters. The home run park factor for right-handed batters was a modest 56, while for left-handed batters it was 67 percent greater at 93. After the installation of the LF bleachers in the 1913–1919 seasons, the home run park factor for right-handed hitters (237) was nearly double the average for left-handed batters (120).[20]

One interesting aspect of the history of Shibe Park occurred in 1916. In 1916, the Philadelphia Athletics were in a rebuilding mode after the breaking up of the championship teams earlier in that decade. In the 1916 season, the A's compiled the worst record of any ML team since 1900 with a record of 36 and 117. That record put them in last place, an amazing 40 games out of seventh place. However, Shibe Park cannot be blamed for this dismal record; the A's actually won 23 games at home that season (23–53). Their downfall was on the road where they won only 13 games (a rate of about two road wins per month) while losing 64!

The batting park factors and home-run data are shown in four tables below.

HOME RUNS BY TYPE AT SHIBE PARK

Years	Total	OTF	Bounce	IPHR
1909–1912	55	31	5	24
1913–1919	232	214	35	18

OTF HOME RUNS BY FIELD AT SHIBE PARK (EXCLUDES BOUNCE)

Years	Total	LF	CF	RF	Unknown
1909–1912	26	0	0	26	0
1913–1919	179	116	6	57	19

INSIDE-THE-PARK HOME RUNS BY FIELD AT SHIBE PARK

Years	Total	LF	LC	CF	RC	RF	Unknown
1909–1912	24	3	8	13	0	0	0
1913–1919	18	2	0	15	0	1	0

BATTING PARK FACTORS AT SHIBE PARK

Years	BA	OBP	SLUG	2B*	3B*	HR*	BB**
1909–1912	99	100	100	94	128	66	105
1913–1919	99	100	100	90	95	186	102

*Per AB
**Per Total Plate Appearance (AB+BB+HP)

11

Pittsburgh

Pittsburgh became a ML city in 1882 when its baseball team (the Allegheny Baseball Club) was one of six teams to form the American Association. Pittsburgh remained a member of American Association for five seasons. In 1887, the Alleghenies dropped out of the American Association and joined the NL. Pittsburgh has had a franchise in the NL ever since. The NL team was first called the Alleghenies (1887–1889), then the Innocents for only the 1890 season, and began using the name Pirates thereafter. The name Pirates came about as a result of the end of the Players League after its only season of operation in 1890. The Pittsburgh NL team merged with the Pittsburgh team of the Players League. All players in the 1890 Players League were expected to return to the clubs for whom they had played in the 1889 season. As expected, the Pittsburgh NL team (called the Innocents in 1890) reacquired several players that had left to join the Players League. In addition, Pittsburgh also acquired top-rated second baseman Louis Bierbauer. This player had not played for Pittsburgh in the 1889 season (before playing for Brooklyn in the Players League in 1890, Bierbauer had spent the prior four seasons with the Philadelphia Athletics of the American Association). Pittsburgh managed to obtain the services of Bierbauer for the 1891 season, and the Athletics and other American Association teams objected loudly and accused Pittsburgh of being "pirates." As a result, the team soon began to be called the Pirates. The nickname stuck; thus, the team went in a single season from being the Innocents to being the Pirates.[1]

Unlike the case in many other NL cities where numerous short-lived ballparks were used, Pittsburgh utilized only two NL ballparks in the nineteenth century. Recreation Park was used from 1883 to 1890. The second ballpark, denoted as Exposition Park III, was used from 1891 to late in the first decade of the twentieth century. There were two earlier ML ballparks at the same site called Exposition Park. Located at the confluence of the Allegheny and Monongahela Rivers, the park was subject to repeated floods. To escape the flooding and to obtain more seating capacity, the Pirates left Exposition Park and moved into the largely steel-and-concrete Classic ballpark (Forbes Field) in mid-season 1909.

The Pirates were one of the dominant NL teams in the early years of the Deadball Era. Pittsburgh won the NL pennant in 1901, 1902, and 1903, and again in 1909. The Pirates got off to such a good start in the Deadball Era because of the contraction of the NL from 12 to eight teams after the 1899 season. At that time, the Louisville franchise was merged with the Pittsburgh franchise, and the best players from the Louisville team were added to the Pirates roster. Included among the Louisville players transferred to Pittsburgh was Honus Wagner, the future Hall of Fame shortstop. Wagner, one of the greatest stars of the Deadball Era, helped the Pirates with eight batting championships in his 18 years with the Pirates.

Pittsburgh was one of the four ML cities (the others were Brooklyn, Chicago, and St.

Louis) that had both NL and Federal League teams in 1914–1915. The Pittsburgh Rebels, who used old Exposition Park III, were the Pittsburgh Federal League entry. The 1914–1915 seasons were the first time since 1890 there had been two ML teams in Pittsburgh.

During the entirety of the Deadball Era and for 15 years thereafter, there was no professional Sunday baseball in Pittsburgh, as Sunday baseball was illegal in the state of Pennsylvania until 1934.[2] As a result, each season the Pirates had a number of one-day road trips to various Midwest cities (most often Cincinnati) where Sunday baseball was allowed.

Exposition Park III

Pittsburgh National League: 1891–1909

Exposition Park III was the third ML ballpark in Pittsburgh built on the same site. This park site was very near the junction of the Allegheny and Monongahela Rivers (which meet in Pittsburgh to form the Ohio River) in what at the start of the twentieth century was in the city of Allegheny and now is within the city limits of Pittsburgh. The ballpark got its name from the site being used by traveling circuses and other expositions. The earlier ML ballparks on this site were Exposition I Lower Field and Exposition II Upper Field. These two ballparks were used by the American Association and Union Association teams from 1882 to 1884. The Lower Field was the diamond closest to the river and was the ballpark that was in general use. The other ballpark, Exposition II Upper Field, was a hastily built ballpark used only for the start of the 1883 season because of flooding on the Lower Field. The ballpark was used for less than two months before games were moved back to the Lower Field. Exposition Park III was built for the 1890 Players League Pittsburgh franchise. The Pittsburgh Burghers and the rest of the Players League lasted only one season. The NL team, called the Pirates moved into the ballpark and stayed until mid-season 1909. Exposition Park III was located on the north side of the Allegheny River across from downtown Pittsburgh. The ballpark was separated from the river by a railroad marshalling yard. Exposition Park's playing field sloped from the grandstand and infield (located in the northeast corner of the site) down to the outfield on the south side. The Pirates used innovative ground rules to deal with the occasional floods. On July 4, 1902, the Allegheny River flooded, and there was more than a foot of water in the outfield. As there was a doubleheader scheduled that day and the teams did not wish to miss out on the large crowds, a special ground rule was adopted. All balls hit into the water in the outfield were good for one base. At the park site, the surrounding streets were South Ave. on the north, School St. on the east, and Grant St. on the west. The park site was larger than average for pre–Classic ML ballparks and amounted to 6.4 acres. Unlike many other ML ballparks in this era, the dimensions of the park were not limited by the size of the park site or the pattern of surrounding streets.

When the park opened in 1890, the seating capacity was only 6,500. The large amount of area in the outfield made it possible to accommodate several thousand extra fans as outfield standees. Attendance for game seven of the 1903 World Series amounted to 17,038, nearly three times the ballpark's regular-season seating capacity. The ballpark was built entirely of wood, but, unlike many of it contemporaries, it never burned. In the park's original and only configuration, there was a single-deck covered grandstand with bleachers down both foul lines and a small set of shallow bleachers in fair LF. Both the third-base and first-base bleachers were angled towards the playing field and thus converged with the foul lines. The grandstand was made up of three sections: the first-base and third-base sections extended to about

Exposition Park III, regular season, 1904. The above photograph (dated August 23, 1904), taken from deep right-center field, shows the overflow crowd of standees in right field, the third-base bleachers, and the single-deck covered grandstand. Note the smoke rising from a chimney behind the grandstand (Pittsburgh was called the Smokey City for a reason) and the substantial distance between the right-field fence and the ring of standees. The generous dimensions of Exposition Park meant there was still ample room between the outfielders and the overflow crowd. (Photograph by the George R. Lawrence Co., Panoramic Photographs Collection, Library of Congress.)

the edge of the infield, and the third section was a diagonal between them that formed the backstop. The shallow LF bleachers reached on the right end from almost LC to nearly the LF foul line. However, these bleachers did not extend into the LF corner; instead, there was a notch, about 20 feet wide, between the LF foul line and the left end of the LF bleachers. The total seating capacity of 6,500 made Exposition Park III the smallest in terms of capacity of any of the regular-use ML pre–Classic ballparks. Given the small seating capacity of the ballpark and the problems with recurring flooding, the Pirates were one of the first clubs to build a new Classic steel-and-concrete ballpark, Forbes Field. The Pirates left the old wooden ballpark and moved into Forbes Field on June 30, 1909. Exposition Park III had no further ML use until the Federal League Pittsburgh team used the park for the 1914–1915 seasons. At that time, the seating capacity of the ballpark was increased to 16,000.

The Basis of Exposition Park's Configuration and Dimensions

The park's Opening Day 1901 dimensions (LF 400, CF 515, RF 380) were derived from *Green Cathedrals* and a 1906 Sanborn Fire Insurance Co. map of the ballpark.[3] The 1906 Sanborn map confirmed the dimensions of the park site and provided the location and extent of the grandstand, bleachers, and perimeter fences. A diagram of the park was drawn on the Sanborn map. Home plate was located to fit the LF dimension of 400 listed in *Green Cathedrals*, with the LF foul line parallel with the park's RF perimeter fence, and both foul lines were located such that they just cleared the angled first-base and third-base bleachers (as the bleachers were shown on the Sanborn map and in photos). The RF dimension (380) was determined by calculating the distance from home plate to the RF perimeter wall. This home-plate location resulted in an estimated distance of 65 feet from home plate to the backstop that was made up by the diagonal section of the grandstand. The other outfield dimensions were calculated from the park diagram.

In summary, all of the Exposition Park's dimensions were calculated from the Sanborn map and the resulting park diagram. As neither the foul lines nor the home plate location were shown on the map, these dimensions contain a small amount of uncertainty. All dimensions were checked against, and are consistent with, the available photographic evidence and the home-run data.

Park data and dimensions for Exposition Park III are shown below.

DIMENSIONS (calculated from park diagram)

Years	LF	SLF	LC	CF	RC	SRF	RF
1901–1909	400	393	475	515	439	393	380

FENCE HEIGHTS (estimated from photos)

Years	LF	CF	RF
1901–1909	3–10*	10–20	10

*The three-foot height was the front of the LF bleachers

AVERAGE OUTFIELD DISTANCES

Years	LF	CF	RF
1901–1909	401	484	400

CAPACITY: 6,500 (1890–1909)

Park Size/Composite Average Outfield Distance: 428

Park Site Area: 6.4 acres

Deadball Era Run Factor: 101 (Rank: NL 7)

The Impact of the Park's Configuration and Dimensions on Batting

Exposition Park III in its Deadball years (1901 to mid-season 1909) was by far the largest park in the NL (by about 30 feet as measured by the composite average outfield distance). However, the ballpark, despite its large size, was actually slightly above average as a hitter's park. For the years 1901–1909, Exposition Park's run factor was 101 (one percent above average), as were the park factors for both batting average and on-base. The 1902 Pirates team that won the NL pennant was a good hitting team, leading the NL in batting average, on-base, and slugging. In that 1902 season, the Pirates posted the highest team home-park batting average (.305) of any NL team in the 19 seasons of the Deadball Era. As the largest park in the NL with generous dimensions in LF, CF, and RF, Exposition Park was noted as a haven for triples and IPHR. The park factor for triples was 169, nearly 70 percent more than the average NL ballpark. When it came to home runs, Exposition Park was below average with a home run park factor of 68. While the number of IPHR hit at the park was higher than the NL average, OTF home runs at this ballpark were very rare. In the eight-and-a-half seasons Exposition Park was used in the Deadball Era, there were only six OTF home runs, and five of the six were of the bounce variety. The only home run in the Deadball Era to clear any of the outfield fences on the fly was hit by Tim Jordan of Brooklyn (over the RF fence) on July 22, 1908. This rare event was first-page news the next day in the Pittsburgh newspapers. An interesting aspect of batting in the Deadball Era can be seen in the batting park factors for Exposition Park. For the ballpark, the batting average park factor was 101, and the extra-base-hit park factors were a mixed bag: doubles 94, triples 168, and home runs 66. In contemporary times, such a combination of park factors would produce a below-average park factor for slugging. In the Deadball Era, with far fewer home runs and many more triples, Exposition Park actually had a noticeably higher-than-average slugging park factor of 105.

Home Runs by Type at Exposition Park III

Years	Total	OTF	Bounce	IPHR
1901–1909	109	6	5	103

OTF Home Runs by Field at Exposition Park III (Excludes Bounce)

Years	Total	LF	CF	RF
1901–1909	1	0	0	1

Inside-the-Park Home Runs by Field at Exposition Park III

Years	Total	LF	LC	CF	RC	RF	Unknown
1901–1909	103	26	3	49	9	6	10

BATTING PARK FACTORS AT EXPOSITION PARK III

Years	BA	OBP	SLUG	2B*	3B*	HR*	BB**
1901–1909	101	101	105	94	168	66	99

*Per AB
**Per Total Plate Appearance (AB+BB+HP)

Forbes Field

Pittsburgh National League: 1909–1919

Forbes Field opened on June 30, 1909. The ballpark is considered to be the first of the NL Classic ballparks. This distinction is based on the status of Sportsman's Park IV that opened in April 1909 as a not-yet-Classic ballpark. The new double-deck grandstand at Sportsman's Park in St. Louis was built of steel and concrete. However, because Sportsman's Park in 1909 retained (from Sportsman's III) a substantial portion of the existing wooden stands, it was at that point in time not considered a Classic ballpark. Forbes Field was described as "A Gem When It Opened" and was a substantial improvement over the Pirates flood-prone Exposition Park III.[4] The new ballpark had more than three times the seating capacity of the all-wooden Exposition Park III and was larger than either the Polo Grounds in New York or the Cubs' West Side Park in Chicago. Forbes Field was named for General John Forbes, a British general who captured Fort Duquesne and renamed it Fort Pitt during the French and Indian War.

The park site amounted to seven acres and was located three miles from downtown Pittsburgh. The park site was purchased by the Pirates from the estate of Mary Schenley and was adjacent to the park (Schenley Park) named after her. Schenley Park was visible from the ballpark behind the LF wall. The streets surrounding Forbes Field were Sennott St. on the northwest behind the third-base bleachers, Boquet St. on the southwest, and Joncaire St. behind RF on the southeast. The grandstand and home plate were located near the southwest corner of the site. The park site of seven acres was typical of the size of park sites for Classic ballparks.

On Opening Day, June 30, 1909, the park consisted of a double-deck grandstand that extended a short distance beyond both first base and third base, a large (43 rows of seating) steel-and-concrete set of bleachers (called a pavilion but not ever roofed) down the LF line, and a set of wooden bleachers that extended from RC to almost dead CF. These wooden bleachers in CF were replaced later that season by a permanent set of steel-and-concrete bleachers after the ground had settled. There was no pavilion or bleachers and thus not any permanent seating between the first-base end of the grandstand and the RF fence. For important games, temporary bleachers were erected, or standing room crowds were allowed in this area. When neither temporary bleachers nor standing room crowds were in place, there was a vast amount of in-play foul area down the RF line. The ballpark's total seating capacity was 23,000, of which 18,000 were in the grandstand. The seating capacity of Forbes Field was increased slightly in late July when the permanent CF bleachers replaced the wooden bleachers in use on Opening Day.

Forbes Field was reconfigured in May 1911, with the relocation of home plate some 26 feet towards the backstop and the rotation of the playing field towards RF. This reconfiguration made no change to any of the ballpark's seating areas, but did have the effect of improving the sight lines by moving the infield closer to the grandstand.

Forbes Field continued to be used by the Pirates until mid-season 1970 when they moved

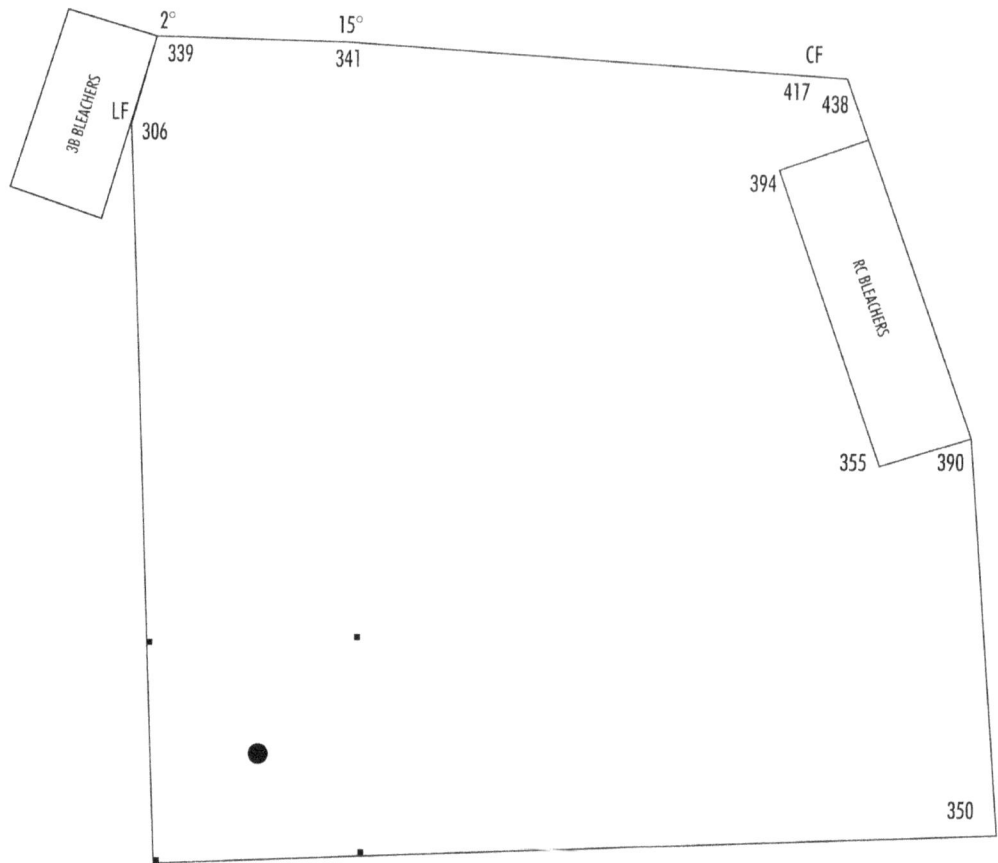

Early Forbes Field — the first configuration, 1909–1911.

into Three Rivers Stadium. The Classic ballpark was torn down in July 1971, and the site is now part of the campus of the University of Pittsburgh.

The Basis of Forbes Field's Configurations and Dimensions

The Opening Day configuration of the playing field was far different from the configuration in later years. Photos from the Library of Congress show the LF foul line intersecting the third-base bleachers some 40–50 feet before the junction of the front of these third-base bleachers with the LF wall.[5] Home plate was located a huge distance from the diagonal portion of the grandstand that formed the backstop (110 feet as listed in *Green Cathedrals*).[6] The location of home plate and the alignment of the diamond that caused the intersection of LF foul line with the third-base bleachers meant the actual LF distance was a great deal less than the LF distance of 360 listed in *Green Cathedrals*. Because the foul line intersected the third-base bleachers, as one moved away from the foul line the LF distances increased very rapidly until the junction with the perimeter LF fence. At this point (two degrees), the estimated distance was 339. Straightaway LF was about the same. This configuration of LF explains the 16 home runs that were hit over the LF fence at Forbes Field in less than two full seasons (most of 1909, all of 1910, and eight games in early 1911). The 1909 Opening Day configuration with the location of home plate 110 feet from the grandstand made the

Early Forbes Field. A view from the left-field corner of Pittsburgh's Forbes Field. The photograph shows the 1909–1911 configuration of the ballpark. Note the position of the left-field foul pole adjacent to the third base bleachers, the large double-deck grandstand, and the absence of any stands to the left of the first base end of the grandstand. This area of the ballpark remained empty until the 1925 expansion that extended the grandstand down the right-field line and into fair right field. (Photograph by the Detroit Publishing Co. [No. 015637], Library of Congress.)

actual RF distance (estimated at 353) less than the later well-known RF distance of 376 (as listed in *Green Cathedrals*). The dead CF distance was also less due to the large home plate-backstop distance and the existence of the RC-CF bleachers (not removed until the 1925 expansion) that reduced the distances to both RC (363) and the right side of CF. The deepest CF point (slightly to the left of the left end of the CF bleachers) was estimated at 435–440. There was a good-sized scoreboard set into the LF wall and located about 20 feet off the foul line.

The short down-the-line LF distance (estimated to have been 306 feet) resulted in a very interesting home run. Bill Abstein of the Pirates hit a fair ball in a game on September 7, 1909, that landed far down in the third-base bleachers and bounced back into LF. Unsure of the situation, Abstein prudently stopped at second base. The umpires directed him home when they correctly ruled his hit a home run.

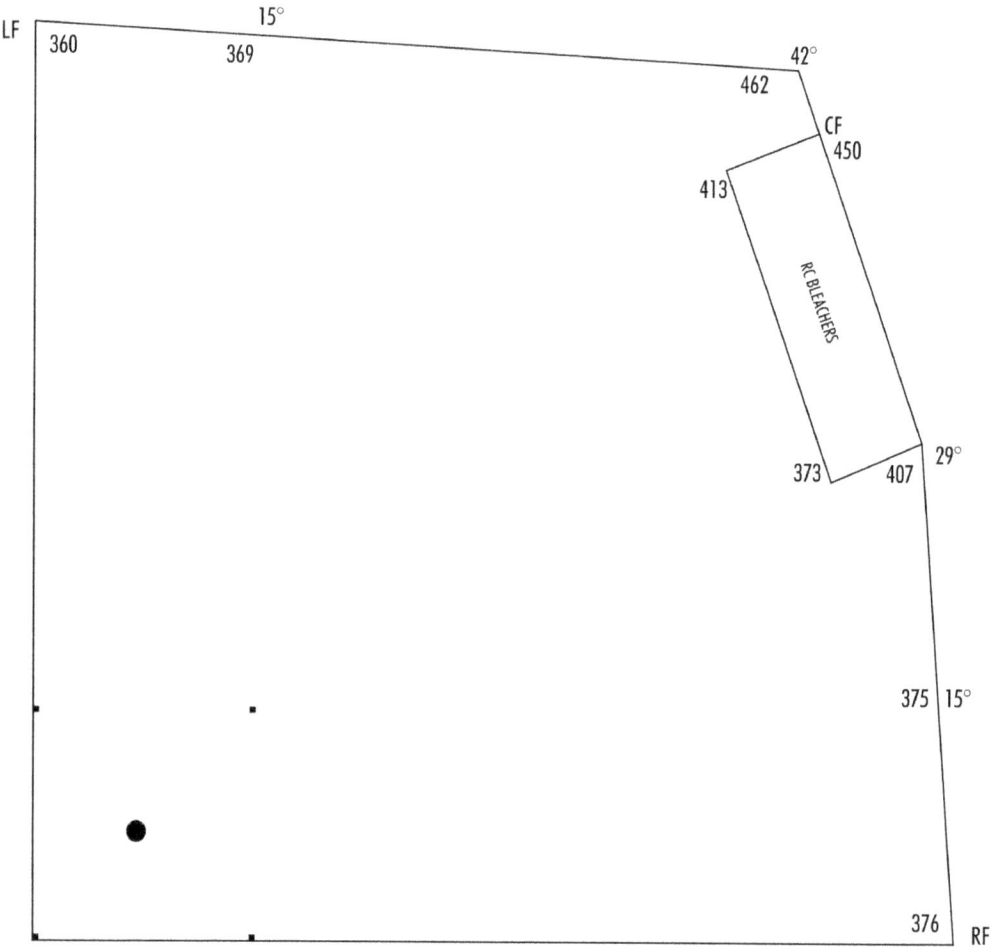

Forbes Field — the second configuration, 1911–1924.

The Pirates reconfigured Forbes Field in May 1911.[7] While the team was on a lengthy road trip, home plate was moved back towards the grandstand an estimated distance of 26 feet, and the field was rotated slightly towards RF. These changes resulted in the LF foul line now hitting the LF fence at the junction of the third-base bleachers and the LF fence. This new 1911 Forbes Field configuration can be seen in a photo in *Ballparks Then And Now*.[8] This fine photo shows the LF foul line, the LF foul pole, and the LF corner. Of course, moving home plate altered all the dimensions of the ballpark. LF was now 360, CF was only 409 because of the CF bleachers, slightly left of dead CF it was 462, and RF was 376. In addition, LC was now more than 400 feet, and the ballpark was now much more conducive for triples. The best description of the changed configuration and dimensions was provided by the *Cincinnati Enquirer* on the occasion of the Red's first trip to Pittsburgh after the change in the configuration of Forbes Field:

> Since the team was here in April, Forbes Field has been greatly enlarged ... LF lengthened more than 20 feet in the foul corner, and more than 50 feet out towards center. The field is now one of the largest in the league. LF is now so far from home plate, it will be very unusual for a ball to be driven over it, and a batter will get full value for his line drives to left-center which was not true before.[9]

DIMENSIONS (calculated from park diagrams)

Time Periods*	LF	SLF	LC	CF	RC	SRF	RF
1909–1911	306	341	366	417	363	375	359
1911–1919	360	369	403	409**	373	375	376

*The park's new configuration and dimensions were effective on May 26, 1911
**Deepest point was to the left of dead center at 462

FENCE HEIGHTS (estimated from photos)

Time Periods	LF	CF	RF
1909–May 8, 1911	3–20*	8–11**	11
May 26, 1911–1919	11–20*	8–11**	11

*The three-foot height was the front of the third-base bleachers; the 20-foot height was the scoreboard
**The eight-foot height was the front of the CF bleachers

AVERAGE OUTFIELD DISTANCES

Time Period	LF	CF	RF
1909–May 8, 1911	344	385	367
May 26, 1911–1919	373	407	382

ARCHITECT: CHARLES W. LEAVITT JR.

CAPACITY: 23,000 (JUNE 30, 1909), 24,000 (JULY 26, 1909), 25,000 (1915–1919)

PARK SIZE/COMPOSITE AVERAGE OUTFIELD DISTANCE: 365 (1909–MAY 8, 1911), 387 (MAY 26, 1911–1919)

PARK SITE AREA: 7 ACRES

DEADBALL ERA RUN FACTOR: 100 (RANK: NL 8)

The Impact of the Park's Configurations and Dimensions on Batting

Forbes Field, in its original configuration that was in use for slightly less than two full seasons (June 30, 1909-May 8, 1911), was actually a pretty good hitter's park, except for home runs. The park factors in this time period were above average for batting average, on-base, and slugging (102, 101, and 104). In this configuration, Forbes Field had a doubles park factor of 103 and 130 for triples. Only the Forbes Field home run park factor was below the league average at 77. Forbes Field was actually slightly smaller than the average NL ballpark. The park's modest LF dimensions were noticeably conducive to OTF home runs, as 16 such home runs were hit in less than two full seasons.

In the new larger configuration (effective with the game of May 26, 1911), Forbes Field became a below-average park for doubles, slightly better for triples, and average for batting average, on-base, and slugging (park factors of 100, 99, and 100). The revised configuration appears to have had only a small impact on home runs. The number of home runs per game in the original configuration was 0.32, and it was 0.37 in the immediately subsequent time period (most of the 1911 and all of the 1912 seasons). As 1911 was the first NL season with the use of the cork-center ball, home runs increased dramatically (up 48 percent) in the NL. In this context, the revised configuration of Forbes Field actually reduced the number of home runs, as total home runs/game increased only 15 percent. The mix of home runs was significantly altered. The larger playing area of the revised configuration decreased the absolute number and the proportion of OTF home runs, and increased the number and the proportion of IPHR. In the 135 games played (a bit less than two full seasons) in the original configuration, 16 home runs cleared the Forbes Field LF fence. In the next nearly four full seasons, that feat was accomplished only four times.

Home Runs by Type at Forbes Field

Time Periods	Total	OTF	Bounce	IPHR
1909–May 8, 1911	44	22	2	22
May 26, 1911–1919	143	28	9	115

OTF Home Runs by Field at Forbes Field (Excludes Bounce)

Time Periods*	Total	LF	CF	RF	Unknown
1909–1911	20	16	2	0	2
1911–1919	19	10	0	9	0

*The park's configuration and dimensions were changed on May 26, 1911

Inside-the-Park Home Runs by Field at Forbes Field

Time Periods*	Total	LF	LC	CF	RC	RF	Unknown
1909–1911	22	5	0	4	3	9	1
1911–1919	115	7	13	73	1	20	1

*The park's configuration and dimensions were changed on May 26, 1911

Batting Park Factors at Forbes Field

Time Periods*	BA	OBP	SLUG	2B**	3B**	HR**	BB***
1909–1911	102	101	104	103	134	77	93
1911–1919	100	99	100	89	144	52	93

*The park's configuration and dimensions were changed on May 26, 1911
**Per AB
***Per Total Plate Appearance (AB+BB+HP)

12

St. Louis

St. Louis was one of the original NL franchises, but the NL stayed in St. Louis for only two seasons: 1876–1877. The NL again had a franchise in St. Louis for two years in 1885 and 1886, before again leaving. The NL returned to St. Louis for good in 1892, and there has been a NL team in the city until the present day. The NL team was called the Browns (a shortened form of Brown Stockings) until 1897, the Perfectos in 1898–1899, and the Cardinals starting in 1900. From 1892 until 1900, the NL team played in only two ballparks. Sportsman's Park II was used for only a single season, 1892. Sportsman's II was one of a series of ML ballparks on the same site (Sullivan Ave. and Spring St.) with the same name. The second ballpark used by the NL was named Robison Field after the Cardinals' owners and was used for nearly thirty years from 1893 to 1920. Located at Vandeventer Ave. and Natural Bridge Ave., the ballpark was also known as Vandeventer Lot. The Cardinals' use of this park ended when the team moved to share Sportsman's Park IV with the AL St. Louis Browns in mid-season 1920.

In 1902, the AL moved its Milwaukee franchise to St. Louis, and the team built a new ballpark (Sportsman's Park III) on the site of two former ballparks called Sportsman's Park. The ballpark built by the Browns was located only four blocks from the NL's Robison Field. The new AL team played at Sportsman's Park III for seven seasons (1902–1908). In 1909, the Browns rebuilt and re-oriented the ballpark. Included in the rebuilding was a state-of-the-art double-deck steel-and-concrete grandstand. Sportsman's Park IV, after the replacement of the holdover wooden stands from the prior park, was considered one of the Classic ballparks. The Browns stayed in Sportsman's Park IV until the club was sold and the franchise was moved to Baltimore after the 1953 season.

In the Deadball Era, the AL Browns were the top team in St. Louis. The Cardinals did poorly and by the 1910s played in a rundown wooden ballpark (Robison Field). In contrast, the Browns after 1908, while not capturing any AL pennants, often had first-division teams and played in a far newer and better ballpark. The lot of both the Browns and Cardinals became more difficult with the start of the 1914 season. The upstart Federal League placed a team in St. Louis and played in a new ML ballpark, Handlan's Park. The presence of the Federal League for the 1914–1915 seasons meant there were three ML teams in the not overly large city of St. Louis. In the competition for fans and attendance in St. Louis, the NL Cardinals were mostly overlooked until the farm system initiated by Branch Rickey began to pay off in the mid–1920s. After the mid–1920s, the Browns declined to a very low level of performance that was captured in a colorful title of a book about the Browns, *Still Last in the American League*.[1]

In the Deadball Era, playing professional baseball on a Sunday was not a problem in St. Louis. Sunday baseball had been legal in the city since the late nineteenth century.[2] In combination with the prohibition on Sunday baseball in some Midwestern and all ML Eastern cities, the ability to play Sunday baseball positively impacted the economics of professional baseball in St. Louis. The AL and NL both scheduled teams from Eastern cities to play as many Sunday games as possible in the Midwestern cities (one of which was St. Louis) where Sunday baseball was legal.

Robison Field

St. Louis National League: 1893–1919

Robison Field was the home park of the St. Louis Cardinals for all 19 seasons of the Deadball Era. For the first decade of the Deadball Era, the ballpark was a large capacity largely wooden pre–Classic ballpark. Robison Field is neither famous, nor well thought of, nor well remembered. The park was also called League Park until about 1911 and Cardinals Park from 1918 until 1920. The ballpark acquired the name Robison Field from the then Cardinals owners Frank and Stanley Robison (1898–1911).

When Robison Field opened in 1893, it was representative of ML ballparks in its time. By the park's last years (1916–1920), the ballpark was far behind other ML ballparks in size and standards of comfort and safety. The ballpark's reputation for safety was not helped by a fire on May 4, 1901, that burned down parts of the grandstand, pavilion, and offices.[3] The Cardinals had to move the next day's game to Sportsman's Park II, then being used only for bicycle racing. Despite the damage from the fire, the Cardinals missed only one game at Robison Field.

Robison Field was located on a large rectangular lot (reported in 1893 to have been 714 feet north to south and 514 feet east to west) that consisted of most of one entire city block located north of downtown St. Louis. The park was bounded by on the northeast by Natural Bridge Ave., on the southwest by Lexington Ave., on the southeast by Prairie Ave., and on the northwest by other properties and then Vandeventer Ave. The grandstand and home plate were located in the northwest corner of the site. The park site amounted to about 7.8 acres. Despite having a large park site, the design, location, and alignment of the grandstand, pavilion, and RF bleachers meant the distance along Lexington Ave. on the south and Natural Bridge Ave. on the north, always limited the size of RF at Robison Field.

When opened in 1893, the ballpark consisted of a single-deck curved grandstand (164 feet long and 60 feet wide), and two pavilions (100 feet by 60 feet) that ran from the ends of the grandstand along first and third base. The small grandstand did not extend as far as either first base or third base. Later in the nineteenth century (most likely before the 1899 season), bleachers were added in both fair LF and RF. The rectangular RF bleachers were about 50 feet in depth and extended from the RF foul line beyond RC and ended at the junction with the diagonal CF fence. The rectangular LF bleachers were also about 50 feet in depth and extended from the LF corner to beyond LC and ended at the junction with the diagonal CF scoreboard. The scoreboard was about 20 feet high and was raised slightly above the level of the field. As a result, any batted balls that rolled under the scoreboard could not be retrieved and were home runs. The clubhouses (one for the home team and, untypical in that period, one for the visitors) in the park's original 1893 configuration were located on ground level near first base. By 1901, the clubhouse was in deep CF behind the CF fence and scoreboard. Later in the life (installation date unknown) of the park, down the LF line were a set of rectangular bleachers that converged with the foul line and actually intruded slightly into fair LF 20–30 feet before the LF corner.

Grandstand and bleachers at Robison Field, 1916. The player is Rees "Steamboat" Williams, a pitcher with the St. Louis Cardinals. In the background are a portion of the wooden grandstand and the right edge of the first base bleachers. Both structures date to 1893 and were enhanced with steel and concrete before the 1909 season. Robison Field was notable for having a small grandstand and four sets of bleachers in left field, right field, and down both foul lines. (Prints and Photographs Division [No. LC-B2-3814-6], Library of Congress.)

What was curious about the layout of the stands at Robison Field was their placement and alignment. The curved grandstand was set well back from home plate (82 feet), and the grandstand end of the first-base pavilion was set back even further from the foul line (about 120 feet) as was the nearby first-base end of the grandstand. On the third-base side, the 1909 grandstand was about 100 feet from third base. The grandstand end of the third-base bleachers was even further from the foul line! In 1909, these bleachers were angled towards the LF foul line and actually protruded into fair LF near the LF corner. With the substantial setback of the stands from the foul lines, Robison Field had a tremendous amount of foul territory. With the grandstand, pavilion and three sets of bleachers, the final capacity of Robison Field was 21,000. This capacity made it one of the largest wooden pre–Classic ML ballparks.

The Cardinals continued to use Robison Field until mid-season 1920 when they moved to Sportsman's Park IV and became tenants of the Browns. After the Cardinals left, the ballpark was demolished, and the land broken into parcels. The largest parcel was sold (at a goodly profit) to the St. Louis School Board and used for a new high school.

The Basis of Robison Field's Configuration and Dimensions

Not a lot of information has been available about this ballpark. Recent research has unearthed some additional data which greatly increases our understanding and knowledge about this long-gone ballpark. The basis for the Robison Field dimensions and configuration are a 1901 photo of LF and CF at Robison Field from the *St. Louis Star*, a 1909 Sanborn Fire Insurance Co. map of the ballpark, and press coverage of the park's first Opening Day in 1893.[3] The 1901 photo of Robison Field from the *St. Louis Star* showed the packed LF bleachers, the CF scoreboard, and the left side of the clubhouse. In this photo, both the scoreboard and the roof of the clubhouse were covered with precariously perched fans. This photo established that the LF bleachers existed in 1901 and perhaps earlier, and that safety was *not* a prime concern at Deadball Era ballparks! The 1909 Sanborn map covered the entirety of the park site and showed (unlike most Sanborn maps) the location of the infield and foul lines. From the Sanborn map, it is not clear if there was a CF fence extending from the right edge of the scoreboard to the left-front corner of the RF bleachers. The 1901 photo sheds no light on this issue, as the large crowd of standees in CF masked the view of the front of the clubhouse. Research into home runs hit at Robison Field uncovered the existence of a picket fence located in front of the CF scoreboard and clubhouse. A home run in the game on April 24, 1901, rolled "to CF a few yards in front of the clubhouse, struck picket fence and dropped dead."[4] The dimensions shown below in the first table are based on including such a CF fence. In later years when there was no picket fence, the deepest point in the ballpark was the left-front corner of the RF bleachers (to the right of the scoreboard) 475 feet from home plate. Of course, in the Deadball Era, the impact on the play of the game between the deepest CF points having been 428 feet from home plate vs. 475 feet away was zero.

The 1893 Opening Day game article in *St. Louis Dispatch* listed the dimensions of the park site as 714 by 514. From the Sanborn map, the dimensions of the park site were 664 by 578. The author used the dimensions from the Sanborn to calculate the park site area. That same Opening Day article stated the stands consisted of a grandstand and two pavilions. From the dimensions listed for the stands, the total capacity of the ballpark would have been about 5,500. In contrast, the Sanborn gives the capacity of the ballpark as 20,000 in 1909. If the 1893 Opening Day article is correct, then additional stands (in particular, the LF and RF bleachers) must have been built before the 1901 season. Before the 1899 season, improvements were known to have been made to the ballpark. In addition, the ballpark was modernized with steel-and-concrete improvements after the 1908 season.[5] These improvements likely involved an expansion of the grandstand (known to be much larger in 1909 vs. 1893). In addition, the expansion of the first-base pavilion, as well as the construction of third-base bleachers, must have been done either before the 1899 season or the 1909 season.

The dimensions for Robison Field were derived from the park diagram drawn on the 1909 Sanborn. Selected dimensions in feet were:

- LF: 410
- CF: 441
- RF: 312
- Deepest point in the park: left of dead CF: 475
- Back of CF scoreboard at front of clubhouse: 545
- Depth of RF and LF bleachers: 50
- Back of LF bleachers at foul line: 460
- Back of RF bleachers at foul line: 362
- Home plate to backstop: 82

The LF dimension listed in *Green Cathedrals* for 1893 was 470.[6] Given the 1893 Opening Day press coverage that mentioned no outfield bleachers, the 1893 LF dimension would have been 460, quite close to the 470 figure listed in *Green Cathedrals*. However, the 1901 photo that established the existence of the LF bleachers at least as early as the 1901 season meant that in the twentieth century LF at Robison could never have been 470.

In summary, all of the Robison Field's dimensions were calculated from the Sanborn map and park diagram. As the location of both the foul lines and home plate were shown on the map, these dimensions contain very little uncertainty. All dimensions were checked against, and are consistent with, the available photographic evidence and the home-run data.

Park data and dimensions for Robison Field are shown below.

DIMENSIONS (calculated from park diagram)

Time Period	LF	SLF	LC	CF	RC	SRF	RF
1901	410	424	428	425	360	323	312
1902–1919	410	424	458	441*	360	323	312

*The deepest point in the ballpark, to the left of dead CF, was 475

FENCE HEIGHTS (estimated from photos and contemporary descriptions)

Years	LF	CF	RF
1901	8	3	10
1902–1919	8	8–15	10

AVERAGE OUTFIELD DISTANCES

Years	LF	CF	RF
1901	425	411	328
1902–1919	429	430	328

ARCHITECT: BEINKE & WELLS

CAPACITY: 5,500 (1893–1898 EST.), 15,000 (1899–1908 EST.), 20,000 (1909–1920)

PARK SIZE/COMPOSITE-AVERAGE OUTFIELD DISTANCE:
396 (1901); 396 (1902–1919)

PARK SITE AREA: 7.8 ACRES

DEADBALL ERA RUN FACTOR: 97 (RANK: NL 12)

The Impact of the Park's Configuration and Dimensions on Batting

Robison Field in the Deadball Era was a below-average offensive ballpark with a run park factor of 97. The ballpark was below average in nearly offensive category except triples and, in 1901–1910, home runs. The reasons for the below-average batting park factors are the large LF and CF average distances (both more than 425) and the huge amount of foul territory in the infield. The dimensions down the LF line, to LC, and to CF were both substantial and conducive to triples. Only the modest dimensions to RC (360) and down the RF line (312) inhibited triples. The decrease in the home run park factor from 108 in 1901–1910 to 81 for 1911–1919 warrants comment. Robison Field had the same dimensions and configuration in both time periods. However, park factors are relative measures; they measure the ratio of a given ballpark (Robison Field in this case) to the average of all league ballparks. In the 1911–1919 time period, the other NL ballparks generally became smaller and more conducive to home runs. For example, at Philadelphia's Baker Bowl home runs per season jumped from 12.8 in 1901–1910 to 56.2 in 1911–1919. Thus, the home run park factor at Robison Field decreased while the park's configuration remained unchanged.

The majority (71 percent) of home runs at Robison Field in the Deadball Era were IPHR. This proportion of IPHR was nearly double the proportion at other NL ballparks. It should not be surprising to learn that nearly all of the IPHR were hit to the generous areas of LF or CF. There was on average one IPHR per season to RC or RF at the ballpark. Bounce home runs were even rarer, only seven in 19 seasons. In the Deadball Era, there were only two home runs hit on the fly into the LF or CF bleachers. The RF bleachers were the destination for numerous OTF home runs. Despite the over 100 OTF home runs hit at the ballpark, there was a relative rarity of home runs hit completely out of Robison Field. There were only five such home runs (all hit over the RF bleachers) in the 19 seasons of the Deadball Era. At Robison Field, the distance to straightaway RF (15 degrees) was 323; at the back of the RF bleachers (still at 15 degrees), the distance was 375, and this point the back of the bleachers was at an estimated height of 30 feet.

The home-run data and batting park factors for Robison Field are shown below.

HOME RUNS BY TYPE AT ROBISON FIELD

Years	Total	OTF	Bounce	IPHR
1901–1910	212	34	5	178
1911–1919	226	92	2	134

OTF HOME RUNS BY FIELD AT ROBISON FIELD (EXCLUDES BOUNCE)

Years	Total	LF	CF	RF	Unknown
1901–1910	29	0	0	26	3
1911–1919	90	1	1	83	5

Inside-the-Park Home Runs by Field at Robison Field

Years	Total	LF	LC	CF	RC	RF	Unknown
1901–1910	178	53	19	89	4	4	9
1911–1919	134	32	9	70	10	3	10

Batting Park Factors at Robison Field

Years	BA	OBP	SLUG	2B*	3B*	HR*	BB**
1901–1910	98	97	99	80	124	108	92
1911–1919	100	100	98	85	109	81	101

*Per AB
**Per Total Plate Appearance (AB+BB+HP)

Sportsman's Park III

St. Louis American League: 1902–1908

Sportsman's Park III was built before the 1902 season for the newly arrived AL club. In 1901, the club had played in Milwaukee as the Brewers in the inaugural ML season of the AL. Upon moving to St. Louis, the franchise adopted the name Browns and acquired the site of a former major league ballpark near downtown St. Louis. The first ballpark located on this site, Sportsman's Park I, was used in 1875–1878 by the St. Louis teams in the National Association and the NL. The next ballpark on the same site was also called Sportsman's Park (II). This park was used by the American Association and NL teams from 1882 to 1892. All three of the ballparks named Sportsman's Park occupied most of a rectangular city block bordered on the west, north and east by city streets. A peach orchard and other properties in the same city block made up the southern boundary of the park site. The five-acre park site of Sportsman's Park III was larger in the east-west dimension than in the north-south dimension. This park site area was smaller than typical of the wooden pre–Classic ML ballparks used in the Deadball Era. The field was oriented with the grandstand and home plate in the northwest corner of the site, which made LF the sun field for the typical afternoon game.

For the 1902 AL season, the Browns built a new ballpark; replacing the existing run-down stands of the former bicycle track/ballpark on the site with a new wooden grandstand and three sets of wooden bleachers. The park's seating areas consisted of a single-deck covered grandstand that curved behind home plate and stretched between first and third bases, third-base bleachers that ran down the LF foul line and converged with the foul line in the LF corner, a curved first-base pavilion that extended from the first-base end of the grandstand to the foul portion of the RF fence and extended such that the seats faced home plate, and a separate set of bleachers in LF that ran from near the LF foul line to nearly the clubhouse in the CF corner. The RF area had no seating in fair territory and was bounded by a fence (the southern boundary of the park) that was parallel to the park's northern boundary, Sullivan Ave. At the east (CF) end of the LF bleachers was a diagonal scoreboard located in front of the clubhouse, which in the newspaper game accounts (using the terminology of the day) was called a bulletin board. Note that because of the alignment of the playing field, the LF bleachers extended beyond dead CF. However, given the reporting conventions of the day, any ball hit into these bleachers was referred to as a home run into the LF bleachers. The reported planned dimensions of the park were LF 342 and RF 300.[7] The LF foul line intersected the LF bleachers at less than 90 degrees, while the RF foul line hit the RF fence at more than 90 degrees. Seating capacity was reported as close to 15,000 in 1902.

There was a modest addition to the park's capacity after the 1906 season. The gap between the third-base bleachers and the LF bleachers (an area that was behind a short segment of fence in 1902–1906) was filled in before the 1907 season with additional bleacher seating. This addition of a few hundred seats did not affect any of the park's dimensions. At the same time, small additions were made to the grandstand and foul-area bleachers that resulted in a total increase in the ballpark's capacity of about 2,000 seats.

No balls were hit over the LF perimeter fence at the back of the LF bleaches or over any part of the CF fence during the ballpark's history. If a player could have cleared the CF scoreboard with a mighty drive, such a home run landing in front of the clubhouse and behind the scoreboard would have been in play. No game accounts mention what would have been a tremendous blast and a memorable occurrence.

The Basis of Sportsman's Park III's Configuration and Dimensions

The data available on the dimensions of Sportsman's Park III are either scanty, or wrong, or both. For example, *Green Cathedrals* (1992 edition) lists the LF fence as being 15 feet in height, and as will later be shown, this dimension is largely wrong.[8] Research in the St. Louis newspapers of the day provided the Opening Day 1902 dimensions for LF (342) and RF (300).[9] The starting point used to derive other estimated dimensions for Sportsman's Park III was the park diagram of Sportsman's Park IV that included the playing field, the stands, and surrounding streets found in the 1986 edition of *Green Cathedrals*.[10] The Sportsman's Park III park site was bounded by Sullivan Ave. on the north, Grand Blvd. on the East, and Spring St. on the west. On the south, another parcel situated between the park and Dodier St. formed the southern boundary. The wonderfully detailed diagram in *Green Cathedrals* provided the overall size of the city block as east-west 500 feet and north-south 621 feet. In addition, the diagram showed that the southernmost 74 feet of this city block was not part of the park site in 1909. This portion of the city block was used for other purposes, including an office building. Therefore, it can be concluded that Sportsman's Park IV occupied the remaining 547 feet of the north-south dimension of the city block. The north-south dimension of Sportsman's III was based on a the 1902 Opening Day dimensions from the *St. Louis Star* article and a park diagram derived from a 1909 Sanborn map.[11] For Sportsman's Park III, the overall land plot had an estimated north-south dimension of 438 feet, and the east-west dimension was the known distance of 500 feet. Based on these two dimensions, the size of the park site of Sportsman's Park III amounted to an estimated 5.0 acres.

Because home plate was in the northwest corner of the field, the LF foul line ran in an east-west direction. The following analysis is the basis for the LF foul line not being parallel with the northern boundary of the park (Sullivan Ave.). A 1909 Sanborn fire insurance map showed the LF bleachers of Sportsman's IV (which were the third-base bleachers of Sportsman's III) to abut the northern boundary of the park. A 1907 photo from the Library of Congress and another in *Baseball Memories: 1900–1909* clearly show the convergence of the foul line and the third-base bleachers in the LF corner.[12] These photos established that the third-base bleachers were built parallel to the park's northern perimeter, and the playing field and LF foul line were angled to the left that converged with the third-base bleachers. One result of this field alignment was that the LF fence intersected the foul line at less than 90 degrees.

A second result of this field alignment was that the curved first-base pavilion must have diverged from the park's western boundary (Spring St.) to have converged with the RF foul line in the RF corner. Another photo shows the end of the first-base pavilion quite close to the RF foul line and RF fence.[13] This photo revealed that the end of the first-base pavilion in the RF corner hooked around to face the infield. To be consistent with the photographic evidence, the park must have had the first-base pavilion curved away from Spring St. and towards the RF foul line.

The overall east-west dimension of Sportsman's III was the same as for Sportsman's Park IV (500 feet.). Newspaper game accounts and numerous photos show the existence of the LF bleachers. In particular, a 1908 photo (of the Browns' Rube Waddell with the LF bleachers in the background) shows the bleachers to have had a depth of 20 rows.[14] Game accounts mention home runs being hit over (or under) a short fence and/or gate located between the third-base and LF bleachers.[15] A 1907 photo shows the bleachers wrapping around the foul pole with no gap, gate, or fence between the third-base and LF bleachers. From this photographic evidence, one concludes the LF bleachers must have been modified and expanded before the 1907 season to extend to and join with the third-base bleachers, as shown in the 1907 photo. This means the LF dimension for 1907–1908 would have remained unchanged at 342 feet. This modification of the LF bleachers (pre–1907 season) is consistent with the other 1907 park modifications (the pavilion and grandstand being expanded slightly in 1907) listed in the publication of the St. Louis SABR National Convention.[16]

The LF fence itself was about eight feet in height, perhaps 10 feet in the LF corner where there was a billboard. In the 1908 photo of Rube Waddell and the LF bleachers, a LF screen (two to three feet in height) atop the short LF fence at the front of the LF bleachers is visible. The total height of the LF fence, including the short screen on top, was therefore estimated to be eight feet. From this, one concludes the 15-foot height of the LF fence listed in *Green Cathedrals*, except for the LF scoreboard, is definitely in error for 1907–1908 and most likely for 1902–1906 as well.

The RF fence was about 10–12 feet in height and ran at more than 90 degrees to the RF foul line. There was a two-story clubhouse in CF that met the RF fence. In front of the clubhouse was a diagonal scoreboard that connected to the CF end of the front of the LF bleachers.[17] There was a carriage entrance off Grand Ave. between the end of the LF bleachers and the clubhouse. In addition, there was a carriage-way drive near the scoreboard in CF. A game account from September 29, 1904, reported that a home run was hit over the screen into the LF bleachers. This indicates that as early as the 1904 season, there was known to be a short screen in front of the LF bleachers.

The park data and dimensions for Sportsman's Park III are shown in the following tables.

DIMENSIONS (largely calculated from park diagram)

Years	LF	SLF	LC	CF	RC	SRF	RF
1902–1908	342	333	350	390*	400	331	300

Backstop–home plate: 60
*Deepest points were the scoreboard (428) and the CF corner (468)

FENCE HEIGHTS (estimated from photos and contemporary descriptions)

Years	LF	CF	RF
1902–1908	8–10	8–15*	10

*The 15-foot height was only the scoreboard

AVERAGE OUTFIELD DISTANCES			
Years	LF	CF	RF
1902–1908	337	390	336

CAPACITY: 15,000 (1902–1906), 17,000 (1907–1908 EST.)

PARK SIZE/COMPOSITE AVERAGE OUTFIELD DISTANCE: 354

PARK SITE AREA: 5.0 ACRES

DEADBALL ERA RUN FACTOR: 93 (RANK: AL 18)

The Impact of the Park's Configuration and Dimensions on Batting

Sportsman's Park III was not a hitter's park. The ballpark was smaller than the average AL ballpark by 20–25 feet in terms of the average outfield distance. Despite this, the Deadball Era runs park factor was 93, which ranked eighteenth in the AL. The most important factor leading to the modest home run totals and the park's low run factor (third worst in the AL among 20 ballparks) is believed to be the poor batter's background that existed because of the LF bleachers that extended all the way to beyond dead CF. This poor batter's background, caused by the predominance of white-shirted fans in the bleachers, is also likely the cause of the lower-than-average park factors for batting average, on-base, slugging, triples, and walks.

In the seven seasons (1902–1908) the Browns played in Sportsman's Park III, the offensive performances were definitely of the Deadball type. The average game played in Sportsman's III produced 6.98 runs — not a bad scoring average until you learn that 6.98 runs/game was the total for both teams! The Browns and their opponents combined for an average of 7.59 runs per game in the other seven AL parks. Thus the run factor for Sportsman's Park vs. other AL parks was 93. Truly, Sportsman's Park III was no haven for hitters. The story for home runs in the park was a little different. The total home runs for both teams averaged 19.3 per season, while the home run park factors ranged from 53 to 170 and averaged 104 (the average AL ballpark was by definition 100). This means that Sportsman's Park III was slightly better than average for home runs. Unlike contemporary times, the impact of more home runs on total runs scored was minimal. The above average rate of home runs at Sportsman's Park III added all of about 3 runs per *season* to the total runs scored!

As one of the smaller AL ballparks, Sportsman's was not a good park for triples or IPHR. There were only 5.7 IPHR per season at the park, while in the same time period the average AL ballpark saw more than twice that number of IPHR. In relative terms, IPHR accounted for 30 percent of the total home runs hit at Sportsman's Park III, while in the same 1902–08 time period, IPHR accounted for 52 percent of total home runs at all AL ballparks. This result is consistent with Sportsman's Park III being one of the smaller AL ballparks. The close LF and RF fences limited nearly all IPHR to CF, as that was the only deep part of the ballpark.

There were never any home runs hit over the LF or CF perimeter fences during the life of the park. The data on the distribution of OTF home runs by field are biased. Because the park's fences were rectangular, the game accounts of home runs refer to home runs hit into the LF bleachers or over the RF fence. However, because of the alignment of the playing field, balls hit into the far right side of the LF bleachers were actually home runs to CF. Thus the park's reported total of zero OTF home runs to CF is wrong. One known home run (by Cleveland's Nap Lajoie on June 30, 1902) that was reported as being hit high up and near the CF end of the LF bleachers was actually a home run to dead CF. The longest home run hit at Sportsman's Park III, it traveled an estimated distance of 400–410 feet. What remains unknown is how many other OTF home runs to CF were erroneously described as being to LF.

The ballpark averaged exactly one bounce home run per season, as the screen at the front of the LF bleachers deterred such home runs. The overall home run park factor for Sportsman's Park during its seven seasons was 104, a modest value for what was a much-smaller-than-average-size AL ballpark. The park's smaller-than-average dimensions certainly curtailed IPHR, and the almost complete lack of bounce home runs held down home run totals.

The Browns and the visiting teams combined for 135 home runs in the seven seasons played at Sportsman's Park III. Of these, 40 were IPHR, and an additional seven were bounce home runs. There were 95 OTF home runs; this total included the seven bounce home runs. The reported distribution of OTF home runs was quite simple: half to LF and half to RF. In the seven-year life of the park, there were no reported OTF home runs to CF, and there are no game accounts of any home runs clearing the LF bleachers on the fly. Nearly all IPHR (over 90 percent) were hit to CF.

The home-run data and batting park factors for Sportsman's Park III are shown below in four tables.

Home Runs by Type at Sportsman's Park III

Years	Total	OTF	Bounce	IPHR
1902–1908	135	95	7	40

OTF Home Runs by Field at Sportsman's Park III (excludes Bounce)

Years	Total	LF	CF	RF	Unknown
1902–1908	88	44	0	43	1

Inside-the-Park Home Runs by Field at Sportsman's Park III

Years	Total	LF	LC	CF	RC	RF	Unknown
1902–1908	40	2	1	32	1	3	1

Batting Park Factors at Sportsman's Park III

Years	BA	OBP	SLUG	2B*	3B*	HR*	BB**
1902–1908	97	97	96	101	77	104	96

*Per AB
**Per Total Plate Appearance (AB+BB+HP)

Sportsman's Park IV

St. Louis American League: 1909–1919

Sportsman's Park IV was the Classic ML ballpark used by Browns and Cardinals from 1909 to 1966. The name Sportsman's Park IV was the designation given to the new Classic ballpark which resulted from the drastic alteration, expansion, and realignment of Sportsman's Park III after the 1908 season. The playing field was reoriented with home plate and the infield moving from the northwest corner to the southwest corner of the site. This change made RF the sun field, particularly sunny in the late innings of afternoon games. In addition, the southern boundary of the park site was extended about 110 feet towards Dodier St. The park site now amounted to 6.3 acres, typical in size for Classic ballparks. The Browns used this added area to build a new state-or-the-art (for 1909) double-deck steel-and-concrete grandstand. This involved removing the first-base bleachers from the prior park to make room for the new grandstand. Never ones to waste money, the Browns' management retained both the former LF bleachers and the curved covered grandstand (previously facing the infield) from Sportsman's Park III. Thus, what had been the LF bleachers in the old park became the RF bleachers in the new park, while the curved grandstand became the third base-LF pavilion that wrapped around the LF corner.

However, the 1909 Opening Day game revealed a problem: the location of home plate resulted in the view from a portion of the third base-LF pavilion being blocked by the new grandstand. In May, home plate was moved 18 feet towards LF to correct this problem. Although the new grandstand was double-decked and had as extensive a footprint as the former first-base bleachers it replaced, the park's reported capacity (17,600) for the 1909 Opening Day was about the same as for Sportsman's III.[18] The Opening Day newspaper story provided details of the new park. The headline was "Park in Good Condition." The story revealed, "Only the upper deck of the grandstand will not be in shape for the fans to enjoy — not needed in view of the immense seating capacity of the new park." Later in the 1909 season, the upper deck of the grandstand was opened. *Green Cathedrals* lists the park's capacity as 24,040 in June 1909.[19]

For the 1911 season, the curved third base-LF pavilion and the LF bleachers — both retained from Sportsman's III — were replaced by a new set of third-base bleachers and a new set of LF bleachers. These new LF bleachers wrapped around in CF to meet the RF bleachers. Also for the 1911 season, a new first-base pavilion was built down the RF foul line.[20] The park's total capacity was estimated to have been more than 25,000.

From the game accounts of the 1913 season, one learns of an IPHR hit to CF ("busted to the flag pole") that showed the CF flagpole to be in the field of play. On July 21, 1915, a long home run was hit over the RF bleachers onto Grand Ave.[21] This home run was noted in the SABR Home Run Log as traveling a minimum of 420 feet. The batter was a left-handed Red Sox pitcher named Ruth.

The Basis of the Ballpark's Configurations and Dimensions

The dimensions of Sportsman's IV are much better documented than those of Sportsman's III. The *St. Louis Globe Democrat* provided data, descriptions, and dimensions about the new park in their 1909 Opening Day stories.[22] On Opening Day 1909, the dimensions (based on the 1909 Sanborn map and the newspaper stories) were LF 368, CF 445, and RF 315.[23] Home plate was moved 18 feet towards LF in the next month to improve the viewing angle from the curved third base-LF stands. The revised May 1909 dimensions became LF 350, CF 445, and RF 315. There was a small curved section of the old pavilion that formed

Opposite: Sportsman's Park IV, 1910. Frank LaPorte of the St. Louis Browns stands on the outfield grass. In the background are the wooden left-field bleachers and scoreboard added by the Browns before the 1912 season. The bleachers were in use through the 1925 season, when expansion and renovation brought new steel-and-concrete bleachers. (Prints and Photographs Division [No. LC-USZ62-133654], Library of Congress.)

the fence in the LF corner. The LF bleachers, which formed the large majority of the LF fence, ran at 90 degrees to an extension of the foul line. The next major change to the park's configuration was the replacement of the third base-LF pavilion and the old LF bleachers that had been retained from Sportsman's III, and the building of a new first-base pavilion.

Game accounts of the 1912 season report a number of home runs hit into the RF bleachers. In addition, there are game accounts of two home runs being hit onto the roof in RF. The first occurrence was in the first game of a doubleheader played on September 27, 1912, and the second home run was in the second game of another doubleheader played the next day; both home runs were hit by Gus Williams of the Browns. How could home runs be hit both into the uncovered RF bleachers and onto the roof in RF? SABR member Robert Tiemann supplied the answer: the first base pavilion (by definition roofed) was angled, faced towards second base, and extended about 15 feet into fair territory near the RF corner.[24] Thus, there were both roofed and unroofed stands in the fair RF area.

This new construction changed the dimensions of the park in two areas of the outfield. The new and more extensive LF-CF bleachers resulted in a reduction in the CF distance from 445 to 420, while down the RF line the intrusion of the first-base pavilion reduced the RF distance to an estimated 270 feet. The RF bleachers remained at 90 degrees to an extension of the RF foul line. The 270 foot RF dimension is misleading, as behind the first-base pavilion the RF dimension was 315.

The majority of the evidence indicates that the above denoted changes occurred before the 1911 season. However, *Green Cathedrals* lists the changes as occurring before the 1912 season, and Tiemann also dates the park's changes as effective for the 1912 season.[25] Another SABR source, from the 1992 SABR convention held in St. Louis, gives the date as 1911 for the building of the new LF bleachers and first-base pavilion.[26] Contemporary newspaper game accounts provide clues to one aspect of the park's configuration. A game account from the 1911 season is potentially helpful; in the game of August 22, 1911, a home run by Frank LaPorte was hit "into the new stands in LF."[27] This clearly indicates that the LF bleachers were in place during the 1911 season. If the LF bleachers and first-base pavilion were built at the same time, as appears likely, then the first-base pavilion was also built before the 1911 season. In addition, during the 1912 season, one game account reported a home run hit over the LF fence and against the scoreboard (by the Browns Del Pratt in the first game of a doubleheader on September 27).[28] This report confirmed the existence during the 1912 season of a new scoreboard in LF, located at the back of the bleachers and near the LF line as shown in later photos.

The report of a home run by Roy Hartzell "over screen into the RF bleachers" is consistent with the reports and photographs of a low screen on top of the LF bleachers of Sportsman's Park III, as the LF bleachers of Sportsman's III became the RF bleachers of Sportsman's IV.[29]

The following tables show the park data and dimensions for each of the three configurations of Sportsman's Park IV (1909–1919).

DIMENSIONS (from park diagrams)

Time Periods	LF	SLF	LC	CF	RC	SRF	RF
April 1909	368	390	435	445	364	326	315
May 1909–1910	350	372	414	445	364	326	315
1911–1919	350	362	404	420	364	326	270*

*RF corner at the front of the RF bleachers was 315

FENCE HEIGHTS (estimated from photos and contemporary descriptions)

Time Periods	LF	CF	RF
April 1909	4–8	8–12	8
May 1909–1910	4–8	8–12	8
1911–1919	8	8	8

AVERAGE OUTFIELD DISTANCES

Time Periods	LF	CF	RF
April 1909	395	432	332
May 1909–1910	376	424	332
1911–1919	368	409	328

ARCHITECT: OSBORN ENGINEERING

CAPACITY: 17,600 (APRIL–MAY 1909), 24,040 (JUNE 1909–1910), 25,500 (1911–1919 EST.)

PARK SIZE/COMPOSITE AVERAGE OUTFIELD DISTANCE: 386 (APRIL 1909), 377 (MAY 1909–1910), 368 (1911–1919)

PARK SITE AREA: 6.3 ACRES

DEADBALL ERA RUN FACTOR: 94 (RANK: AL 16)

The Impact of the Park's Configurations and Dimensions on Batting

Sportsman's Park IV in the Deadball Era was not a hitter's park. The ballpark was slightly smaller than the average AL ballpark by 10–12 feet in terms of the average outfield distance. Despite this, the Deadball Era runs park factor was 94, which ranked sixteenth in the AL. The most important factor leading to the modest home run totals and the park's low run factor (fifth worst in the AL among 20 ballparks) is the poor batter's background that existed because of the bleachers in CF. The park's below-average triples park factor was caused by the modest dimension to RC (364) and straightaway RF (326).

In comparison with the previous park, the dimensions of Sportsman's IV were greater in LF and RF and about the same in CF. Not surprisingly, during the 11 seasons during the Deadball Era at Sportsman's IV (1909–1919), home runs averaged 18 per season vs. 19.3 home runs per season for Sportsman's III. A better comparative measure, the home run park factors for Sportsman's Park IV in the Deadball Era were also less than for the prior park. The range of home run park factors was 57–129, and the average was 90 vs. the average home run park factor of 104 for Sportsman's III. IPHR accounted for 18 percent of total home runs at Sportsman's IV during the Deadball Era (1909–1919). By comparison, at all AL and NL ballparks in the same time period, IPHR accounted for 37 percent of total home runs. This comparison suggests that Sportsman's IV was somewhat smaller than the average ML ballpark during the second decade of the Deadball Era. Of the 160 OTF (excluding bounce) home runs, 16 percent were to LF, 81 percent to RF, zero to CF, and 3 percent to a field unknown. Clearly the closer and more reachable RF bleachers attracted a disproportionate share of the OTF home runs. Of the 36 IPHR, 80 percent were to CF.

The home-run data and batting park factors for Sportsman's Park III are shown below in four tables.

Home Runs by Type at Sportsman's Park IV

Years	Total	OTF	Bounce	IPHR
1909–1910	17	8	2	9
1911–1919	183	156	2	27

OTF Home Runs by Field at Sportsman's Park IV (Excludes Bounce)

Years	Total	LF	CF	RF	Unknown
1909–1910	6	2	0	4	0
1911–1919	154	23	0	126	5

Inside-the-Park Home Runs by Field at Sportsman's Park IV

Years	Total	LF	LC	CF	RC	RF	Unknown
1909–1910	9	1	0	6	0	2	0
1911–1919	27	1	0	23	2	1	0

Batting Park Factors at Sportsman's Park IV

Years	BA	OBP	SLUG	2B*	3B*	HR*	BB**
1909–1910	95	97	93	101	81	50	101
1911–1919	98	98	97	106	75	114	100

*Per AB
**Per Total Plate Appearance (AB+BB+HP)

13

Washington

The NL operated in Washington, D.C., from 1886 to 1889 and from 1891 to 1899. The NL team was first called the Statesmen, then the Nationals, and finally the Senators. The NL used two ballparks in these years: Swampoodle Grounds (1886–1889) and Boundary Park (1891–1899). After the 1899 season, the NL reduced from 12 to eight teams, and Washington was one of the four teams that were disbanded.

For the 1900 season, the AL operated as a minor league. In 1901, the AL declared itself a major league for the 1901 season and moved several of its existing minor league franchises to other cities. Washington was one of the new AL cities. The AL team built a completely new ballpark. This ballpark, built on the site of a former brickyard, was called American League Park I. The Senators stayed at American League Park I for three seasons. The team (generally known as the Nationals starting with the 1904 season) moved to a new ballpark at a new location with an old name. This new ballpark, also called American League Park, has been designated American League Park II, as it was the second park used by the AL in Washington. The Nationals remained at this ballpark until the end of the 1910 season. The reason the Nationals discontinued their use of the park was that American League Park II burned down in March 1911. A new Classic ballpark, known for most of its life as Griffith Stadium (the name was not actually adopted until 1922), was quickly built on the site. Griffith Stadium remained in use by the AL through the 1961 season.

There were prohibitions on Sunday baseball in Washington in the early years of the twentieth century. As a result, the AL tried to schedule as many Sunday games in the cities where Sunday baseball was allowed. Thus the Nationals played Sunday games on the road until May 14, 1918, when the prohibitions on Sunday baseball in Washington were removed.[1]

American League Park I

Washington American League: 1901–1903

The first ballpark used by the AL in Washington was called American League Park. An all-wooden ballpark built before the start of the 1901 season, it was located in what is now downtown Washington, D. C., at 14th St. and Florida Ave. Northeast.[2] Home plate and the covered grandstand were located in the southwest corner of the site. Seating consisted of a covered grandstand in three sections between first base and third base, and bleachers located down both the LF and RF foul lines. One colorful aspect of the ballpark was an in-play clubhouse located in the RF corner. In addition, there was a scoreboard in RF. In 1902, the park was the scene of the first announcement of lineups by a public address announcer (E. Lawrence

Phillips). The planned capacity was about 7,000. The site of the ballpark had previously been used as a brickyard.[3] From this, it is clear that this ballpark was not the same one as was used by the Washington entry in the NL between 1892 and 1899 (called Boundary Park or National Park). American League Park I was used for only three seasons before the Senators/Nationals moved a few blocks to a new park, American League Park II. The wooden stands of American League Park I were torn down and reused at the new park. No photos of this ballpark could be located.

The Basis of American League Park I's Configuration and Dimensions

Dimensional data for this ballpark are virtually non-existent. The totality of the entry for this park in *Green Cathedrals* consists of the duration of the occupancy of the park (April 29, 1901-September 29, 1903), and the fact that the stands were torn down and moved to the second Washington AL ballpark (also named American League Park) for the 1904 season. The basis for the configuration of American League Park I was the ballpark perspective in *Baseball Memories: 1900–1909*.[4] In this illustration, LF was noticeably shorter than RF. The LF and RF fences met in CF at a right angle. In addition, the LF fence was at more than 90 degrees and the RF fence at less than 90 degrees to the foul lines. There were two newspaper articles about the park in the *Washington Post* before the 1901 Opening Day. The first article provided the overall dimensions of the park site, 400 by 500 feet.[5] The configuration from *Baseball Memories: 1900–1909* was combined with the park site's dimensions to produce a ballpark diagram. The location of home plate and the alignment of the foul lines were estimated consistent with the data on home runs at the park. The shorter of the park site's two dimensions (400 feet) was the north-south distance, which severely limited the LF dimension. The second article about the park listed the planned dimensions (LF 295, CF 550, and RF 455). However, the CF and RF dimensions listed in that article were physically impossible given the limits of the park site.

Based on the home run data, the LF dimension was estimated to have been 290. In the three seasons the park was in use, there were a total of 13 home runs to RF; only two were OTF home runs, and the 11 other were IPHR. Of the two OTF home runs to RF, one was due to special circumstances. On July 16, 1902, Doc Casey of Detroit hit a ball into a crowd of fans crossing deep RF on their way to one of the park's exits. The Senators right fielder was unable to retrieve the ball; and the hit was thus ruled a home run. RF distances for American League Park I were developed based on an analysis of AL home run data for the 1901–1903 seasons. The author used the SABR Home Run Log and newspaper game accounts to compile home run data for all AL ballparks during the 1901–1903 seasons. The time period for each park was selected to encompass seasons where there was no change in the average RF distances. One obvious conclusion: with 11 IPHR to RF and only one truly OTF home run to RF, the RF dimensions must have been markedly greater than the LF dimensions and likely similar to the RF dimensions of other AL parks with similar levels of OTF home runs to RF. The above comparison suggested the average RF distance at American League Park I was similar to the distance at Baltimore's Oriole Park IV and less than the 380 feet average RF distance at Detroit's Bennett Park. The RF dimension at American League Park I was estimated to have been 368. Given the estimated LF and RF distances, the CF corner distance (that coincidently was also dead CF) was derived as the junction of the LF and RF fences.

Park data and dimensions for American League Park I are shown below.

13. Washington

DIMENSIONS (calculated from park diagram)

Years	LF	SLF	LC	CF	RC	SRF	RF
1901–1903	290	315	362	465	397	368	368

FENCES HEIGHTS (from pre-season newspaper article)

Years	LF	CF	RF
1901–1903	14	14	14

AVERAGE OUTFIELD DISTANCES

Years	LF	CF	RF
1901–1903	319	420	373

CAPACITY: 7,000

PARK SIZE/AVERAGE OUTFIELD DISTANCE: 371

PARK SITE AREA: 4.6 ACRES

DEADBALL ERA RUN FACTOR: 104 (RANK: AL 7)

The Impact of the Park's Configuration and Dimensions on Batting

American League Park I was a great park for power hitters, particularly for right-handed hitters with at least modest power. The home run park factors for the three seasons of the park's use were 160, 210, and 199. What led to these large home run park factors? A review of the home run data led to some interesting discoveries. Home runs at the park totaled 53, 74, and 39 for 1901–1903. Unlike at many other ballparks in the first decade of the Deadball Era, the proportion of IPHR was relatively low. In the 1901–1903 seasons at the other seven AL cities, IPHR accounted for 55 percent of total home runs. In the three seasons at AL Park I in Washington, there were 34 IPHR (20 percent of the total). OTF home runs, which included two bounce home runs, accounted for 80 percent of the total. Of the 130 OTF home runs (excluding the two bounce home runs), 119 were to LF, 2 to CF, and 2 to RF (there were another seven OTF home runs where the field was unknown). Game accounts in the *Washington Post* frequently mention cheap home runs over the short LF fence. This characterization of home runs to LF may have been related to the propensity of visiting batters to come to town and drop numerous home runs over the short LF fence. In just four games on (August 9–10, 1901, the Philadelphia A's, led by Nap Lajoie's four homers, knocked out nine home runs to the Senator's zero. Of these nine A's home runs, eight were over the close and batter-friendly LF fence. For variety, the ninth home run (by Harry Davis) was hit over the CF fence. Instances like this may explain why, when the Nationals built Griffith Stadium in 1911, the LF dimension was a generous and pitcher-friendly 407 feet. As shown in the table below, OTF home runs per season to LF at the park were more than four times as great as at any other full-season AL ballpark.

Despite the proliferation of home runs over the close LF fence, the ballpark was only four percent above average in runs scored and was actually a below-average park for batting average, with a three-season park factor for batting average of 98. In 1902, the Senators posted an impressive team batting average of .304 at the park, but hit only .262 on the road.

After including the opponent's batting performance (batting average of .263 at AL Park and .316 at their home parks), the park factor was actually a below-average 98. Despite the short dimensions in LF and LC, the ballpark posted a triples park factor of 130. In 1903, the ballpark's park factor for walks was 130. This was the highest single-season park factor for base on balls in the Deadball Era. No explanation for this very high base on balls park factor was discovered.

Home-run data for the park and comparisons with other AL parks, as well as batting park factors, are shown below in six tables.

HOME RUNS BY TYPE AT AMERICAN LEAGUE PARK I

Year	Total	OTF	Bounce	IPHR
1901	53	43	2	10
1902	74	58	0	16
1903	39	31	0	8

OTF HOME RUNS BY FIELD AT AMERICAN LEAGUE PARK I (EXCLUDES BOUNCE)

Year	Total	LF	CF	RF	Unknown
1901	41	35	1	0	5
1902	58	54	1	1	2
1903	31	30	0	1	0

INSIDE-THE-PARK HOME RUNS BY FIELD AT AMERICAN LEAGUE PARK I

Year	Total	LF	LC	CF	RC	RF	Unknown
1901	10	1	0	3	0	5	1
1902	16	1	2	9	0	3	1
1903	8	1	3	1	0	3	0

OTF HOME RUNS TO LEFT FIELD BY PARK (1901–1903)

City–Park	Years	Home Runs*	Average LF Distance**
BAL–Oriole Park IV	1901–1902	0	391
BOS–Huntington Ave	1901–1903	0.3	395
CHI–South Side	1901–1903	1.0	370
CLE–League III	1901–1903	5.7	351
DET–Bennett	1901–1903	0.7	392
NY–Hilltop	1903	3.0	368
PHL–Columbia II	1901–1903	7.0	358
STL–Sportsman's III	1902–1903	9.5	335
WAS–American League I	1901–1903	39.7	317

*Per Season (excludes Bounce)
**Adjusted for Fence Height and Home Run Distributions

OTF HOME RUNS TO RIGHT FIELD BY PARK

City–Park	Years	Home Runs*	Average RF Distance**
BAL–Oriole Park IV	1901–1902	2.5	396
BOS–Huntington Ave	1901–1903	0.3	372

City–Park	Years	Home Runs*	Average RF Distance**
CHI–South Side	1903	4.0	347
CLE–League III	1901–1902	1.5	336
DET–Bennett	1901–1903	0	380
PHL–Columbia II	1901–1903	11.3	295
STL–Sportsman's III	1902–1903	7.0	331
WAS–American League I	1901–1903	0.3	375

*Per Season (excludes Bounce)
**Adjusted for Fence Height

BATTING PARK FACTORS AT AMERICAN LEAGUE PARK I

Years	BA	OBP	SLUG	2B*	3B*	HR*	BB**
1901–1903	98	100	105	93	130	187	112

*Per AB
**Per Total Plate Appearance (AB+BB+HP)

American League Park II

Washington American League: 1904–1910

The second ballpark used by the AL in Washington was called League Park or American League Park. As this was the second ballpark in Washington to be used by the AL, it has been designated American League Park II in various ballpark books. The site of American League Park II was previously used for a major league ballpark by the NL Washington Senators for the 1892–1899 seasons. That prior ballpark at this location was called Boundary Park or National Park.

American League Park II was a wooden ballpark located in downtown Washington, D.C., near the corner of Seventh St. and Florida Ave. Northwest.[6] Home plate and the grandstand were located in the southwest corner of the park site with the LF line being canted a few degrees to the west of a north-south orientation. There was an in-play clubhouse in RC and a modest-sized scoreboard in LF. The all-wooden seating facilities consisted of a single-deck grandstand which ran from first base to about halfway between home and third base (see photo above), a covered pavilion that ran from the third-base end of the grandstand about 50 feet beyond the infield down the LF line, and bleachers that angled toward the RF foul line and extended the majority of the length of that foul line. There was no seating in the fair portion of the outfield. The grandstand at American League Park I had been disassembled and moved to American League Park II in March 1904. This rebuilding of the grandstand took place only two weeks before Opening Day.[7] The rushed nature of the building of this ballpark can be gauged by the fact that the opening of the gates to fans on Opening Day (April 14, 1904) was delayed while workers completed the ramp leading from the main gate to the grandstand.[8] The planned capacity of the park in 1904 was about 7,000. A big game during the 1905 season (May 6, 1905) drew 9,300, including numerous standees in LF, and from the attendance data for that game the 1905 seating capacity was estimated to have been about 8,000. This ballpark, like many of its wooden contemporaries, suffered a sad fate; it burned down on March 17, 1911.

American League Park II: Philadelphia vs. Washington, 1905. A view from the right-field corner of Washington's American League Park II. The date was May 6, 1905, and the opponent was the Philadelphia Athletics. Note how small the grandstand was, and the overflow crowd in front of the left field fence. Attendance was 9,300 in a ballpark with a seating capacity of about 8,000. (Panoramic Photographs collection [LC-USZ62-88346], Library of Congress.)

The Basis of American League Park II's Configuration and Dimensions

Dimensional data for this ballpark are virtually non-existent. The only relevant information for this park in *Green Cathedrals* (1992 edition) consists of the duration of the National's occupancy of the park, April 14, 1904–October 6, 1910. The initial basis for the configuration of American League Park II was a 1910 Sanborn fire insurance map of the park.[9] This Sanborn map showed the northern, eastern, and southern boundaries of the park site. The park was set back on its western boundary from another property (Maryland House) that fronted on 7th St. The Sanborn map did not show the property line between Maryland House and the park site. That boundary line was estimated on the basis of the illustration in *Baseball Memories: 1900–1909*.[10] The Sanborn map and ballpark photos from the Library of Congress and *Baseball Memories* were used to develop a park diagram. The location of the stands was based on these photos and the depiction of the park in *Baseball Memories*. Home plate was an estimated location with the LF foul line perpendicular to the LF fence. From the photos of the ballpark and the Sanborn map, it was clear that the RF foul line intersected the RF fence at more than 90 degrees. From the photo in *Baseball Memories*, CF was bounded by a multi-angle kinked fence, and thus there was no CF corner. The home-run data was used to cross-check the estimated dimensions, and no necessary adjustments were identified. All in all, these outfield dimensions are estimates that contain a moderate-to-large amount of uncertainty.

DIMENSIONS (estimated from park diagram)

Years	LF	SLF	LC	CF	RC	SRF	RF
1904–1910	356	368	410	442	433	380	328

FENCES HEIGHTS (estimated from photos)

Years	LF	CF	RF
1904–1910	10	10	10

AVERAGE OUTFIELD DISTANCES

Years	LF	CF	RF
1904–1910	375	438	386

CAPACITY: 7,000 (1904), 8,000 (1905–1910 Est.)

PARK SIZE/COMPOSITE AVERAGE OUTFIELD DISTANCE: 400

PARK SITE AREA: 6.1 ACRES

DEADBALL ERA RUN FACTOR: 96 (RANK: AL 14)

The Impact of the Park's Configuration and Dimensions on Batting

American League Park II was not a great offensive park. The park's run factor was 96, or four percent below average, while the home run park factor was 50 (see Batting Park Factors in the fourth table below). What led to this modest home run park factor? A review of the home run data led to some interesting discoveries. Home runs of all types amounted to only nine per season. Excluding the 18 bounce home runs, there were only five OTF home runs in seven seasons (four to LF and one to RF). In the park's seven-year history, no one ever hit a ball over the CF fence. This home-run data suggested the park was spacious and the average outfield distances greater than the typical AL ballpark. In addition, the OTF home run data are consistent with LF having a smaller average distance than RF. Like at many other ballparks in the first decade of the Deadball Era, the proportion of IPHR was high, amounting to 63 percent of the total home runs hit in the history of the ballpark.

Despite the park's run factor of 96, the batting average park factor was 100. The on-base park factor was 99, and slugging was 97. Despite the generous dimensions in LC, CF and RC, the ballpark posted a below-average triples park factor of 83. The reason the park had a batting average park factor of 100 and at the same time a lesser run factor of 96 was due to the low park factors for triples, home runs, and walks. Home-run data for the park and batting park factors are shown below in four tables.

Home Runs by Type at American League Park II

Years	Total	OTF	Bounce	IPHR
1904–1910	63	23	18	40

OTF Home Runs by Field at American League Park II (Excludes Bounce)

Years	Total	LF	CF	RF	Unknown
1904–1910	5	4	0	1	0

Inside-the-Park Home Runs by Field at American League Park II

Years	Total	LF	LC	CF	RC	RF	Unknown
1904–1910	39	17	4	5	2	7	4

Batting Park Factors at American League Park II

Years	BA	OBP	SLUG	2B*	3B*	HR*	BB**
1904–1910	100	99	97	103	84	50	95

*Per AB
**Per Total Plate Appearance (AB+BB+HP)

Griffith Stadium

Washington American League: 1911–1919

The third ballpark used by the AL in Washington was Griffith Stadium. In the Deadball Era, the park was known as National Park IV. The name Griffith Stadium was adopted in 1920 by the new owner of the Washington Nationals, Clark Griffith. Prior to the building of Griffith Stadium in 1911, the park site had previously been used for the location of American League Park II. Griffith Stadium was located in downtown Washington near the corner of Seventh St. and Florida Ave. Northwest. In 1911, the park site was bounded on the north by Howard University and on the west by another property (Maryland House) that fronted on Seventh St. On the southern boundary (behind RF), there was another property, then an alley, then Spruce St. (later renamed U St.). On the east, Fifth St. made up the final boundary of the park and adjoined the back of the LF bleachers.

Right field at Griffith Stadium, 1913. An early view of Washington's Griffith Stadium shows the park before it was expanded by the acquisition of the property behind the right-field wall. The player leaping in the photograph is Eddie Foster — an infielder with the Washington Senators from 1912 to 1919. (Photo Prints and Photographs Collection [LC-B2-2729-14 (P&P)], Library of Congress.)

The previous ballpark on the site, American League Park II, burned down on March 17, 1911, destroying most of the stands.[11] Only the first-base bleachers in the old park escaped the fire. One of the earlier Classic ballparks, Griffith Stadium was built largely of steel and concrete, and had a planned capacity of about 15,000. The ballpark was only partially complete in time for Opening Day on April 12, 1911. At that time, the upper deck of the grandstand and the roof were not completed, and the permanent seats in the pavilions were not yet installed.[12] Temporary wooden seats were used in the pavilions for Opening Day.[13] When completed later that season, the park's seating facilities consisted of a double-deck grandstand which ran from beyond first base to beyond third base, two concrete pavilions (that were not yet roofed on Opening Day) that ran from the ends of the grandstand down the LF and RF lines, and a large set of bleachers in fair LF that extended into CF. There was no seating in fair RF. There was an in-play clubhouse in RC and a modest-sized scoreboard (installed in May 1911) located in RF. Home plate and the grandstand were located in the northwest cor-

Griffith Stadium grandstand, 1912. The player taking batting practice is outfielder Tilly Walker of the Washington Nationals. Note the double-deck grandstand extended only to about third base and the left edge of the third-base pavilion. (George Grantham Bain Collection, Library of Congress.)

ner of the park site with the LF line being canted a few degrees to the north of an east-west orientation. The ballpark was completed on July 24, 1911.

The park site and playing field were both expanded after the 1913 season. The Nationals acquired the adjacent property (a storage plant) located behind the RF fence. This property was situated on the north side of the alley behind U St. The purchase of this parcel permitted an increase in the size of RF and the construction of a new and higher concrete wall to act as the RF barrier.

The Basis of Griffith Stadium's Configurations and Dimensions

Dimensional data for Griffith Stadium from *Green Cathedrals* are LF 407, LC 391, and CF 421.[14] No 1911 RF dimension was found. A clue to the park's RF dimension in the 1911–1913 seasons was found in an account of a home run at Cleveland on July 27, 1912. The National's Danny Moeller hit a home run over the RF wall and screen at Cleveland's League Park IV.

The game account noted that the RF distance at the Cleveland ballpark (290) was about the same distance at the foul line as at Washington (Griffith Stadium).[15]

The basis for the initial configuration of Griffith Stadium was a 1911 Sanborn fire insurance map of the park.[16] This Sanborn map showed the park's boundaries and the location of the stands and perimeter fences. The Sanborn map and ballpark photos from the Library of Congress were used to develop a park diagram. Home plate was placed at an estimated location in the northwest portion of the park consistent with a LF dimension of 407 and a CF dimension of 421. In this alignment, the LF foul line hit the LF bleacher fence at far less than 90 degrees. From the photos of the ballpark and the Sanborn map, it was clear that the RF foul line must intersect the RF fence at more than 90 degrees. Given the location of home plate, the resulting RF dimension was 280, roughly consistent with the earlier noted comparison with Cleveland's League Park IV. The short fence in RF was an item of discussion in the 1911–1912 seasons. Early in the 1912 season, the *Washington Post* noted that a high screen had been promised on top of the RF fence.[17] The story in the *Post* stated that there were visiting batsmen to whom the short, low fence was a cinch. In May 1912, the Washington club closed a deal to acquire the storage plant behind the existing RF fence.[18] That same story stated that one of the chief objections against the local grounds was the fact that the RF fence was short. The home run data for 1911–1913 proved how true that statement was: nearly all of the OTF home runs (34 of 38) were hit over the RF fence. The acquisition of this additional parcel allowed the RF dimension to be increased to 320 for the 1914 season, and a higher concrete RF wall was constructed. However, home run research in later seasons showed that a portion of the RF wall was not at the new increased height. During the 1917 season, and again late in the 1919 season, there were accounts of home runs over the "low section of the RF wall."[19] Based on the known height of the RF wall in the late 1920s, the height of the main portion of the RF wall in 1914–1919 was estimated to have been 20 feet.

The CF fence made a nearly 90-degree turn to the right at the CF end of the LF bleachers because the park site excluded a few properties in what would have been the CF corner. The CF fence in 1911–1913 ran from the right end of the LF bleachers to the RF corner, passing behind an in-play clubhouse in RC. After the 1914 expansion of the ballpark, the RF fence ran at more than 90 degrees to the foul line to RC where there was a kink, and the CF fence continued in a diagonal section until it met the CF end of the LF bleachers. At the time the new RF wall was built before the 1914 season, it is likely the clubhouse was removed from its in-play location in fair RF, as there was no further mention of it in the Deadball Era.

Given the known LF and CF dimensions and the existence of a Sanborn map, the Deadball Era dimensions contain only a small amount of uncertainty. The following tables show the dimensions, fence heights, and average outfield distances in the Deadball Era for each configuration of Griffith Stadium.

DIMENSIONS (largely estimated from park diagrams)

Years	LF	SLF	LC	CF	RC	SRF	RF
1911–1913	407	388	393	421	405	315	280
1914–1919	407	388	393	421	419	365	320

FENCES HEIGHTS (estimated from photos)

Years	LF	CF	RF
1911–1913	11	11	11
1914–1919	11	11–20	11–20

Average Outfield Distances

Years	LF	CF	RF
1911–1913	392	413	325
1914–1919	392	415	367

CAPACITY: 11,000 (APRIL 1911 EST.), 15,000 (JULY 24, 1911–1919)

PARK SIZE/COMPOSITE AVERAGE OUTFIELD DISTANCE:
377 (1911–1913), 391 (1914–1919)

PARK SITE AREA: 6.1 ACRES (1911–1913), 6.5 ACRES (1914–1919)

DEADBALL ERA RUN FACTOR: 98 (RANK: AL 12)

The Impact of the Park's Configurations and Dimensions on Batting

Griffith Stadium in its first configuration (1911–1913) was not a great offensive park. The park's run factor was 98 (two percent below average), while the home run park factor was 85 (see Batting Park Factors in the fourth table below). This close-to-average home run park factor was enhanced by the 18.3 per season IPHR in the park's first three years. After the expansion of RF before the 1914 season, the park became spacious in all fields, with average outfield distances greater than the typical AL ballpark. The 1914 expansion produced a major impact on home runs at the park. Total home runs dropped from 31.7 per year to 7.5 from 1914 to 1919. OTF home runs at the park became rare — about two per season — and there were none to LF or CF. From 1914 forwards, Griffith Stadium became known as the least favorable AL ballpark for hitting home runs. Unlike at many other ballparks in the second decade of the Deadball Era, the proportion of IPHR remained high, amounting to 62 percent of the total home runs hit in the ballpark's nine Deadball seasons.

Consistent with the park's run factor of 98, the batting average and on-base park factors were in the range of 98–99, and the slugging park factors were 93–95. Despite the generous dimensions starting in 1914 in LC, CF, and RC, the ballpark posted only an average triples park factor of 101. Home-run data for the park and batting park factors are shown below in four tables.

Home Runs by Type at Griffith Stadium

Years	Total	OTF	Bounce	IPHR
1911–1913	95	40	2	55
1914–1919	45	13	0	32

OTF Home Runs by Field at Griffith Stadium (excludes Bounce)

Years	Total	LF	CF	RF	Unknown
1911–1913	38	1	2	34	1
1914–1919	13	0	0	13	0

Inside-the-Park Home Runs by Field at Griffith Stadium

Years	Total	LF	LC	CF	RC	RF	Unknown
1911–1913	55	16	6	23	6	2	2
1914–1919	32	9	2	14	3	2	2

Batting Park Factors at Griffith Stadium

Years	BA	OBP	SLUG	2B*	3B*	HR*	BB**
1911–1913	98	98	93	100	85	85	96
1914–1919	99	99	95	82	101	40	96

*Per AB
**Per Total Plate Appearance (AB+BB+HP)

14

Summary

The Impact of Ballparks on Batting in the Deadball Era

There were a total of 34 ballparks used by the AL and NL in the Deadball Era. What can one say about the impact of the various ballparks on batting in this time period? Individual ballparks and several ballparks in individual seasons did show pronounced effects on batting. One ballpark in particular, Burns Park, the Sunday-only ballpark of the Detroit Tigers in the 1901–1902 seasons, was a very good hitter's park. Burns Park in 1901 posted park factors for batting average (118), slugging (125), and doubles (199) that were never exceeded by any ballpark in the Deadball Era and most probably never exceeded by any ML ballpark since 1901.

The highest and lowest single-season park factors in both the AL and NL for each of seven offensive categories are shown below in two tables.

Deadball Era Highest and Lowest Park Factors — AL (YR 19xx)

Category	High	Park/City/YR	Low	Park/City/YR
Batting Average	118	Burns/DET/01	78	S. Side/CHI/10
On-Base	113	League/CLE/17	84	S. Side/CHI/10
Slugging	125	Burns/DET/01	71	S. Side/CHI/10
Doubles*	199	Burns/DET/01	74	Comiskey/CHI/10
Triples*	174	Huntington/BOS/04	18	S. Side/CHI/10
Home Runs*	344	Hilltop/NY/04	09	S. Side/CHI/04
Base on Balls**	130	AL I/WAS/03	79	AL II/WAS/04

*Per At Bat
**Per Total Plate Appearance

Deadball Era Highest and Lowest Park Factors — NL (YR 19xx)

Category	High	Park/City/YR	Low	Park/City/YR
Batting Average	112	Palace of Fans/CIN/06	90	Braves/BOS/18
On-Base	110	S. End/BOS/10	92	Forbes/PIT/14
Slugging	117	Baker/PHL/15	87	Braves/BOS/15
Doubles*	164	Weeghman/CHI/16	67	Palace of Fans/CIN/11
Triples*	213	Palace of Fans/CIN/07	33	Baker/PHL/16

Category	High	Park/City/YR	Low	Park/City/YR
Home Runs*	315	Polo/NY/05	19	Expo/PIT/05
Base on Balls**	115	Expo/PIT/02	81	W. Side/CHI/02

*Per At Bat
**Per Total Plate Appearance

Note that in both the AL and NL the highest and lowest park factors for doubles, triples, and home runs were far more extreme than for the other offensive categories. A couple of qualifying comments regarding the data in the two above tables are in order: in 1901 Burns Park (Detroit) had only 13 games; in 1910 South Side Park (Chicago) had 28 games; and in 1915 Braves Field (Boston) had 26 games. Thus some of the highest and lowest single-season batting park factors may have been due in part to the data reflecting partial seasons at the three aforementioned ballparks. For full seasons, the most extreme effect of ballparks on batting was on home runs in the 1904 AL season. At Hilltop Park in New York, the high home run park factor was 344, while at South Side Park in Chicago the low home run park factor was a mere nine. This meant that home runs were roughly 35 times more likely at Hilltop Park that season than at South Side Park. At South Side Park, the home team White Sox hit zero home runs, while visiting teams combined for the grand total of two home runs.

In individual seasons, ballparks had impacts on batting—particularly on extra-base hits—that ranged from moderate to extreme. However, what was the typical range of effects on batting during the entirety of the Deadball Era? The following methodology was developed to measure the ballpark-related variances in batting among all of the ballparks in use during each of the Deadball seasons. For each season and for each league, the ballparks with the highest and lowest park factors for each of seven offensive categories were identified. The averages of the highest park factors for each batting category over the 19 seasons were calculated separately for each of the two leagues. In the same manner, the averages of the lowest park factors during the 19 seasons were also calculated. This data set was used to determine the range of average highest and average lowest park factors. The range of average high vs. low park factors illustrated the extent of the impact of ballparks on batting. The ratio of the average high park factor to the average low park factor was determined for each batting category. This last statistic (ratio of average high to average low park factor) was the unit of measurement chosen for assessing the impact of ballparks on batting in the Deadball Era. The following table presents both the ranges of average high and low park factors and the ratios of the high to the low average park factors.

AVERAGE DEADBALL ERA HIGH AND LOW PARK FACTORS

Offensive Category	AL Range	NL Range	AL Ratio	NL Ratio
Batting Average	92–109	93–107	1.19	1.14
On-Base	95–107	95–106	1.13	1.11
Slugging	90–112	93–110	1.24	1.18
Doubles*	80–132	78–137	1.65	1.75
Triples*	62–143	54–164	2.32	3.04
Home Runs*	30–228	37–221	7.60	5.89
Base on Balls**	95–112	90–111	1.18	1.23

*Per At Bat
**Per Total Plate Appearance

To illustrate, the range of AL park factors for the category of batting average (92–109) means that on average the lowest batting average park factor each season over the 19 Deadball seasons was 92 and the highest was 109. To translate park factors into common everyday terms, this meant that on average the worst ballpark in the AL was eight percent worse than the average AL ballpark that season. In the same manner, the best AL ballpark for batting average was typically nine percent better than the average AL ballpark. The ratios are the average high park factors divided by the average low park factors. Thus, for the AL, the best ballpark for batting average was (on average) 19 percent better than the worst ballpark for batting average. This, in the author's judgment, is the best measurement of the impact of Deadball Era ballparks on batting average.

For the general offensive categories of batting average, on-base, slugging, and base on balls, the ratios of highest to lowest park factors ranged from 1.11 to 1.24. Thus, typically ballparks had an impact on these batting categories of less than 25 percent from the best to the worst hitter's ballpark. However, for extra-base hits the situation in the Deadball Era was strikingly different. The ratios of average highest to average lowest park factors for extra-base hits ranged between 1.65 and 7.60. For example, the Phillies and their opponents combined for 16 home runs at the Baker Bowl in 1909, whereas in the 1911 season that total had risen nearly 400 percent to 74 home runs. The causes of the increase were twofold: the adoption of the livelier cork-center ball in the NL in 1911, and the installation of LF bleachers in Baker Bowl for the 1910 season. At Baker Bowl, changing the configuration of the ballpark only in LF led to the home run park factor increasing from 84 in 1909 to 210 in 1911.

In conclusion, ballparks in the Deadball Era had moderate impacts on the general measures of batting (batting average, on-base, and slugging). The impact on extra-base hits was far more pronounced. In the Deadball Era, teams averaged 179 doubles, 70 triples, and 22 home runs per season. The impact of the ballparks on extra-base hits was greater the less common the type of hit. The average ratio between the highest and lowest park factors for doubles was 70 percent, for triples 268 percent, and for home runs 675 percent. In particular, the impact of Deadball Era ballpark dimensions and configurations on home runs was obvious, immediate, and overwhelming.

Chapter Notes

Preface

1. Detroit used a neutral site for one game at Ramona Park in Grand Rapids, MI (1903), two at Armory Park in Toledo, OH (1903), and two at Neil Park II in Columbus, OH (1905). Cleveland played two games in 1902 at Jailhouse Flats I in Fort Wayne, IN, one game in 1902 and one in 1903 at Neil Park I in Columbus, OH, one in 1902 and two in 1903 at Mahaffey Park in Canton, OH, and one at Fairview Park in Dayton, OH. In the NL, Boston played a game at Rocky Point Park in Warwick, RI (1903), and St. Louis played one game at Sportsman's Park II in 1901 after a fire the previous day at their home park of Robison Field.

Introduction

1. David Vincent, *Home Run: The Definitive History of Baseball's Ultimate Weapon* (Washington, D.C.: Potomac Books, 2007).
2. Philip J. Lowry, *Green Cathedrals* (New York: Walker Publishing Company, 2006).
3. *Total Baseball*, ed. John Thorn and Pete Palmer (New York: Viking Penguin, 1995).
4. Frank Vaccaro, *All Games Baseball, Volume One 1871–1924* (College Point, NY: All Games Baseball, 2005). Designed and edited by Frank Vaccaro of SABR, this database lists all major league games, their scores, and number of innings.

Chapter 1

1. Charlie Bevis, *Sunday Baseball* (Jefferson, NC: McFarland, 2003).
2. Philip J. Lowry, *Green Cathedrals* (Reading, MA: Addison-Wesley, 1992), p. 109.
3. Sanborn Fire Insurance Co. map, Baltimore 1902.
4. Michael Gershman, *Diamonds: The Evolution of the Ballpark* (Boston: Houghton Mifflin, 1993).
5. Marc Okkonen, *Baseball Memories: 1900–1909* (New York: Sterling, 1992), p. 29.
6. This statement must be qualified because AL home-road BA data (actual or reliable estimates) are available for 1901–1919, 1930–1939, and 1957–2004. The highest full-season team BA in AL history was 1921 Detroit, with a .316 mark. The Detroit home batting average was .311. Using the home-road estimation methodology presented earlier in the Introduction produced an estimated team home BA of .332 for 1950 Boston, a team that scored an incredible 223 more runs in home games than in an equal number of road games. The 1901 Baltimore home BA is not the ML's top mark, as the NL Philadelphia Phillies hit .344 at home in 1930.

Chapter 2

1. *Boston Globe*, July 15, 1894.
2. *Boston Globe*, January 13, 1895.
3. *Boston Globe*, January 7, 1908.
4. Lowry, *Green Cathedrals*, p. 109.
5. Sanborn Fire Insurance Co. map, Boston Base Ball Grounds, Boston 1895 (sheet 58).
6. Eric Enders, *Ballparks Then And Now* (San Diego: PRC Publishing, 2002), p. 25.
7. *Boston Globe*, January 7, 1908.
8. *Boston Globe*, December 21, 1911.
9. *Boston Globe*, January 20, 1912.
10. *Boston Globe*, February 13, 1912.
11. Sanborn Fire Insurance Co. map, Boston Base Ball Grounds, Boston 1914 (volume 2 sheet 58).
12. Alan E. Foulds, *Boston's Ballparks & Arenas* (Boston: Northeastern University Press, 2005).
13. "Just The Place," *Boston Globe*, January 23, 1901.
14. Bill Nowlin, *Red Sox Threads* (Burlington, MA: Rounder Books, 2007).
15. "Huntington Av Grounds," *Boston Globe*, February 3, 1901.
16. Foulds, *Boston's Ballparks & Arenas*.
17. "Changes At Huntington Av Grounds," *Boston Globe*, March 29, 1905.
18. *Chicago Tribune*, September 17, 1909.
19. Lowry, *Green Cathedrals*.
20. "Just The Place," *Boston Globe*, January 23, 1901.
21. "Crowd Leaving The Baseball Grounds," *Boston Globe*, September 15, 1904.
22. Enders, *Ballparks Then and Now*.
23. "Changes At Huntington Av Grounds," *Boston Globe*, March 29, 1905.
24. Gershman, *Diamonds*, p. 100.
25. "New Home of the Red Sox," *Boston Globe*, October 15, 1911.
26. "Section of Centre Field Crowd & Tris Speaker," *Boston Globe*, April 21, 1912.

27. "New Stands and Boxes at Fenway Park," *Boston Globe*, September 20, 1912.
28. "New Home of the Red Sox," *Boston Globe*, October 15, 1911.
29. "Section of Centre Field Crowd & Tris Speaker," *Boston Globe*, April 21, 1912.
30. "If You're Going To Fenway Park Next Week," *Boston Globe*, October 4, 1912.
31. "New Stands and Boxes at Fenway Park," *Boston Globe*, September 20, 1912.
32. John Boswell and David Fisher, *Fenway Park: Legendary Home of the Red Sox* (Boston: Little, 1992).
33. "Braves Field Will Be Open Wednesday," *Boston Globe*, August 15, 1915.
34. Lowry, *Green Cathedrals*.
35. Lawrence S., Ritter, *Lost Ballparks* (New York: Penguin, 1992), p. 20.
36. Sanborn Fire Insurance Co. map, Boston 1925.
37. *Boston Globe*, August 24, 1915, July 12, 1919.
38. Bill Price, "Braves Field," *Baseball Research Journal* 7 (1978).
39. Lowry, *Green Cathedrals*.
40. *Boston Globe*, May 29, 1925.
41. *Boston Globe*, August 24, 1915, July 12, 1919.

Chapter 3

1. Bevis, *Sunday Baseball*, p. 194.
2. Lowry, *Green Cathedrals*, p. 116.
3. "Brooklyn Club's New Grounds," *Brooklyn Daily Eagle*, March 15, 1898.
4. Peter Morris, *A Game of Inches* (Chicago: Ivan R. Dee, 2006), p. 75.
5. Okkonen, *Baseball Memories*, p. 37; Sanborn Fire Insurance Co. map, Brooklyn 1906 (volume 1, sheets 38–39).
6. "Brooklyn Club's New Grounds," *Brooklyn Daily Eagle*, March 15, 1898.
7. *Brooklyn Daily Eagle*, September 5, 1901.
8. Lowry, *Green Cathedrals*, p. 116.
9. *Brooklyn Daily Eagle*, September 5, 1901.
10. Lowry, *Green Cathedrals*, p. 116.
11. *Ebbets Field: The Original Plans*, ed. Rod Kennedy Jr. (New York: The Brooklyn Dodgers Hall of Fame, 1992).
12. *New York Times*, April 29, 1913.

Chapter 4

1. Sanborn Fire Insurance Co. map, Chicago 1917 (volume 7, sheet 71).
2. "Death Closes Roof Stands," *Chicago Tribune*, July 19, 1908.
3. "Rain Floods Park; Cubs Again Idle," *Chicago Tribune*, May 12, 1908.
4. Lowry, *Green Cathedrals*.
5. *Chicago Tribune*, April 13, 1905.
6. *Chicago Tribune* August 29, 1910.
7. "Old Sox Park Only A Memory," *Chicago Tribune*, October 3, 1910.
8. Library of Congress American Memory Collection, South Side Park photos.
9. *Chicago Tribune*, June 27, 1901.
10. Sanborn Fire Insurance Co. map, Chicago 1911 (volume 2, sheet 127).
11. *Chicago Tribune*, July 30, 1901; April 30, 1903.
12. *Chicago Tribune*, April 30, 1903.
13. Okkonen, *Baseball Memories*.
14. *Chicago Tribune*, May 14, 1907.
15. "Notes of the White Sox," *Chicago Tribune*, May 18, 1907.
16. Much of the information on the configuration of the stands and, in particular, the roof seats at the ballpark came from research by SABR member and Chicago ballpark expert Mark Fimoff.
17. Christy Mathewson, *Pitching in a Pinch* (Lincoln: University of Nebraska Press, 1994), p. 296.
18. Sanborn Fire Insurance Co. map, Chicago 1917 (volume 7, sheet 71).
19. George W. Hilton, "Comiskey Park," *Baseball Research Journal* 3 (1974), pp. 2–11.
20. Lowry, *Green Cathedrals*.
21. Library of Congress American Memory Collection, Comiskey Park photo (digital ID ichicdn s0088 390).
22. *Chicago Tribune*, July 15, 1915.
23. *St. Louis Post Dispatch*, January 26, 1914.
24. *Baseball In Chicago*, Special Issue of the *Chicago Tribune Sunday Magazine*, May 23, 2004.
25. *Chicago Tribune*, April 28, 1914.
26. *Chicago Tribune*, July 8, 1916.
27. Lowry, *Green Cathedrals*.
28. *Chicago Tribune*, April 4, 1914.
29. *Chicago Tribune*, April 30, 1914.
30. Library of Congress American Memory Collection (digital ID s060168, s060191).
31. William Hartell, *A Day At The Park-In Celebration of Wrigley Field* (Coal Valley, IL: Quality Sports Publications, 1995), p. 9.
32. Sanborn Fire Insurance Co. map, Chicago 1923 (volume 9, sheet 116).
33. Lowry, *Green Cathedrals*.
34. SABR Home Run Log from SABR member David Vincent.

Chapter 5

1. Bevis, *Sunday Baseball*, p. 104.
2. Morris, *A Game of Inches*, p. 48.
3. Lowry, *Green Cathedrals*, p. 137.
4. Sanborn Fire Insurance Co. map, Cincinnati 1891 (sheets 106–108).
5. Okkonen, *Baseball Memories*, p. 46.
6. *Cincinnati Enquirer*, June 13, 1901.
7. *Cincinnati Enquirer*, June 11, 1901.
8. *Cincinnati Enquirer*, June 11, 1901.
9. Sanborn Fire Insurance Co. map, Cincinnati 1904 (sheet 203); Richard Miller and Gregory Rhodes, "The Life and Times of Old Cincinnati Ballparks," *Queen City Heritage* 46, no. 2 (Summer 1988), p. 25; Lowry, *Green Cathedrals*, p. 137.
10. Gershman, *Diamonds*, p. 170.
11. Sanborn Fire Insurance Co. map, Cincinnati 1950 (sheet 203); Miller and Rhodes, "The Life and Times of Old Cincinnati Ballparks," *Queen City Heritage* 46, no. 2 (Summer 1988), p. 25; Lowry, *Green Cathedrals*, p. 138.

12. Lowry, *Green Cathedrals*, p. 138.
13. *New York Times*, September 11, 1913.

Chapter 6

1. Lowry, *Green Cathedrals*.
2. Sanborn Fire Insurance Co. Map, Cleveland 1896, Sheet 292.
3. *Cleveland Leader*, July 6, 1909.
4. *Cleveland Plain Dealer*, June 5, 1908.
5. *Cleveland Leader*, July 6, 1909.
6. This figure excludes five home games played at neutral sites.
7. Lowry, *Green Cathedrals*.
8. Lowry, *Green Cathedrals*.
9. . Lowry, *Green Cathedrals;* Sanborn Fire Insurance Co. map, Cleveland 1911; Ritter, *Lost Ballparks*.
10. Bob Boynton, "Cleveland Ballparks," SABR-L, March 29, 2001.

Chapter 7

1. Richard Bak and Charles Vincent, *The Corner* (Chicago: Triumph Books, 1999); Gershman, *Diamonds*, p.230; Lowry, *Green Cathedrals*.
2. Sanborn Fire Insurance Co. map, Detroit 1897 (volume 2, sheet 28).
3. Gershman, *Diamonds*; Okkonen, *Baseball Memories*, p.52.
4. Michael Benson, *Ballparks of North America* (Jefferson, NC: McFarland, 1989).
5. Richard Bak, *A Place For Summer* (Detroit: Wayne State University Press, 1998).
6. Richard Bak and Charles Vincent, *The Corner*, pp.158–59.
7. Research by the author from game accounts in the *Detroit Free Press*.
8. *Detroit Free Press*, April 17, 1910.
9. Bob Hercules, dir., *The Story of America's Classic Ballparks* (Questar, 1990), VHS.
10. Peter Morris, *Level Playing Fields* (Lincoln: University of Nebraska Press, 2007), p. 116.
11. Morris, *Level Playing Fields*, p. 116.
12. Bak, *A Place For Summer*.
13. *Detroit Free Press*, May 19, 1902.
14. Gershman, *Diamonds;* Lowry, *Green Cathedrals;* Bak and Vincent, *The Corner*.
15. Bak and Vincent, *The Corner*.
16. Sanborn Fire Insurance Co. map, Detroit 1897.
17. Gershman, *Diamonds*, p. 230; Bak, *A Place for Summer*, pp. 124–25.
18. Lowry, *Green Cathedrals*.

Chapter 8

1. Bevis, *Sunday Baseball*, p. 43.
2. Okkonen, *Baseball Memories*, p.55.

Chapter 9

1. Bevis, *Sunday Baseball*, p. 194.
2. Bevis, *Sunday Baseball*.

3. Lowry, *Green Cathedrals*, p. 116.
4. *New York Times*, April 30, 1907.
5. Lowry, *Green Cathedrals*; Sanborn Fire Insurance Co. map, New York City 1909; *New York Times*, April 30, 1907.
6. *New York Times*, game accounts 1901–1908.
7. *New York Times*, 6 April 1903, p. 6. "For baseball grounds the field is certainly heroic in its proportions, as the following measurements will show: On One Hundred and Sixty-fifth Street the enclosure (sic) measures 535 feet 7 inches; on Broadway its eastern boundary, it is 702 feet; along One Hundred and Sixty-eighth Street, on the north, it is 675 feet, and along Fort Washington Road, the western boundary, the length is 675 feet. There is plenty of room inside the enclosure (sic) for home run drives, and it will require a mighty batsman to knock a fair ball over the fence."
8. Joe Vila, *New York Sun*, March 6, 1923, p.20.
9. Lowry, *Green Cathedrals*; Ritter, *Lost Ballparks*.
10. Lowry, *Green Cathedrals*; Ritter, *Lost Ballparks*.
11. *New York Times*, 6 April 1903, p. 6.
12. Sanborn Fire Insurance Co. map, New York City 1909 (map no. 82).
13. Research by the late SABR member Larry Zuckerman from newspapers of the day was verified by the author for each season.
14. Author's research using SABR's Tattersall-McConnell Home Run Log and game accounts from the *St. Louis Globe Democrat* 1902–1908.
15. Ritter, *Lost Ballparks*, p. 94.
16. SABR Home Run Log data supplied by David Vincent.
17. *New York Times*, game accounts 1901–1908.
18. Research by Larry Zuckerman from newspapers of the day.
19. Philip J. Lowry, *Green Cathedrals*, 1st ed. (Cooperstown, NY: Society for American Baseball Research, 1986), p. 104.
20. Sanborn Fire Insurance Co. map, New York City 1909 (map no. 82).
21. Research by Larry Zuckerman from newspapers of the day.
22. Research by Larry Zuckerman from newspapers of the day.
23. Research by Larry Zuckerman from newspapers of the day.
24. *New York Times*, April 29, 1913.
25. *New York Times*, May 19, 1911; May 31, 1917.
26. Sanborn Fire Insurance Co. map, New York City 1909 (map no. 68).
27. *New York Times*, June 16, 1915.

Chapter 10

1. Bevis, *Sunday Baseball*, p. 260.
2. Rich Westcott, *Philadelphia's Old Ballparks* (Philadelphia: Temple University Press, 1996), p. 76.
3. Lowry, *Green Cathedrals*, p. 207; Sanborn Fire Insurance Co. map, Philadelphia 1921 (volume 13, map 1224).
4. Westcott, *Philadelphia's Old Ballparks*, p. 39.
5. Westcott, *Philadelphia's Old Ballparks*, p. 47.
6. Lowry, *Green Cathedrals*.

7. Westcott, *Philadelphia's Old Ballparks,* p. 49.
8. Data courtesy of noted baseball researcher and SABR member Bill Deane.
9. *Washington Post,* July 5, 1903.
10. Lowry, *Green Cathedrals,* p. 209; Gershman, *Diamonds,* p. 247.
11. *Philadelphia City Atlas 20th and 29th Wards* (Philadelphia: Elving Smith, 1907), plate 1.
12. *Philadelphia Inquirer,* May 8, 1902; June 26, 1906; April 22, 1907.
13. "Panoramic View of the Opening Game of the American League Season at Columbia Park," *Philadelphia Inquirer,* April 27, 1901.
14. Westcott, *Philadelphia's Old Ballparks,* p. 104.
15. "Panoramic View of Shibe Park," *Philadelphia Inquirer,* December 3, 1908.
16. Lowry, *Green Cathedrals,* p. 210; Sanborn Fire Insurance Co map, Philadelphia 1921 (map 122–123).
17. John Pastier, *Historic Ballparks* (Edison, NJ: Chartwell Books, 2006).
18. *Philadelphia Inquirer,* June 23, 1912; October 4, 1912.
19. Library of Congress, George Grantham Bain Collection; photo 14440 dated October 8, 1917.
20. SABR member Vic Wilson, unpublished study of Home Run Park Factors for Right-handed and Left-handed Batters.

Chapter 11

1. Frederick Ivor-Campbell, "Team Histories," *Total Baseball,* ed. John Thorn and Pete Palmer (New York: Viking Penguin, 1995).
2. Bevis, *Sunday Baseball,* p. 260.
3. Lowry, *Green Cathedrals,* p. 215; Sanborn Fire Insurance Co. map, Pittsburgh 1906 (map 84).
4. Donald G. Lancaster, "Forbes Field Praised as a Gem When It Opened," *Baseball Research Journal* 15 (1986), pp. 26–29.
5. Forbes Field photos from the Library of Congress American Memory Collection (ID det 4a10302, det 4110304, det 4a10305, det 4a10306, and det 4a10306).
6. Lowry, *Green Cathedrals,* p. 216.
7. *Cincinnati Enquirer,* May 27, 1911.
8. Enders, *Ballparks Then and Now,* p. 128.
9. *Cincinnati Enquirer,* May 27, 1911.

Chapter 12

1. William Borst, *Still Last in the American League* (West Bloomfield, MI: A & M Publishing, 1992).
2. Bevis, *Sunday Baseball,* p. 40.
3. *St. Louis Star,* July 13, 1901; Sanborn Fire Insurance Co. map, St. Louis 1909 (map section 5183); *St Louis Post Dispatch,* April 23, 1893.
4. *St. Louis Globe-Democrat,* April 25, 1901.
5. Joan Thomas, ballpark articles in *Senior Circuit* 2000–2003.
6. Lowry, *Green Cathedrals,* p. 227.
7. *St. Louis Star,* April 13, 1902.
8. Lowry, *Green Cathedrals,* p. 229.
9. *St. Louis Star,* April 13, 1902.
10. Philip J. Lowry, *Green Cathedrals* 1st ed.
11. *St. Louis Star,* April 13, 1902; Sanborn Fire Insurance Co. map, St. Louis 1909 (volume 7, sheet 46).
12. Library of Congress American Memory Collection (digital ID ichicdn s0005709); Okkonen, *Baseball Memories,* p. 75.
13. Library of Congress American Memory Collection (digital ID ichicdn s0005713).
14. Borst, *Still Last in the American League,* p. 97.
15. *St. Louis Globe-Democrat,* July 3, 1902; July 8, 1902; August 4, 1902; June 23, 1906. The newspaper reports the games on the previous day.
16. *St. Louis's Favorite Sport,* ed. Robert L. Tiemann (Cleveland: Society for American Baseball Research, 1992).
17. Library of Congress American Memory Collection (digital ID ichicdn s0005700, and s0005 713).
18. *St. Louis Globe-Democrat,* April 11, 1909.
19. Lowry, *Green Cathedrals,* p. 228.
20. *St. Louis's Favorite Sport.*
21. *St. Louis Globe-Democrat,* July 22, 1915.
22. *St. Louis Globe-Democrat,* April 14, 1909.
23. *St. Louis Globe-Democrat,* April 14, 1909; Sanborn Fire Insurance Co. map, St. Louis 1909 (volume 7, sheet 46).
24. Interview with SABR member Robert Tiemann at the SABR National Convention, July 11, 2003.
25. Lowry, *Green Cathedrals*; Interview with Robert Tiemann, July 11, 2003.
26. St. Louis's Favorite Sport.
27. *St. Louis Globe-Democrat,* August 23, 1911.
28. *St. Louis Globe-Democrat,* September 28, 1912.
29. *St. Louis Globe-Democrat,* July 13, 1911.

Chapter 13

1. Bevis, *Sunday Baseball,* p. 193.
2. Lowry, *Green Cathedrals,* p. 243 .
3. *Washington Post,* February 16, 1901.
4. Okkonen, *Baseball Memories.*
5. *Washington Post,* April 30, 1901.
6. *Washington Post,* March 24, 1904.
7. "Tearing Down The Stands," *Washington Post,* March 31, 1904.
8. "Senators Lose First," *Washington Post,* April 15, 1904.
9. Sanborn Fire Insurance Co. map, Washington 1910 (volume 4, sheet 325).
10. Okkonen, *Baseball Memories,* p. 78.
11. *Washington Post,* March 18, 1911.
12. *Washington Post,* April 9, 1911.
13. *Washington Post,* April 13, 1911.
14. Lowry, *Green Cathedrals.*
15. *Washington Post,* July 28, 1912.
16. Sanborn Fire Insurance Co. map, Washington 1911 (volume 3, sheet 17).
17. "Noted of the Nationals," *Washington Post,* May 9, 1912.
18. *Washington Post,* May 31, 1913.
19. *Washington Post,* June 17, 1917; September 28, 1919.

Bibliography

Bak, Richard. *A Place For Summer*. Detroit: Wayne State University Press, 1998.

_____, and Charles Vincent. *The Corner: A Century of Memories at Michigan and Trumbull*. Chicago: Triumph Books, 1999.

Baseball in Chicago. Special Issue of the *Chicago Tribune Sunday Magazine*, May 23, 2004.

Benson, Michael. *Ballparks of North America*. Jefferson, NC: McFarland, 1989.

Bevis, Charlie. *Sunday Baseball*. Jefferson, NC: McFarland, 2003.

Borst, William. *Still Last in the American League*. West Bloomfield, MI: A & M Publishing, 1992.

Boswell, John, and David Fisher. *Fenway Park: Legendary Home of the Red Sox*. Boston: Little, Brown, 1992.

Boynton, Bob. "Cleveland Ballparks." SABR-L, March 29, 2001.

Ebbets Field: The Original Plans. Edited by Rod Kennedy Jr. New York: The Brooklyn Dodgers Hall of Fame, 1992.

Enders, Eric. *Ballparks Then and Now*. San Diego: PRC Publishing, 2002.

Foulds, Alan E. *Boston's Ballparks and Arenas*. Boston: Northeastern University Press, 2005.

Gershman, Michael. *Diamonds: The Evolution of the Ballpark*. Boston: Houghton Mifflin, 1993.

Hartell, William. *A Day at the Park: In Celebration of Wrigley Field*. Coal Valley, IL: Quality Sports Publications, 1995.

Hercules, Bob, dir. *The Story of America's Classic Ballparks*. Questar, 1990. VHS.

Hilton, George W. "Comiskey Park." *Baseball Research Journal* 3 (1974): 2–11.

Ivor-Campbell, Frederick. "Team Histories." In *Total Baseball*, edited by John Thorn and Pete Palmer, 15–69. 4th ed. New York: Viking Penguin, 1995.

Lancaster, Donald G. "Forbes Field Praised as a Gem When It Opened." *Baseball Research Journal* 15 (1986): 26–29.

Lowry, Philip J. *Green Cathedrals*. Cooperstown, NY: Society for American Baseball Research, 1986.

_____. *Green Cathedrals*. 2nd ed. Reading, MA: Addison-Wesley, 1992.

_____. *Green Cathedrals: The Ultimate Celebration of Major League and Negro League Ballparks*. 3rd ed. New York: Walker Publishing, 2006.

Mathewson, Christy. *Pitching in a Pinch*. Lincoln: University of Nebraska Press, 1994.

Miller, Richard, and Gregory C. Rhodes. "The Life and Times of Old Cincinnati Ballparks." *Queen City Heritage* 46, no. 2 (Summer 1988): 25–41.

Morris, Peter. *A Game of Inches*. Chicago: Ivan R. Dee, 2006.

_____. *Level Playing Fields*. Lincoln: University of Nebraska Press, 2007.

Nowlin, Bill. *Red Sox Threads*. Burlington, MA: Rounder Books, 2007.

Okkonen, Marc. *Baseball Memories: 1900–1909*. New York: Sterling, 1992.

Pastier, John. *Historic Ballparks*. Edison, NJ: Chartwell Books, 2006.

Philadelphia City Atlas 20th and 29th Wards. Philadelphia: Elving Smith, 1907.

Price, Bill. "Braves Field." *Baseball Research Journal* 7 (1978): 1–6.

Ritter, Lawrence S. *Lost Ballparks*. New York: Penguin, 1992.

St. Louis's Favorite Sport. Edited by Robert L. Tiemann. Cleveland: Society for American Baseball Research, 1992.

Sanborn Fire Insurance Co. Maps: Baltimore 1902; Boston 1895, 1914, 1925; Brooklyn 1906; Chicago 1911, 1917, 1923; Cincinnati 1891, 1904, 1950; Cleveland 1896, 1911; Detroit 1897: New York City 1909; Philadelphia 1921; Pittsburgh 1906; St. Louis 1909; Washington 1910, 1911.

The Tattersall-McConnell Home Run Log, provided by David Vincent.

Thomas, Joan M. Ballpark articles. *Senior Circuit* (2000–2003).

Total Baseball. Edited by John Thorn and Pete Palmer. 4th ed. New York: Viking Penguin, 1995.

U.S. Library of Congress. *American Memory*. http://memory.loc.gov/ammem/index.html.

_____. *George Grantham Bain Collection.* http://memory.loc.gov/ammem/awhhtml/awpnp6/Bain_coll.html.

Vaccaro, Frank. *All Games Baseball, Volume One, 1871–1924.* College Point, NY: All Games Baseball, 2005.

Vincent, David. *Home Run: The Definitive History of Baseball's Ultimate Weapon.* Washington, D.C.: Potomac Books, 2007.

Westcott, Rich. *Philadelphia's Old Ballparks.* Philadelphia: Temple University Press, 1996.

Newspapers

Boston Globe
Brooklyn Daily Eagle
Chicago Tribune
Cincinnati Enquirer
Cleveland Leader
Cleveland Plain Dealer
Detroit Free Press
New York Sun
New York Times
Philadelphia Inquirer
Pittsburgh Gazette Times
St. Louis Globe-Democrat
St. Louis Post Dispatch
St. Louis Star
Washington Post

Index

Abstein, Bill 147
American Association 140, 141, 157
American Giants Baseball Park 53
American League Park New York (Hilltop Park) 115
American League Park I, Washington, D.C. 8, 85, 98, 167–171, 180
American League Park II, Washington, D.C. 56, 167, 168, 171–175, 180
Archambault, Edmund 63
Armory Park, Toledo Ohio 90

Bak, Richard 97
Baker, William F. 126
Baker Bowl, Philadelphia 8, 74, 125–133, 180, 182
Beinke & Wells 155
Bennett, Charlie 90
Bennett Park, Detroit 55, 56, 55, 56, 82, 90–98, 100, 168, 171
Bierbaur, Louis 141
Boundary Park (National Park) Washington, D.C. 167, 168, 171
Boynton, Bob 87
Braves Field, Boston 17, 33–36, 136, 180, 181
Briggs Stadium, Detroit 1, 90, 100
Brotherhood Park, New York 108
Brush, John T. 72, 107
Brush Stadium, New York 107
Burns, James T. 97
Burns Park, Detroit 1, 5, 26, 81–82, 90, 97–100, 120, 180, 181

Cantillion, E.M. 63
Cantillion, Joe 63
Cardinals Park (Robison Park) St. Louis 152
Casey, Doc 168
Chouihard, Felix 68
Cobb, Ty 90, 96, 123
Columbia Park I, Philadelphia 132
Columbia Park II, Philadelphia 2, 8, 25, 55, 56, 125, 132–134, 170, 171

Comiskey Park, Chicago 8, 53, 55, 56, 59–63, 180
Comiskey Park II, Chicago 60
Congress Street Grounds, Boston 17
Coors Field, Denver 26, 99
Coots 40
Cravath, Gavvy 131, 132
Crawford, Sam 88, 90, 96
Crosley, Powel 78
Crosley Field, Cincinnati 78
Cruise, Walton 35
Cubs Park, Chicago 65, 66, 69

Davis, Harry 169
Davis, Zachary Taylor 37, 61, 67
Duffy's Cliff 33
Duncan, Pat 80

Eastern Park, Brooklyn 37
Ebbets, Charles H. 37, 43
Ebbets Field, Brooklyn 3, 14, 37, 38, 42–46, 108
Exposition Park I (Lower Field), Pittsburgh 141
Exposition Park II (Upper Field), Pittsburgh 141
Exposition Park III, Pittsburgh 140–145, 181

Federal League 13, 37, 47, 63–65, 68, 125, 141, 143, 151
Fenway Park, Boston 17, 19, 23, 28–33
Flack, Max 68
Forbes, General John 145
Forbes Field, Pittsburgh 8, 140, 145–150, 180
Freeman, Buck 117

Gaffney, James 35
Griffith, Clark 174
Griffith Stadium, Washington, D.C. 136, 167, 169, 174–179

Hake, Harry 79
Handlan's Park, St. Louis 151
Harrison Field, Newark 37, 107

Hartzell, Roy 164
Hickman, Charlie 83
Hilltop Park, New York 2, 27, 55, 56, 91, 109, 113–121, 126, 170, 180, 181
Huntingdon Grounds, Philadelphia 125
Huntington Avenue Baseball Grounds, Boston 17, 22–28, 56, 74, 170, 180

Jennings, Hugh 96
Johnson, Ban 98
Jordan, Tim 144

Lajoie, Nap 81, 161, 169
Lake Front Park I, Chicago 47
Lake Front Park II, Chicago 47
LaPorte, Frank 164
League Park I, Cincinnati 71
League Park I, Cleveland 82
League Park II, Cincinnati 71–75
League Park II, Cleveland 82
League Park III, Cleveland 56, 81–86, 91, 126, 170, 171
League Park IV, Cleveland 81, 86–89, 135, 176, 180
Leavitt, Charles W. 149
Lee, Cliff 130
Lloyd Street Grounds, Milwaukee 103–106

Mack, Connie 22, 125, 133, 136
Manhattan Field (Polo Grounds IV), New York 108
Mathewson, Christy 57
McLaughlin, Charles E. 29, 32
Merkle, Fred 68
Moeller, Danny 176

National League Park, Cleveland 81
National Park IV (Griffith Stadium), Washington, D.C. 174
Navin Field, Detroit 90, 91, 100–102
Neil Park II, Columbus Ohio 90
Nowlin, Bill 22

Oriole Park I, Baltimore 13
Oriole Park II, Baltimore 13
Oriole Park III, Baltimore 13
Oriole Park IV, Baltimore 2, 13–16, 26, 27, 168, 170
Osborn Engineering. Co. 31, 32, 35, 87, 102, 165

Palace of the Fans, Cincinnati 71, 74–78, 180
Palmer, Pete 9, 10
Philadelphia Baseball Grounds, Philadelphia 125
Players League 107, 108, 140, 141
Polo Grounds I, New York 107, 108
Polo Grounds II, New York 107, 108
Polo Grounds III, New York 107, 108
Polo Grounds IV, New York 3, 8, 103, 107–113, 121, 145, 181
Polo Grounds V, New York 3, 38, 107, 109, 121–124
Pratt, Del 164

Ramona Park, Grand Rapids Michigan 90
Recreation Park, Detroit 90
Recreation Park, Philadelphia 125
Recreation Park, Pittsburgh 140
Redland Field, Cincinnati 71, 78–80
Riverfront Stadium, Cincinnati 78
Robison, Frank 152
Robison, Stanley 152
Robison Field, St. Louis 8, 130, 151–157
Ruth, Babe 8, 33, 80, 162
Ryan, Jimmy 48

SABR Home Run Log 9, 116, 168
Sanborn Maps: Boston 14, 19, 31, 34; Brooklyn 39; Chicago 48, 49, 53, 55, 56; Cincinnati 72, 75, 78, 79; Cleveland 82, 86, 87; Detroit 93, 95, 98; Milwaukee 104; New York 109, 116, 117; Philadelphia 128, 129, 137; Pittsburgh 143; St. Louis 154, 158; Washington 173, 177
Schenck, Phil 115
Schendly, Mark 145
Shannon, Paul 25
Shea Stadium, New York 107
Shibe, Ben 135
Shibe Park, Philadelphia 2, 8, 125, 128, 133, 135–139
Sisler, George 88
Snyder, Frank 35
Somers, Charles 22
South End Grounds II, Boston 17
South End Grounds III, Boston 17–23, 180
South Side Park II, Chicago 47
South Side Park III, Chicago 47, 53–59, 105, 170, 171, 180, 181
Speaker, Tris 88
Sportsman's Park I, St. Louis 157
Sportsman's Park II, St. Louis 151, 152, 157
Sportsman's Park III, St. Louis 55, 56, 117, 118, 145, 151, 157–162, 164, 170, 171
Sportsman's Park IV, St. Louis 145, 151, 154, 161–166
Steele, William 138
Swampoodle Grounds, Washington, D.C. 167

Terrapin Park, Baltimore 13
Three Rivers Stadium, Pittsburgh 146
Thurtle, John G. 75
Tieman, Robert 164
Tiger Stadium, Detroit 90, 100, 101
23rd Street Grounds, Chicago 47

Union Association 141
Union Park, Baltimore 13

Van Buskirk, Clarence R. 44
Vincent, David 7

Waddell, Rube 159
Wagner, Honus 140
Walker, Tillie 33
Washington Park I, Brooklyn 38.
Washington Park II, Brooklyn 37, 38
Washington Park III, Brooklyn 37–41, 107
Washington Park IV, Brooklyn 37
Weeghman, Charles A. 47, 63, 65
Weeghman Park, Chicago 48, 63–70, 180
West Side Grounds, Chicago 8, 47–52, 145, 181
West Side Park, Chicago 47
White Stockings Park, Chicago 47
Williams, Gus 164
Wilmot, Walt 48
Wrigley, William 65, 66
Wrigley Field, Chicago 37, 48, 63

Yankee Stadium, New York 3, 8

Zuckerman, Larry 19, 20, 116

www.ingramcontent.com/pod-product-compliance
Lightning Source LLC
Chambersburg PA
CBHW081209170426
43198CB00018B/2901